WILLIE
BROWN

BASIC BROWN

My Life and Our Times

Simon & Schuster

NEW YORK · LONDON · TORONTO · SYDNEY

SIMON & SCHUSTER
Rockefeller Center
1230 Avenue of the Americas
New York, NY 10020

First Simon & Schuster hardcover edition February 2008

SIMON & SCHUSTER and colophon are registered trademarks
of Simon & Schuster, Inc.

For information about special discounts for bulk purchases,
please contact Simon & Schuster Special Sales at
1-800-456-6798 or business@simonandschuster.com

Designed by Paul Dippolito

Manufactured in the United States of America

10   8   6   5   7   9

Library of Congress Cataloging-in-Publication Data

Brown, Willie L.
Basic Brown : my life and our times / Willie Brown
p.   cm.
Includes index.
1. Brown, Willie L.   2. Brown, Willie L.—Political and social views.
3. California Legislature. Assembly—Speakers—Biography.   4. Mayors—
California—San Francisco—Biography.   5. Legislators—California—Biography.
6. African-American Legislators—California—Biography.   7. California—Politics
and Government—1951–   8. United States—Politics and government—
1945–1989.   9. United States—Politics and government—1989–   I. Title.
F866.4.B76A3 B76   2008
328.797092—dc22   2007044956

ISBN-13: 978-0-7432-9081-4
ISBN-10:   0-7432-9081-X

Photo credits appear on page 339.

To those many opponents who say I speak only bits of the truth. May they find much in these pages to confound themselves.

A Word from Willie Brown

I'd like to thank P. J. Corkery for capturing in these
pages my love of politics and my appetite for life.

Contents

CONTENTS

CONTENTS

Basic
BROWN

Willie Talk: The Hipster of the Breakfast Table

WILLIE BROWN SPENDS hours every day in San Francisco's restaurants. For him, San Francisco's dining rooms, with their fine cuisine, fine company, leather banquettes, and leathery dice cups, are both a setting and a sanctuary. This is where he does business, plots, and lives much of his life. This is the public Willie Brown. That's the Willie Brown I used to see.

For all his time at the table, though, Willie Brown is still a fit, thin man, the same size 40 regular that he was twenty-seven years ago when he was first elected Speaker of the California Assembly. He is gourmet, but he eats abstemiously. He has no fitness regimen to speak of and must be one of the few politicians who can't stand playing golf. Perhaps his terrific condition is due to his fifty-six-year-old habit, begun when he arrived in San Francisco as a seventeen-year-old, of walking constantly around the city he loves. Oh, and he often walks up and down the stairs of the St. Regis Hotel/apartment complex, in San Francisco's South of Market district, in a way that excites the envy of his coresident Al Gore.

He often lunches at Le Central, near the brokerages of Montgomery Street and the boutiques of Grant Avenue, where he and his longtime pal, haberdasher Wilkes Bashford; his dapper society friends like Harry de Wildt and Matthew Kelly; architect Sandy Walker; and the late Herb Caen (celebrated columnist of the *San Francisco Chronicle*), have occupied the window seats for thirty-seven years.

When Willie Brown was mayor and, before that, speaker of the assembly in Sacramento, ninety fast minutes away, he gave over just about every day and night to the whims of his schedulers, except for three hours on Fridays at Le Central. That was his time. It still is. It's there he and his friends play boss dice for an hour and the lunch tab. The dizzying games, an old San Francisco tradition dating back to the tented saloons of the Gold Rush, move at a rate of about three games a minute. The boys once tried playing poker, but it was way too slow.

He also attends political banquets and fund-raisers at night. There are hundreds of these events every year: for example, the Chinese Six Companies, an ancient San Francisco amalgam of six family associations, holds full-dress, full-ritual, presidential inaugurations every two months as the association's presidency rotates. The food at these events in food-crazy San Francisco is hardly grub, but Willie Brown is there to work.

At events like these—four a night is not uncommon for Willie Brown, who is no longer even in office—he addresses the crowd from the dais, then table hops, connects with pals, and hears, notes, files, and contributes to the latest gossip. To those remaining old-school news reporters who actually believe in getting out into the city streets to find news, encountering Willie Brown on his nightly rounds is like running into a one-man CIA, though the reporters do not always acknowledge him as the source of some of the newsiest and juiciest items that make the news.

It's after working the banquets that he and a date and whatever friends happen to be tagging along will visit some new restaurant or some favored hangout for the real evening meal. Then it's off to hear music, dance, hang at a bar. A colorful, flamboyant public man, at home on the public stage and intriguing as such.

Was there ever a private Willie Brown? Did he ever spend a moment when he was not on stage? Well, I had heard about his breakfasts. He takes breakfast in public, not surprisingly, usually dining in a hotel dining room. But typically he didn't entertain an entourage. He had at most one guest, and he took many phone calls. This was the sanctum of the great political chief. Then one day he invited me to breakfast. Our talks at those breakfasts are the source of this book.

The Willie Brown of the breakfast table is no less humorous, delightful, insightful, or zany than the Willie Brown of the lunch table with its dice cups to be slammed or the banquet table with its hundreds of hands to be shaken. But at breakfast, he is more reflective, less given to the small talk. It is at the breakfast table that he tries out new ideas and deals privately with political concerns. It is there that he receives confidential calls on his iPhone. (When he was mayor, he refused to carry the then bulky cell phones of the day. Then his bodyguards carried his cell phones. The reason? The fat phones disturbed the lining and draping of his $5,000 Brioni suits. The iPhone offers no such sartorial threat.) The calls come in from the Barack Obama camp, the Hillary Clinton camp, the Rudy Giuliani camp, from Speaker Nancy Pelosi, from Senator Dianne Feinstein, from Mayor Gavin Newsom, from Los Angeles mayor Antonio Villaraigosa, even from Republican governor, and personal pal, Arnold Schwarzenegger. He has sharp and sincere advice and guidance for them all, and he also picks up the news.

I am not quite sure why these breakfast sessions with me, these seminars, these Willie Brown Think-and-Action Tank Institute breakfasts started. I had asked him, as a fan of American political literature from William Riordon's account of Tammany Hall boss George Washington Plunkitt to William Kennedy's Albany novels to Edwin O'Connor's *The Last Hurrah*, to consider writing a memoir.

I really hadn't much of a hope for the idea. Not because the mayor isn't a spellbinding communicator. He is. Nor was it because he isn't well read. He is. He has read or listened to audio editions of almost every political book and memoir published. But like most notable politicians, he once sagely observed, what makes him strongest is what makes for weaker memoirs. Sharp American politicians aren't intent on hiding details. It's just that they move so fast, that an account of a bygone play must, to them, sound wooden, inept, half-wise and maybe half-dangerous: you could unwittingly slight the contribution of a teammate. American politicians are players to whom the almost indescribable, hydra-headed action, the moment, is everything. For British politicians, whose memoir writing is the literary standard, the memoir itself is a tool in the continuation of their rhetoric-proud parliamentary version of the political game, which is heavy on ideological thrust, betrayal, and back-lobby gossip. It's just not in the blood of the fast-moving American pol to overcontemplate how the play went down. History writing—at least the writing of full, interesting history—is rarely the forte of American politicians.

And Willie Brown, though a very reflective man, is also a quipster. He is out of the Fillmore, the black San Francisco neighborhood once called "the Harlem of the West," where quipping (also valued in all San Francisco bars) is rated higher than history.

It was also apparent to me that the mayor's career and life were hardly over. "I'm on the 'J,' " he frequently says on the phone to a caller. "I'm on the job." He's hardly a guy to look back. He's involved and looking forward. I knew he wasn't interested in recounting the minutiae of every day of his life, even though he remembers all of it. But he likes to talk. So he invited me to breakfast. And then once again. And then almost every Saturday morning for many months, I had breakfast with him.

In a leisurely fashion, he began to talk and spill out his observations of politics today, what makes things work, how money operates, who influenced him, how to handle scandals, and how flamboyance in a politician doesn't mean an avoidance of serious political issues. Over time, the material began to organize itself— not as a standard biographical work, but as a set of related glimpses and flashes into the making of modern politics and a modern political life. That's what he was intent on doing through our breakfasts. He had a few things to say.

And so from a master of American politics, here are the quips, themes, lessons, and points of politics that struck him at a San Francisco breakfast table. In the first of these pages, Willie Brown talks of the political life. Then he describes salients from his life as a teenager arriving in San Francisco from segregated Texas, to his rise in politics and his own important and different family life. From his years in the legislature, he limns the dynamics of political power and how luck and setbacks both intervened in his rise to the top. From his years as Speaker of the California Assembly, he describes the high and low efforts required to make new laws and to stay safe personally from the ravages of out-of-control investigators. He also tells of how and why he maintained his speakership as a Democrat in a chamber controlled by Republicans. Last, he draws some lessons from a job he never expected to hold: big city mayor. He concludes with some unusual advice for young politicians.

As I talked and listened to Willie Brown, increasingly he struck me not as a man looking back on to the closed past, but as a player looking into past plays from the vantage point of someone who is still in the game. He is the politician as quarterback or point guard. You can learn a lot from conversations with a guy who thinks like that.

—*P. J. Corkery*

PART ONE

Willie Brown Talks the Talk

Willie Brown discourses on the political life, how to succeed, and how to handle money and scandal.

CHAPTER ONE

"Willie Brown, Who Are You Kidding?"

ONE FOGGY SAN FRANCISCO Saturday morning not long ago, a dapper, tweedy, old-school fellow—a real East Coast establishment type—came up to me in the Big 4, a clubby restaurant in the Huntington Hotel atop San Francisco's Nob Hill. The restaurant with its dark green leather banquettes and dim lighting pays homage to the secret dealings of four of the great railroad barons who lived and plotted in San Francisco's bonanza days back in the 1880s. It still attracts deal making, high society, high-level gossip, and, occasionally, frank talk.

This old Brahmin was new to me. He obviously wasn't a San Franciscan. At the outset, I wasn't sure that he was a fan.

"Willie Brown," he said, wasting no time on preliminaries, "who are you kidding?

"Look at you," he said, going right into it, "wearing three-thousand-dollar suits, a five-hundred-dollar shirt, a French foulard tie." I was a little insulted: the Brioni suit I was wearing cost at least six grand. The Wilkes Bashford shirt was about eight hundred dollars, and my Hermès necktie would have exhausted a trust fund baby's monthly stipend.

And he didn't mention the beautiful Russian blonde, Sonya Molodetskaya, on my right, which I thought was unchivalrous. But he was making a point and I didn't take offense. He went on.

"The way you dress, the way you carry on—it's pure power, wealth, and privilege. And yet at the same time, you do this number about having started out poor, underprivileged. You do this whole 'I was born in a log cabin' routine . . . Complete hypocrisy, Mr. Mayor. I don't believe there's a sincere bone in your body."

He wasn't being mean. He was merely confused by me. He figured that anyone with polish couldn't possibly be a brutha, someone from the rough-and-tumble. He figured I was a highborn fella who found it politically convenient to pretend to be from the streets. He supposed I was more likely to be at home in the celebrated woodsy grove of San Francisco's Bohemian Club on a Saturday rather than in a barbershop in San Francisco's black 'hood, the Western Addition. If I told him I was from Mineola, he would have thought I was from Mineola, a Long Island suburb, and not from hardscrabble Mineola, Texas, where I was actually born. Mineola, Texas, the humble home of the pinto bean! He figured if I weren't the product of one of the red-brick Ivies like Harvard or one of the Silicon Ivies like Stanford, then at least I had gone to Howard or Morehouse, not humble San Francisco State College.

I'll say this for the old boy: he didn't start to rant and rave that I was corrupt, on the take, for sale to the highest bidder. Maybe he was just being courteous, maybe he didn't believe the old libel, or maybe he shied away from the theme of corruption because it might strike close to home. I recognized him as the heir to a great American industrial fortune—on the way to building that pile of cash, there had been a lot of chicanery. The man was also a major Republican contributor.

I said to him, "Brother, I'll let you in on the secret."

He jolted at being addressed as "brother," but he liked the idea of being in the know, of learning the secret behind a player. The powerful like being in on the know.

"You're right," I said. "I wasn't born in a log cabin."

"I knew it," he said.

"No," I said, "I was born *under* a log cabin."

It's true. I didn't just come from poor circumstances, I came from something worse: segregated rural Texas in the Depression. But I rose in the world to sleep in the Lincoln Bedroom of the White House and to host the Queen of England in Sacramento and I intend to get back to the Lincoln Bedroom (I'd like to bring a date) by helping the Democrats regain the White House. The old Republican who accosted me in the Big 4 might not be thrilled with the idea, but I can tell you that my mother and grandmother, who raised me and my sisters and brother, certainly would be.

My mother worked "in service," as they used to say, as a cook in a Dallas home, eighty miles distant. She rarely changed employers and lived in. Her name was Minnie Collins Boyd. Her grandmother had been a slave. Another grandparent had been a runaway slave. We also had Cherokee blood in us. We may not have been a typical family by white standards, but we were a mighty family. And mother was the most important person in my life, even though I saw her only on weekends. We children always called her by her first name, Minnie.

She was always fixed on us, her five children, and made sure we behaved well. We were not allowed to be flakes. She raised well-disciplined, orderly children.

Like so many black families, ours was a kind of matriarchy. The women kept the family operation together, functioning as a survival unit. My father, Willie Lewis Brown, Sr., but known as Lewis

11

Brown, was gone early. He and I never spent even one night together under the same roof.

If ever there were bad feelings between my parents about either of them or what might have happened to their relationship, it was not communicated to me. But it wasn't until I was in grade school that I learned that I shared my father's name. I knew, of course, that I was his son. People around Mineola used to point to me and say, "That's Lewis Brown's son." But I was seven or eight before I knew my name was Willie L. Brown Jr. I thought my name was Lawson Brooks Brown. People called me Brookie. To this day contemporaries back in Mineola still call me Brookie. Lawson Brooks was the leader of a roadhouse blues band that was playing in my grandmother's tavern the night I was born! My mother had wanted to go and hear the band, but instead she went into labor with me. Someone commemorated the event by calling me Brookie.

In later life, when I became an influential California politician and my father was living in Los Angeles, he would sometimes show up at political banquets, announce himself as the father of the speaker of the assembly, and ask the banquet organizers to be seated. They would ask me and I always consented. Sometimes he was seated at the head table. Despite any feelings I had about his absence during my childhood, I never gave way to them and never gave him away. I looked after him financially, and when the time came, buried him with respect and reverence.

Back in Mineola, my grandmother, Anna Collins, also looked after us, making us study and work. Grandmother was quite a character. She took nothing off no one, black or white. My mother, her daughter, believed the best way to handle society's hypocrisy was to comply assiduously with its often absurd rules and regulations. She believed in working to change them, but meanwhile she wasn't going to let society have the slightest chance of laying a hand on her. She made a point of meeting with society's rules. There'd be no opening against her. My grandmother came to a different kind of accommodation with the local establishment. She made arrangements with it. She and my uncles had to. My mother and uncles called grandmother "mot' dear," short for "mother dear." We children did the same.

You see, in our little town, Grandmother and my uncles ran a speakeasy. It was called the Shack, an apt description of the property. Inside you could buy bootleg liquor called "chock" and listen to blues bands that made the circuit through Texas. I'm not the only popular politician to have a bootlegger in the family closet. Old Joe Kennedy moved lots of scotch through Boston, I'm told.

The Shack was never raided, as far as I know, so grandmother's arrangement with the sheriff must have been an effective one.

The Shack brought in money, but as kids we all had to have jobs. At age ten, I picked beans in the fields—and was glad to have the cash mother let me keep from my pay. With that I was able to buy some little kid toys and even shoes. A few years later, I shined shoes outside a railroad hotel (fishing nickels out of the spittoon by the stand into which white customers gleefully pitched their coins and phlegm). I made six wet dollars a week. Our primary school was terrible: a one-room schoolhouse. But we were lucky to have that and a high school: Mineola Colored High School. I played point guard for the basketball team, but we played on a dirt outdoor court. Indoor courts were for the white schools.

When my sisters and brother took the train to Dallas to see our mother, we did what the conductor told us to do, which was to pull down the shades on the windows in the colored car when passing through the town of Grand Saline. The good white people of Grand Saline didn't want to have even a glimpse of black people. It was the law of that town that the colored riders on the train had to pull down the shades when passing through.

• • •

From that limited and limiting environment, or perhaps because of it, I grew up to become one of America's most adept politicians. For fifteen years, I was Speaker of the California Assembly and controlled one of the largest and most complex governmental budgets in the globe. I even got Ronald Reagan, the icon of right-wing Republicanism, to sign liberal legislation! Then I served and thrived through two terms—all that the law allows—as mayor of the most politics-ridden city in America, my fabulous San Francisco.

To commentators, I'm something of a conundrum because I'm a black Democrat. I opposed the War in Vietnam in 1962, long before the teach-ins of Vietnam Summer in 1967 turned opposition to the war into an acceptable political stance. I worked for Bobby Kennedy in the 1968 presidential campaign. As a legislator I won, through long, intricate political fights over many years, battles for gay rights, women's rights, immigrants' rights, and against guns. I fought at the 1972 Democratic Convention for George McGovern. I chaired Jesse Jackson's presidential campaign in 1988. What makes me a seeming contradiction is that I've also been unusually popular with Republicans. They helped make me speaker of the assembly in 1980, and when the Republicans finally gained control of the assembly in 1994, they didn't elect a Republican to be speaker, they elected me! I've been out of public office since I left the mayoralty of San Francisco in 2004, but I'm still very close to Republicans. Arnold Schwarzenegger is one of my best friends. Ronald Reagan and I got along just fine.

People come to me for political and legal advice all the time. That's how I earn my living these days—as a political consultant and lawyer. I'm very good at both, but something in the way

I've done things—from working with Republicans while being a liberal—and in my demeanor—I can't resist a cutting line—makes people wonder, "Willie Brown, are you kidding?"

Sometimes I've had to make it very clear that when it comes to maintaining power, I'm not kidding.

CHAPTER TWO

Willie Brown Is NOT Kidding

IN 1988 I HAD been speaker—Ayatollah—of the assembly for eight years. I would go on to serve seven more years as speaker. I would still be speaker today were it not for term limits, a destructive idea introduced by mean-spirited wretches from Southern California who sought to deprive the people of San Francisco of the right to reelect me as their assemblyman. You know, even Ronald Reagan opposed term limits. He and Nancy Reagan wrote a letter that was to have been used in the ballot campaign against term limits. But due to the indolence of Democratic colleagues of mine in the California State Senate, the letter wasn't mailed out to the voters, and I and scores of other legislators were "termed-out" because the voters never learned of the Reagans' opposition to the idea.

Back in 1988, however, I was unchallenged as speaker until suddenly a handful of members of the assembly decided it was time for me to go. They became known as the "Gang of Five." Their story shows that while the use of power can be elegant (at least when Willie Brown is wielding it), politics itself ain't pretty.

You already know one of the Gang of Five: Gary Condit, who

in 2003 lost reelection to his seat in the U.S. Congress after having become involved in the scandal around the disappearance and murder of his congressional intern, Chandra Levy. Condit was not implicated in Ms. Levy's brutal slaying, but in denying that he had had an intimate relationship with her, he lied to her family, the press, and investigators. That finished his career. Back then, in 1988, he was an assemblyman from the San Joaquin Valley, the massive agricultural heart of California.

With four cohorts in the assembly—Jerry Eaves, Rusty Areias, Chuck Calderon, and Steve Peace—Condit attempted to oust me from the speakership, even though I had been generous to them, appointing them to powerful committee chairmanships and providing them with campaign funds and perks galore. Indeed, I had been training them to one day succeed me in the ranks of the powerful in the assembly. They got pushy, though.

Without revealing their agenda, they asked one day to meet with me. Assembly members always came first with me, so I stopped what I was doing, brought them to my inner office, and served them coffee. They came right to the point.

"We think it's time," said Condit, "for you to give us your exit date." They said, you know, we really love you, you've set the record, you're going to go down in history: you've been speaker for seven and half years, longer than anyone else, and you're the first black speaker, but we want to take over. I was surprised but not fazed.

I said, "You young fellows, you really impress me with your skills and your ability. Each of you is the chair of a major committee, each of you holds an important position, so when people like you say something like this, I have to listen. But, oh boy, this is not something we can decide easily—there are a lot of ramifications. So let me go cancel all my other appointments for this afternoon and we'll talk about this in depth." I stepped out of my office.

17

Whew. Now, a challenge to a speaker's hold on his chair can never be unexpected. In fact, in California challenges to previous speakers were common. As speaker you're holding a job that not only has no built-in tenure, but your job security depends on your constantly pleasing a majority of the membership. Politics and ambition being what they are, somebody is always unhappy. Somebody is always thinking of toppling you.

But you don't expect a coup attempt from your own side, especially from members to whom you had given chances for advancement. What was it my mentor, Machiavelli, said? "Lavish your allies and underlings with honors and opportunities, and they shall not desire to change princes"? Well, Machiavelli never lived with my legislature. My mistake with the Gang of Five now attempting to oust me was to have shown them, by appointing them to leadership posts, that I thought they themselves might one day make fine speakers of the assembly. They showed their gratitude by telling me to quit.

Their demeanor fascinated me. They wanted me to acknowledge publicly that they were my masters and that they had decided to move things around. They behaved as if they were being charitable towards me by allowing me to be awarded with the record of having been the longest-serving speaker in the history of the California Assembly! And by being the first black speaker. One of them said it looked good on my résumé! I was supposed to be impressed that they were concerned about my record and my future career.

I knew, though, that their coup would not succeed. They had only their five votes—with perhaps a few more members lurking in the shadows. I, however, had more backup, including Republicans as well as Democrats. So while the Gang of Five had a handful of the eighty members of the assembly, when you counted up the numbers (as I did a few times every day), I had over forty-one. And that's all it takes to stay in power. The Gang of Five could not win.

Nonetheless, these five had to be punished for their temerity and ingratitude. So when I left them behind in my office, ostensibly to tell my secretary to cancel my appointments for the rest of the day, I actually told her to get the chairman of the Rules Committee, the late Lou Papan, on the phone.

Lou was a guy who loved dropping bombs. And as chairman of the Rules Committee—*my* chairman of *my* Rules Committee—he was in charge of all the other chairmen and chairwomen, and of the political housekeeping in the assembly.

The message I told my secretary to give Lou Papan was this: "I am immediately removing Condit, Peace, Calderon, Eaves, and Areias from their committee chairmanships, but I'm not stopping with just strippin' them of their titles. I want you to evict them from their offices. I want you to fire all the staff they hired for their committees. And I want you to put their furniture out in the hall."

Even then I planned (as I eventually did) to reassign the five ingrates to lesser positions—I never cut any one out entirely. They might be renegades today, but I regarded myself as in competition for their votes in the future. At that moment, however, they had to be punished.

"And tell Lou," I said to my secretary, "I want it done within an hour. That's as long as I am going to stay in a room with these disloyal bastards. . . . As soon as you tell Lou what I want done, he'll understand what maneuver these five have just tried to pull."

She called Lou, who was *deeeelighted* to invoke the eviction process without notice to these renegades. And I knew my characterization of the Gang as "these disloyal bastards" would be repeated all around the capitol, and to the press corps, within the same hour.

I went back into my office where the renegades were sitting with sick smiles. I didn't tell them I had just denuded them of the robes of power, their offices, even their parking spaces. I told them nothing. I went deadpan. I sat down and listened to them shine me on. After about an hour I knew that Lou had had enough time to carry out the executions. Then I said to the Gang of Five: "Listen, guys, can I have overnight? Let me think about what you've said overnight." And they said, "Oh, yeah, that's easy."

They must have really thought I was chastened by them, hit as a human being because one of them then said, "Why don't you have dinner with us tonight?" I said, "Absolutely. No problem at all. We'll have dinner." They didn't know they were already toast. I got up to signal the end of the session and said, "Why don't you guys go out that side door? More confidential." Sure.

Of course, that side door led right into the microphones, cameras, and notebooks of the waiting press. Every statehouse reporter and camera crew from every TV station from San Diego to Los Angeles to Sacramento and San Francisco—and national TV crews as well—was there. The statehouse scribes had seen all their furniture suddenly being moved out of their offices. They were getting signals from Lou Papan. They knew something was up. As soon as that door to my office opened, the TV reporters were right in the faces of the treacherous five. The members of the Gang were shocked and sickened as the reporters began shouting questions like, "Mr. Condit, how does it feel to no longer be chairman?" "Mr. Calderon, how does it feel to have been stripped of your staff and office?"

The traitors tried to retreat back into my office. I didn't let them in. I let them experience what it was like to run into a real shark. "Guys," I said. "Hey, treachery is fair play. Old age and treachery will always outdo youth and skill. And that's what you just experienced." I sent them back to face the lions of the media. Because eventually I reassigned them to lesser posts in the assembly, I saved them from total abjection—a shrewd use of power.

Anyway, you never need to thoroughly terminate bad actors.

Let the cosmos handle them. Indeed, bad karma followed the Gang of Five for decades. Jerry Eaves was eventually convicted of taking a bribe. Chuck Calderon was fined heavily for violation of campaign funding laws. Rusty Areias, who had been acclaimed in a magazine for being a young guy who had made a million before he was thirty-five, lost everything. He was in the farming business, but the bank took his farm, his dairy, and everything else, and he ended up living for a time in that small, spare Sacramento apartment on N Street that Jerry Brown used as his plebeian version of a governor's mansion.

The two who suffered the worst were Steve Peace and Gary Condit. Steve Peace became the author of energy deregulation in California, a move that was supposed to have resulted in huge savings for Californians, but which actually cost the consumers and the state billions as energy producers and distributors exploited the new legislation. Although billions of dollars were eventually repaid to the customers, Peace's political career never recovered from the deregulation debacle.

These days, I have lunch with Rusty Areias a few times a month. And Chuck Calderon, whose campaign literature mentions nothing of his fines, has just been reelected, after a long absence, to the assembly. But the moral still stands: don't cross Willie Brown, don't spit in the fountain of favors, because he certainly has more votes and moves than you do. And there's always that bad old karma out there. The story of the Gang of Five is still told wherever legislators gather.

So when people ask me if I'm kidding, I tell them this story.

CHAPTER THREE

Consensus and Power

IN JANUARY 2007, I, Willie Brown, a San Francisco liberal Democrat, presided as the master of ceremonies at the gubernatorial inauguration of Arnold Schwarzenegger, a Republican from conservative Southern California. I first got to know Schwarzenegger in 2002 when he was campaigning (victoriously) for a California ballot proposition to build new after-school care and fitness programs. Although he is a Republican, he came to me for help with the ballot proposition. As we talked during the course of that campaign, I began to see that he was interested in being a problem solver, not just a spokesman for a cause. He wanted to know how the levers of power worked. Fun to be with, lively, jovial, quick-witted, quippish, full of the magnetism and glamour of a real star, he often came to have lunch with me and my friends at our hang-out, the restaurant called Le Central, in San Francisco. The folks lined up on the sidewalks to meet him and his wife, Maria, while inside they attended what amounted to a Willie Brown Postgraduate Course on Practical Politics. They're really interested in learning the game. Together, Maria and Arnold are the true heirs of the Kennedy family political legacy. Maybe Arnold isn't as ideologically pure as Uncle Ted Kennedy (and I) would like, but he's no raving right winger and he listens to Maria! You sometimes wonder what the pillow talk must be like around the Schwarzenegger boudoir. But she never takes their political disagreements public. In sum, they have marvelous political instincts. So the Kennedy political genius carries on, but in California. When Arnold became governor of California, he called me up and said, "You've got to help me run the state!" I wasn't interested in taking on any political appointment or job from him, but I'm always available to him for advice, insights, jokes, and jabs to the official conscience. I'm especially interested in seeing that minorities are not forgotten in this administration. We speak at least once a week. And when he asked me to be master of ceremonies at his 2007 inauguration, I couldn't resist the chance to be part of that glamorous show.

Of course, the event was a lot of fun, which political occasions ought to be. I got in some good lines. Arnold had been taking political heat during his reelection campaign when some tapes were disclosed in which he described a Latina assemblywoman as "very hot," due to her "black blood mixed with Latino blood." So at the inaugural I described Maria Shriver, the governor's wife, when I introduced her, as "foxy and sexy," which she certainly is. I could get away with a line like that, I told the crowd, because Arnold, who had broken his leg on a skiing expedition, was on crutches, and couldn't chase me. Later Maria told me, "Watch it, Willie Brown. Arnold may not be able to catch you, but I sure can chase you." Of course, Maria's a lady, so I wouldn't expect her to do such a thing.

Some Democrats, though, seemed to regard my happy participation in Arnold's inauguration as the act of a turncoat. To me, it is a sign of democracy in action. Of course, Arnold is my pal, so I would have appeared at his request anyway, but that's the point: I make friends with everyone, Democrats and Republicans. That's the start of the route to consensus, the basis of any substantive political action.

I have nothing against politicians who are pursuing principled political agendas. But when you first arrive in a political chamber, it's unrealistic to suppose that people will rise up to meet you and take you on your terms—no matter how great your margin of victory. The fact is, *Mr. Smith Goes to Washington* is a fantasy. No matter how righteous your cause, you've got do heavy political lifting to secure the consensus you need to get anything done in the actual political arena like the Congress or the statehouse. You've got to learn to secure votes. You do that through consensus. And if you don't, the voters will be very unhappy. Arnold Schwarzenegger, first elected on a tide of righteous feeling, can tell you that. In first electing him, the voters may have been soulfully indignant about a Democratic state administration that seemed indifferent to them, their needs and wishes, but they didn't want simply to trade in indifference for intransigence, as Schwarzenegger quickly learned. They wanted politicians who could make things work and who could work with each other. I've believed in bipartisanship and cooperation since my early days in the assembly.

As speaker of the assembly, I used to tell freshman legislators that the beginning of their careers in the legislature was not an arrival. It was a leaving. It was not a fulfillment, but a start. They must have thought they had fallen into the hands of some spouting Zen master. I wasn't trying to be cryptic to them, just factual. Getting elected to the chamber is only half the battle. You certainly must not abandon your values or agendas once you enter the political circus that is a capitol or city hall, but you must also learn that new skills may be required to gain success for the ideas you believe in. Righteousness does not, alas, prevail on its own. To be a successful elected official, no matter whether you are a member of a lowly wastewater management district or Speaker of the House, you'll have to learn to be a listener, a diplomat, a deal maker, and a warrior. If you're really good, you'll learn to be an honorable cutthroat as well. Most of all, to your fellow politicians, you have to learn to be what I call "a reliable person."

When I arrived in the legislature in the '60s, I wore a blue serge Nehru jacket and the love beads emblematic of the cool of my Haight-Ashbury district in San Francisco. Those farmers in Sacramento who made up so much of the membership of the assembly at that time had never seen anything like me. They thought I was from another world. But they quickly learned to like my political acumen and willingness to work hard with them even more. I never once breached the commitment to civil rights and to the betterment of my community that brought me to the legislature, but to succeed on those fronts, I made damn sure that I became as cooperative to others as I possibly could be. A few years later when those assemblymen from the Central Valley in their country clothes began affectionately to refer to me as "Farmer Brown in the Afro," I personally blanched. My urban constituents back in San Francisco asked me what I had been doing to gain favor from such anticity folk as the farm representatives. I honestly replied, "Harvesting votes."

So yes, of course, when the Republican governor of California, Arnold Schwarzenegger, called on me to be the master of ceremonies at his inaugural, I agreed. I'm very happy to have the Republican governor of California as one of my constituents. He's not the first of his ilk to be obligated to me. He knows he needs my skills, and not just as a showman.

Governor Schwarzenegger understands that I am that rare thing in politics—the reliable person. Reliable, not because I'm bought and paid for, but because I can be counted upon to know how things work, and, more importantly, can help put a deal together neatly, quickly, and with benefit to all. Get known as a reliable person, a go-to guy, and you are made as an effective politician. Demonstrate that you know how to get something done, big or small, and they'll come back to you. President Clinton, Governor Schwarzenegger, Ronald Reagan, and a thousand others in politics came to Willie Brown because he is the reliable person. People used to assume that another California Republican governor, Ronald Reagan, and I must have had a strained relationship because of our differing ideologies. Not so.

After Ronald Reagan, who had been governor of California from 1967 to 1975, became president of the United States, he was often invited by succeeding Republican governors to revisit the California capital. In fact, he made only one return visit to Sacramento as president and that was at the invitation of Willie L. Brown Jr., Democratic Speaker of the Assembly. So much for the supposed bad relationship that people said existed between Reagan and myself. We had a fine relationship because he knew that I was competent and reliable. As George Shultz, the very senior San Francisco Republican who later became President Reagan's secretary of state, said when endorsing me for mayor of San Francisco, "Willie Brown keeps his word." Furthermore with Reagan, I had taken the time from our earliest days to get to know him.

Back in 1967, the California assembly and senate had summoned the political will necessary to pass some sort of bill decriminalizing abortion. The legislative consensus had been built for the principle, but the bill itself would have to be written along such lines that Reagan would actually be comfortable enough with it to sign it. He was not then the vehement antichoice person he would become as he sought to be embraced by the growing right wing of the party. Still, abortion was difficult for him. Most of the arguments pro and con were on a high philosophical plane. On that level, he could go either way. Having taken the time to get to know Reagan, I realized that if you put things in terms that he could relate to out of his own personal experience, you could move him. I didn't know (and don't know) if he had any personal experience with the question of abortion, but I did know that in his years in Hollywood he had seen the careers, health, and lives of women torn apart because abortion, even when a medical necessity, was then a nasty, expensive, back-alley business, with patients and doctors subject to criminal prosecution and blackmail. If you addressed those concerns in the actual piece of legislation, you could get him to embrace the principle. So I worked with my peers to write a bill that would legalize abortion as a way of protecting the health of patients and removing them and physicians from the threat of prosecution and exposure. This was a civic good that he could relate to. He signed a bill constructed along those lines.

Of course, having Willie Brown be honest with you is sometimes a little more cutting and wry than the typical politician expects. But Reagan and Governor Schwarzenegger are Big Guys. They got the Willie Brown style.

CHAPTER FOUR

Sex Scandals and the Socializing Politician

POLITICIANS ALMOST NEVER EXPRESS regret about their behavior on questions of public policy, but when it comes to their private lives, curiously, they are always ready to apologize. It's bizarre.

Whenever I hear a politician publicly express contrition over some private relationship that has suddenly been exposed, I laugh. And when I hear them promise to seek redemption for having had such a liaison, I just laugh my ass off. This sackcloth-and-ashes routine strikes me as about the most insincere response you could make, and probably the least effective.

Ineffective because the public clearly understands that no disability is created by a relationship between two people that has nothing to do with your public duties and functions.

I don't know why Bill Clinton felt the necessity, at the outset of the Monica Lewinsky scandal, of saying, "I never had sex with that woman." What he should have said to the press was, "This is none of your business. You get nothing out of me. I don't talk about whether I've had a relationship with a lady or not. It ain't your business. Period." Bill Clinton didn't often lose his cool as president, but he did then.

My wife, Blanche, and I have been married for fifty years. We haven't lived together in twenty-five, but we're still close. We talk many times each week. I'll tell you more about her and my family later in these pages. Early on in our marriage, we both recognized a key reality of political life, though.

That reality is this: if you are an attractive person in public life, you're going to have lots of opportunities to have fascinating relationships with women or men. I can think of very few holders of major office in American life, including women, who have not had private relationships along the way. And yet invariably it seems that when these relationships are exposed, the politicians apologize.

Enemies, schemers, the self-righteous are, of course, going to be looking for relationships they think are improper or out of which they think (quite foolishly) they can make political hay. When confronted, you just have to say it's nobody's business but your own.

Personally, I think you ought to glory in any such reputation. My successor as mayor of San Francisco, the talented Gavin Newsom, was caught when a private relationship he had had with a staffer who happened also to be married to one of his top advisors was revealed. He froze. He apologized publicly, especially for hurting his friend, the husband. All well and good, I suppose, but if you're going to apologize for a relationship, apologize to the woman. Frankly, I think he should have leapt at the opportunity to become known as a kind of gallivanting Gavin. I think the public relishes the idea of having someone who's actually alive holding down public office. If you're going to have a reputation, have one for your dashing ways, not for your tears.

A spicy social life really can add to your panache. In San Francisco, the city's hostesses treat me as a star guest because I add flavor to the evening. I've known and appeared with many women during my fifty years of married life and I have never been ostracized or barred from full participation in the social environment because I was with a variety of women. Nancy Bechtle, a superior hostess, enjoys rating my dates. When she invites me to an affair, she invariably asks a day or two before the party, "Whom are you planning to bring? Do we know the name yet?" I always answer her by saying, "I'm still interviewing . . ."

In the course of my life, I have never been accused of any abuse or disrespect or disregard or exploitation of any woman—unlike, say, Newt Gingrich. I've never been brutish to anyone personally involved with me. It isn't my style.

Naturally, it's not easy being the date of Willie Brown either! It's hard to find a companion who can handle dating Willie Brown, because that often means being ignored.

When I walk into a party or public dinner or other social gathering, instantly all the attention is focused on me. Everybody wants to BS with me. My poor date may not know anybody else in the room. My wife, Blanche Brown, will tell you that one of the reasons she ceased stepping out with me was that at parties people would push right past her to get to me. They would knock her over. She was, understandably, offended by such rude behavior.

When I go to a party, I'm not there to float around as part of a couple. I'm a working politician. I work the house. I make sure I talk to everybody there who's significant. And I start with the women! No matter what age they are, I make sure I say hello. I make sure I tell every woman there something about herself. I want them to know how conscious I am of their existence. If I've met them before, I am going to let each one know I remember something about her personally. And that I am continuing to pay attention to her. That's purely sincere. You have to like people and let them know you like and remember them. That goes for the guys in the room too. They want to be remembered.

If you're also locked in to entertaining a date in the course of a party—oh man, that is an impossible duty. So before we go out, I try to explain to my dates what the evening will be like. I tell them, "Now let's get it straight. There's gonna be everybody wanting to take a picture of me. And I may not sit at any one table. I may have to leave you at one table—I'll introduce you to friends there, and they'll look after you. But you may not see me for another half an hour. And I may dance with fifteen people before I can get around to dancing with you. But I love to dance, and we will eventually."

Well, some women don't believe this scenario until they see it. And some don't like it. I have to explain again: I'm busy working. I'm sorry you had to get your own drink. But this isn't an evening out for the two of us. It's a work night for me. And if the lady doesn't get it, then at the next possible opportunity, as gently and as sincerely as I can, I exit the relationship. And I explain to her, "Here's why I'm leaving: you're not ready to put up with my selfish interest in my career. I am selfishly interested in my making sure that everybody in that room knows who Willie Brown is. Because that's who and that's what I'm marketing."

I tell my hurt date, "I can't give up that selfishness. I really love hanging out with you. But henceforth if we are to go out, it is to a movie on a Saturday afternoon where there's no social interaction with other people." I actually go to movies almost every Saturday afternoon to see the newest flicks. That makes a perfect date for me. That and hanging out late at night at a new bar or club—after I've done my evening's work.

Now, conversely, I sometimes run into a woman who wants to be too much a part of Willie Brown, Inc., a woman with her own political ambitions who sees me as a vehicle for them. In that case,

I'm just as selfish about keeping myself and my business a private preserve as I am in demanding the time to pursue that career. There's no room in one political career for two ambitious people. Just one. In Willie Brown, Inc., there's room only for Willie Brown.

I'm often asked: are politicians temperamentally more exposed to extramarital relationships than others? Well, there is something in power that motivates people, women and men, to be more interested in you than they would be otherwise. You can clearly see that in people's behavior towards you when you have power and when you don't have it. You can clearly see the difference. Power is indeed an aphrodisiac. But a limited one.

The opportunities for relationships that present themselves because you have power should not be dismissed. You can meet fascinating women that way, and the world would be awfully dull if you did nothing but the brokering of interests and social networking that is the bulk of life for a modern politician. How you avail yourself of these opportunities depends on your skills at dialogue, your social graces, the breadth of your comprehension of the world, and the curiosity you have about the way we live now.

You can't sustain an acquaintanceship with just the provisions and tenets that power provides. Oh no! If you rely on your power to hold things together in a personal relationship, you will come off as insufferable, as a bore, as an insincere egomaniac. You'll be no fun; the relationship will be just another tedious set of negotiating games. Your date will have no fun.

My friend and mentor, the late Jesse Unruh, former Speaker of the California Assembly and later state treasurer, was a good-looking man but hardly movie-star handsome. He was often overweight, and he had a face full of character lines. But women loved him. Many enemies thought this was only because Jesse wielded power. But his power was merely a door opener. He was clever, funny, charming, and had a brilliant mind. As a result, when it came to women, he had more potential—which he often exercised—than anybody else in the room.

Power and wit open the doors. If you make a speech to a group and do it successfully, you can spot, before you end the speech, the three or four people in the room who want to talk to you personally. Usually they're women. Often attractive women. And they always wait around to talk to you, to shake your hand, to get an autograph. You simply take it from there. Power only opens the door. But for the relationship to be intense, there has to be absolute fascination on your part with the other person too.

Why do so many of these relationships decline in intensity? That's one of the bizarre questions the media likes to ask when they discover that a politician has some interpersonal relationship that isn't on the résumé. Why, the press wants to know, was it fleeting? The press thinks that we must be always looking for a permanent relationship. Well, that's rather puritanical.

The reason why these relationships decline is that they were never built on anything having to do with permanency. They're not permanent relationships—oh, maybe one out of ten might have a shot at permanency—but actually they are fun, quick trips and flights of fantasy for both of you. Frankly, that is the appeal of most interpersonal relationships that politicians stupidly deny: they are flights of fantasy. Totally.

If you want to make a relationship permanent, you can. But don't do so because society suggests you can have only one relationship at a time. I convey to the women who are in relationships with me, "Because we go out, because we date, because we sleep together, that doesn't mean there's supposed to be anything permanent. Do not expect it. Do not demand it."

That sounds mean, but women understand this reality. Level with them and you'll have a friend for life. Out of all the women

I've known, I don't have any ex-girlfriends. I have friends. I keep them. These shamed politicians talk about how they want to be "putting a relationship behind them." I think that's so disrespectful. Relationships change, but I don't believe in apologizing for them or for not recognizing what they are.

CHAPTER FIVE

The Power of Clothes: Don't Pull a Dukakis

I'VE SPENT MORE TIME in the closet than any other straight man in San Francisco, but that's just to choose my wardrobe. I believe that appearance is power, just like money, ideas, and honesty. Politicians should pay diligent attention to assembling an appropriate wardrobe and learning how to wear it. You can tell that most politicians don't think much about clothes—they're always in the same sort of uniform. But I think that clothes are so important (and enjoyable) that I buy all mine myself. I make a point of spending some Saturday afternoons down at the shop of my friend Wilkes Bashford checking out and buying clothes. Most politicians don't have to go to the extremes I do—I have a dozen tuxedos and over a hundred suits. God knows how many pairs of shoes I have. I'm replenishing them constantly and twice a year I clean out my closet and donate the goods to some charity's thrift shop. It's invariably the busiest day of their year when my duds go on sale. Some of the local pols ought to go down and get some of my stuff.

My Uncle Itsie was the man who introduced me to the power of men's fashion. When I arrived in San Francisco in 1951 at age seventeen, he and his wife met my train. I was wearing a pressed cotton short-sleeve shirt and ironed khaki trousers from Sears, Roe-buck. It was a Texas kid's idea of looking good. My uncle took one look at my apparel and was appalled. He decided I desperately needed a makeover. So before we even went home, they took me shopping. That night, in my new duds, we went out to a celebrated black San Francisco nightspot, Jimbo's Bop City. In my new outfit, I was mistaken for Miles Davis. Man, it must have been dark in that nightclub. But I've been hooked on clothes ever since.

A few years later when the young haberdasher (and now my tight friend) Wilkes Bashford opened his men's clothing store, I was among the first three customers. Wilkes recalls, "We kept an eye on this young man who came in on opening day. We knew he wasn't a shoplifter because he had too many questions about the merchandise. He was so inquisitive that we concluded he must have been sent in by the competition. But he's been in almost every Saturday ever since, and he's brought us some wonderful cus-tomers, including Arnold Schwarzenegger, the mayor of Paris, and the vice premier of China. He still knows more about clothes than most of us in the store." Even hats are necessary. They com-plete the look—and given the fact that most men no longer don hats, they make you stand out. I've had a good teacher when it comes to headgear. My fellow Texan and San Franciscan, Mrs. Ruth Garland Dewson, the milliner to high society, stars, and pro athletes, put me into (or under) fine Borsalinos she called "The Willie Brown Snap-Brim." It fit my personality, and I suggest you find a hatter who wants to get to know you, so that you may wear what really suits you.

I regard sharp clothing and good appearance as essential to a politician's success. That a politician be well dressed hasn't always been acceptable, especially in political circles. The great George Washington Plunkitt, one of the bosses of New York's Tammany Hall, immortalized in that century-old handbook of practical politics *Plunkitt of Tammany Hall,* argued against dressing up. He said it made people think you were living on graft. I suppose a few people still think that. They're wrong. But there are some rules a politician, male or female, must follow to be a success in the TV age. Here are some of the things I know about clothes and the politician.

Although you must be well dressed, great pains must be taken to ensure that how you look doesn't diminish or depreciate your value to the voters. Wear the wrong outfit, and your clothes become an obstacle to what you're trying to say. People lose interest in what you have to say when they're taken aback by what you're wearing.

Back when he was a U.S. senator, Tom Daschle showed up one day on the floor of the senate to make an important speech that would be televised. But he was wearing a tan suit and a pink tie. It was cuttin'-edge, high style, but completely inappropriate for the somber well of the Senate. What he was wearing was perfectly okay for a Fourth of July parade or a speech at a summer festival, but not for the floor of the Senate.

Now, I could pull off some high stylin' in the Senate, but even I make sure not to appear dandified when the occasion is somber. Most politicians realize that they can't be cutting-edge in political life, so they go too far the other way, which is why you see so many dull blue suits, white shirts, and red ties on politicians.

That's the tension. You don't see successful candidates wearing cornrows; you don't see candidates for office with diamond studs in their ears. Those things will just make people tune out when they see you. On the other hand, nothing is worse than seeing a politician in an off-the-rack suit with his shirt collar pulling away from him, or the roll of his coat curled up. George W. Bush knows that. You'll never see that happen with George Bush.

Bush is not a clotheshorse. He dresses like a small-town Texas country-club guy, but the people who dress him—his clothes are from Oxxford, a Chicago manufacturer whose clothes offer a more relaxed version of the old Brooks Brothers look—make sure his suits, blazers, and trousers fit terrifically. No collar ever rolls up; no shirt point ever flies away. His problem on the speaking platform isn't sartorial; it's that he can't figure out which door to open when he's exiting—as happened in China.

Bill Clinton was dressed by Donna Karan. He too was always appropriately dressed, though his fluctuating weight sometimes disrupted the fit. He looked very distinguished at times. He was conscious of what he was wearing, as is Hillary Clinton. But Bill was never a fashion plate.

Ronald Reagan had a look completely different than George Bush or Bill Clinton. Always a perfect fit, old-Hollywood style. He was impeccably dressed, fabulously so. He had a wardrobe sense from his days in the movies and on TV. He knew just what to choose. Even as governor of California, he was always meticulously dressed in that high Hollywood glamor style. He didn't look like a dandy dude; he just looked incredibly well turned out. He even wore a pocket square in his coat pocket—the mark of a truly well-dressed man. His pocket squares weren't pointed; they were square and level. But they always had color. And they completed a wardrobe. Reagan was a star!

When it comes to women in politics, the majority are neat in appearance, especially when compared to the guys. But women have to vary their wardrobes or else they get talked about around the office watercooler. People aren't going to mention that Ted Kennedy showed up in the same blue suit again, but they will dissect a woman if she seems inattentive to her appearance and always wears the same sort of outfit. Not that she has to be a fashion leader. Indeed, she can always present a familiar appearance, so long as it doesn't appear that she's wearing a kind of uniform.

Nancy Reagan was a fashion leader—and she had a large budget for clothes, as affluent women often do. Top designers like Oscar de la Renta or Valentino scurried to do a dress for her, and there was always much commentary about what she wore. But Hillary Clinton was not written about in the same way. I don't think many fashion articles were written about what Hillary wore to the inaugurations. You didn't find Hillary being referenced in the popular mind for her apparel. But that doesn't hurt her. In fact, her current appearance is a uniform one. She has lots of clothes, but she strives for a totally nonmemorable look.

Now, Nancy Pelosi, Democratic Speaker of the House of Representatives, clearly reflects the class of women who can spend. She dresses for different events in the course of the day and always looks sharp. Then there's Dianne Feinstein, who also has the resources for high fashion, but that's not her route. She simply doesn't have the clothes mentality. While she never looks sloppy, she sometimes looks hit or miss, as if she were caught between seasons.

Maxine Waters, the congresswoman from Los Angeles, is an example of an attentive dresser. You never notice her clothes, but she's always appropriately attired. You never notice, but her hair is perfect. She's always well groomed and right for the occasion.

The least acceptable female politician I've ever seen, from a sartorial point of view, was Harriet Miers, George W. Bush's White House counsel who had to withdraw her nomination for the U.S. Supreme Court. In those photos of her wandering around Capitol Hill to meet the senators, she looked unprepared. Not like a politician with a message to impart, but like a corporate lawyer in her cubicle. She looked like a corporate nun. She was the reverse of the fashion plate whose clothes overwhelm. But the result was the same. You looked at her and were so taken aback by this "habit" she was in, you completely dismissed what she was saying. She was a disaster on TV.

TV is part of the day. You have to dress for it, even if you're not going to be in a TV studio. So when I'm asked what politicians should wear, I tell them a number of things, but first and foremost to think of the tube.

The key to success on TV is a distinctive but muted appearance. If you're a man, you don't want to wear a white shirt—wear instead a TV shirt: blue or ecru. You want to make sure you don't wear a shirt with bold stripes. You want to be as muted as you can be, but with tones. That's what your tie is for. But use caution with ties: a bright orange tie, for example, stands out on TV like a headlight.

You don't need the physical appearance of a model to look good, credible, and persuasive on TV. Look at John Madden and Al Michaels. They had TV's biggest audience with *Monday Night Football*. And they wore ties and blazers. When it was hot, sure, they'd doff their coats. But they were neat. If John Madden can look good on TV, anyone can. Just be poised, neat, and muted—but with some tone. Be low-key, but not forgettable.

A basic wardrobe is a must. Now, many people, male politicians included, don't devote the time or resources that I do to clothes, but there are four or five items everyone must have.

First, you should have a dark suit for a serious occasion such as a funeral. Make it a blue or dark gray suit, not a black suit even though that might seem like an appropriate choice. The reason is this: it's hard to find a good-quality black suit that doesn't make you look like an undertaker or a bishop.

And at a funeral, even though it might be photographed for TV, you can and should wear a white shirt. You're not making an appearance in your own right—you're there as part of the congregation. A white shirt is right for somber public occasions. Black or gray tie and black shoes, of course. Above all, you must not be a distraction from the seriousness and the sanctity of the occasion.

Then, for an event such as the annual State of the City address in San Francisco's City Hall, or even the State of the Union address, you are moving from the very somber to the upbeat. Do a pinstripe blue suit, with light stripes. For something like that you can wear a television shirt. Pale blue and ecru don't reflect light, so you won't glare. Since these are public events, you can be dressed to face the camera in your own right. Generally, that's a good idea. If there are going to be cameras at the event, dress for them even if you're an extra. This is not to hog the camera, this is to help you, because somebody's going to have you in a picture, and those photos never die. Some mischievous editor will find the worst photo of you that Google or the Getty photo archive can provide and print it.

You must be sure your neckwear doesn't create visual distractions. Stay away from polka dots. Johnnie Cochran, the eminent Los Angeles defense attorney, was a dear friend, but remember those ties he used to wear? Just horrible ties. Just bad taste in ties. You have to take care with neckwear.

Dark blue and gray suits are your evening and dinner wear. You need the proper shirt and tie. After six o'clock (unless you're doing a TV appearance) you wear a white shirt. That's when you can add some color to your neckwear. But again, no polka dots or dizzying stripes. Go for a plain silver or plain gold tie. The yellow adds color to the night.

Of course, along with those two suits, you should also have a blue blazer and gray trousers, and another blue blazer with tan trousers. For spring you can also get a blue blazer with a hint of green—very light. For autumn, get a blazer with fall colors; a hint of gold, brown, or beige. You want these touch notes to be in the threading itself, right in the fabric. And you want them subtle. Avoid plaid blazers.

Your blue blazer is your workhorse. You can add a sportier one for Saturdays, and when you get a little bolder, add a black blazer with another pair of gray trousers.

You'll also want a gray suit. Solid gray, if you're going to have only one. It can be a gray flannel suit, that proverbial garment of the American businessman. It can be light, medium, or dark, but start with a medium or dark.

Then you're almost done. You just have to get into your browns and beiges.

A brown suit is your daytime wear. The brown suit can be of a rougher material, because it's a daytime suit, a daylight suit. I wouldn't wear a brown suit at night. It won't look good. You don't want to get cornered before a TV crew in a brown suit at night. If you're being photographed with a group, you'll look out of place.

And remember: no brown shoes with black or blue suits. You can wear brown shoes with gray suits and, of course, with brown suits.

In my office at City Hall, I kept suits and clothes appropriate for all occasions. You really shouldn't try to get through a public day wearing just one thing. Otherwise, at some time during the day, you'll look inappropriately dressed. Take responsibility for your own clothes for every hour. When I wake up in the morning, I check my schedule and figure out just what I should wear. Sometimes, I change clothes four times a day.

It's a fact, though, that male politicians can get away with wearing the same suit all day, alternating shirts and ties. A woman, however, cannot get away with wearing the same dress or pants suit all the time. If she does, she becomes the subject, the topic of discussion, from watercoolers to message boards and on email chains.

Women have to orchestrate their wardrobes carefully. When a man asks me about a wardrobe, I recommend just what I've told you: a few basics you can build on. With women, I recommend that first they get themselves a good seamstress. Women, unless they have sizable financial resources, have to be smart shoppers. Buying fabrics and patterns for a seamstress to work on is a lot cheaper than couture or even dress shops.

Women in politics need five or six well-fitted sets of pants—gray, brown, black, blue, tan, military green. They also need a complement of blouses or shirts that can be interchanged. And they need a whole series of blazers. For women, the motto is "Acquire, Interchange, Utilize, Complement."

Most important, women in politics should not aspire to dress politically. You have to dress for the occasion, not for a cause. If they're to reach people, they shouldn't appear to be feministic or too feminine.

One thing: women should never wear Nikes, Pumas, or trainers of any kind unless they're also wearing sweatpants. Frankly, Nikes are just ugly. So unless you're in workout clothes, skip the trainers. Opt instead for attractive walking shoes.

That's my advice. My devotion to and interest in clothing has always been such that what I wear—the quality, the fabric, the brand—is what everyone else would like to wear. I actually do program what I am going to wear based on where I am appearing. And I try to make my appearance consistent with the highest standard of the event.

One thing all politicians should avoid: Dukakisism. Remember the photo of Michael Dukakis popping out of an army tank with a helmet on? He looked like a bobble head. Obviously he had to don the uniform to get into the tank, but he should never have been photographed wearing that oversized helmet. He looked like Calvin Coolidge wearing a full Native American headdress or Rudy Giuliani wearing those cowboy boots someone gave him a few years ago.

Don't ever wear a costume or ceremonial garb unless you know already it's going to work for you. If it doesn't look as if it were a natural fit, don't don it. The photo will live forever. I always ask myself: does this look like WLB going to work or going to a masquerade? If the latter, I don't wear it.

Somebody once told me that every candidate should have a personal ethics committee to advise during campaigns. Oh hell no. Instead get someone who majored in wardrobe. Ethics fights can be finessed, but a silly photograph is in your face forever.

CHAPTER SIX

Black Politics and Racism Today

IN 1968, WHEN I was a California assemblyman, I went to Atlanta for the funeral of Martin Luther King Jr. Bill Bagley, a Republican member of the assembly, was in our group. Bill, who now practices law in San Francisco, was a type of Republican you don't see much of anymore: liberal, intelligent, unafraid, open, and collegial. In Atlanta, he drove our little group of legislators around in our rented car. Bill was the only white guy in the car. After the funeral, as we were driving back through the ghetto into the city, Bill noticed that kids on the street were stopping to stare at us as we passed along. Some in our party were nervous about the attention we were garnering. It had been a terrible week in America's cities, with rioting and distress filling the streets in the wake of Dr. King's assassination. But the kids and the grown-ups on the street bore looks of astonishment, not of hostility. Bill asked me, "Why are they staring at us?" I told Bill the truth: "Because they've never before seen a white man chauffeur four black men around." I may have put the expression in a more urban patois when I told Bill what was happening, but my point here on this page is not to shock, but to express a different reality: I was and am a black politician, devoted to the interests of my community, but I also was a very unusual crossover politician. I moved freely in black and white worlds. Indeed, it was not surprising to find myself being chauffeured by white folks, even white Republicans.

In no election that I've run in has more than 15 percent of the electorate been black. But I've never sold out—never become a country-club black person, like former congressman J. C. Watts of Oklahoma or even Secretary of State Condoleezza Rice. I've always kept my membership in the black world. I've worked hard to understand not only the needs of my people, but also how blacks approach politics and how they view candidates.

The black world and its internal social arrangements have, of course, changed significantly in the last two decades. In the old days, your status in the black world had to do with what fraternities and sororities you belonged to. Indeed, it was a common phrase among black people to say disparagingly of someone that he or she "cares a lot more about the Greeks than about Africa." But the Greek fraternities were and are important incubators and social networks. Status in the old black world also, frankly, had much to do with skin shade, hair texture, and economic status. But while those could be factors, they were minor. In terms of electing political leaders, black people were and are much more concerned about your ability to speak up on behalf of black people than they are about your ability to speak up on other issues. What you must show, one way or another, is that you are absent a fear of white people, that you really are unstymied by the white world.

That's one of the reasons, I suspect, why black preachers often have been afforded the mantle of political leadership, even if they weren't always good at politics. Black preachers were viewed as not subject to being influenced or compromised. The perception was that whitey couldn't get to them. The black preachers were financially supported by the black communities, their upkeep provided by love offerings, pastoral aid, housing, and cars. So black people felt that their clergy couldn't be touched by the white world. A minister was seen as a legitimate spokesperson for black people—and that more than anything else determines whether or not you'll get black support.

Ironically, the same perception often keeps black leaders down or left behind in the circles of political power. Once a black person gets into the legislature, the council, the senate, the cabinet, the white power brokers assume that the black member is there just as a spokesperson for the black community. I've had to work hard, have had to show exhaustive and unerring command of subject matter ranging from timber to triage, from education to the environment, just to get taken seriously on these subjects, because at first, other politicians figured I was only interested in one thing: being a spokesman for the black community on issues of concern to the black world. Well, I am, but I am also a very bright student of the whole world. And of political power.

You have to fight against that limitation. You have to fight against the perception that you are only a specialist on black matters. Ron Dellums, for many years a member of Congress (and now the mayor of Oakland), is a brilliant thinker on the armed services and on foreign policy. He had to work doubly hard to be taken seriously as such. Colin Powell moved at the highest levels of military leadership, yet for a long while part of his fight upward involved defeating the perception in the American political establishment that he was just a super-sergeant, a guy whose expertise was on the condition of the black soldier.

The fact of the matter is that as a black politician, you're constantly having to spend energy to integrate yourself into the minds of white power brokers as a real, pure force of politics. You also have to spend as much time reintegrating yourself into the black community. That reintegration is total and completely necessary;

it's also a lot of fun. You have to reintegrate because once blacks see you as distant, as not capable of speaking for them, then you're gone. You lose that membership fairly quickly. As you ascend and make the crossover, you're in grave danger of being no longer seen as hip-hop, as urban. Your world becomes one foreign to your black base.

You'd still be admired, but you lose that camaraderie, even that protection, that comes naturally when people see you as a paid-up member of the community. You can try to keep up by maintaining your membership in the NAACP, by attending the right cotillions, by having your picture in *Jet* magazine or *Ebony*. These, along with the fraternities and festivals, are reaffirmations. But they are nonassertive reaffirmations. And when people suspect that your main point of reference is some white club, or some title like dean at a nonblack university, you have become very distant from the black world. There'd still be pride in your achievements, but not a willingness to transfer the spokesperson responsibilities. Very few have made this crossover, have kept their balance. Ron Dellums is one. I am certainly another. Indeed, I'm unique, given the fact that I've had to run and campaign in districts with very small black electorates. And I also have been courted by the white world—and not as a lackey or a token.

The way you reintegrate as a politician is to keep yourself in play not just as a member of the community, but also as an arbiter. I don't mean a mediator, I mean an arbiter in the barbershop or the beauty shop, the places where people vote unconsciously on your membership.

You've got to go to the barbershop frequently, just so you can maintain your membership. You, if you are to be a successful politician, have to be the one who decides the barbershop questions: "Who was better? Mudcat Grant or Satchel Paige? And why?" You have to know about the Birmingham Barons. You have to know the music. You have to know the movies. You have to know the sports.

You'll need to be in and of both worlds. It's a difficult balance to maintain.

No question but that the level of discourse in American life has sunk far below what it was twenty or thirty years ago. People in public life—pundits as well as politicians—now feel free to indulge their worst prejudices. In the 2006 midterm campaign, the allegedly witty Ann Coulter said of the truly witty Maxine Waters, long-serving member of Congress from Los Angeles (and former colleague of mine in the California legislature), that were it not for the concept known as "affirmative action," Congresswoman Waters would never have held a job "that didn't involve wearing a paper hat." That's a slander, but these days a common and acceptable kind of slander. As the great author and blogger James Wolcott wrote of today's downgraded political discourse, "conservatives will always find a way to reduce [prominent African Americans] to low-paid, low-status, low-skilled caricatured servitude. That's their idea of cutting black personalities down to size and putting them in their place. Whatever uniform they wear, it's still a monkey suit in the eyes and mouths of the white-makes-right contingent . . ."

Well, as I once said to the *Los Angeles Times*, "It's tough being black, mister." The *Times* seemed to regard that as being above my station. Point is, the work and speech of politicians and pundits is often a barometer of feeling in this nation. Racism, once decried, is now back crying out its ugliness. And acting out. When I was mayor of San Francisco, I made sure I appointed supervisors, commissioners, and heads of agencies and departments who were black. But there wasn't an institutional change. On the day I left—within the hour I left—my successors began a consistent, systematic dismantling of that. Now when I walk around City Hall, I see almost no black faces. When I left, blacks were ousted. It had nothing to do with qualifications. It had to do with politics. Either African Americans are not considered to be sufficiently a part of the so-called progressive San Francisco political operation to make them powerful, or the black constituency doesn't carry enough clout with City Hall.

Condoleezza Rice will face the same experience I did. Colin Powell did. Senator Ed Brooke faced the same thing. When the power leaves these people, the changes they made will leave as well. There will be no institutional changes in how people think about black people until people in general change. And African Americans in leadership roles will lose the changes they've effected unless they create a hammer to enforce those changes. It's not a question of failing to seize opportunity; it's a simple fact. A simple fact of politics.

I'm sure the nice people who now inhabit San Francisco's City Hall would react with shock at the thought they might be racist. But the fact is the number of black employees there is nowhere close to representative of our numbers in the population. Racism may not be conscious, but it certainly is back.

The lesson for African Americans, I guess, is that you have to fight every day to maintain the progress you have made. And if you're a black politician you'd better expect to face the charge every day of being above yourself. God forbid you should appoint blacks or friends to high office. Loyalty is something that is allowed only to the country-club set. Well, this isn't racism of an old-fashioned sort, but in America today we are in a kind of denial about race in public life.

CHAPTER SEVEN

Women in American Politics Today

IN TODAY'S UNITED STATES Congress, seventy-four members of the House of Representatives are women. (The Speaker, the first woman Speaker in the House's history, Nancy Pelosi, is a San Franciscan.) In the Senate, sixteen members are women, including the two senators from California: Dianne Feinstein, former mayor of San Francisco, and Barbara Boxer, from Marin County just across the Golden Gate Bridge.

These are impressive numbers, a quantum leap from the '60s when only two or so members of the U.S. Senate were women and there weren't even proper facilities for female members in the gyms and lounges of the institution. Indeed, there are so many women members of Congress today that we no longer bother to count them, which is surely a good sign.

But the fact remains that women still occupy less than 20 percent of the seats in the 535-member Congress. Given that roughly 50 percent of the voting population is female, this means that, despite the progress since the '70s, there really has not been any sea change, any institutional change, in how politics works and how voters think. The politics of America are still excessively dominated by, and set up for success by, white males.

The body politic today routinely produces resources, learning opportunities, and candidacies for male candidates, but it doesn't do that for women. Women candidates still need to look to some special organizations, like Emily's List (which some of us have supported for years) to obtain special resources. Male candidates haven't needed gender-special support. That women candidates still need special help is a sign that although they're growing in numbers, they are still a novelty. Society hasn't changed much.

As a practical matter, it's still much less of a challenge for women to achieve political success if they have had the benefit of a connection to a popular male mate—whether it's Hillary Clinton; Doris Matsui, widow of the late California congressman Bob Matsui; or Mary Bono succeeding Sonny Bono in Congress from down in Palm Springs; or the late Sala Burton, succeeding her husband, the well-beloved but ferocious Phil Burton, in Congress from San Francisco. Indeed Nancy Pelosi, who had built up her bona fides through decades of work and fund-raising for the Democratic Party in Northern California, will be the first to tell you that in her first foray into electoral politics, which was to succeed Sala Burton as a member of Congress, she benefited from the endorsement by Sala Burton, Phil's widow. Pelosi was the designated successor to Phil and Sala.

In a sign of how little things have changed, it's still a fact that women candidates benefit if they are related to a deceased male politician. But if it means showing that you have been an able workmate or heiress to the political gene, why not exploit it? Kathleen Brown, who was elected California state treasurer, benefited from being the daughter of Governor Edmund "Pat" Brown of California and the sister of Governor Jerry Brown. Down in Los Angeles, Janice Hahn, a city council member whose district encompasses 250,000 people, was the daughter of popular Los Angeles politician Kenneth Hahn and the sister of ex–Los Angeles mayor James Hahn.

Some women have had additional or different qualities that marketed them successfully to voters. Consider black women. The four black members of Congress elected from California in 2006—Maxine Waters, Juanita Millender-McDonald (who died in April 2007), Diane Watson, and Barbara Lee—are all women. In San Francisco we've had more black females serve on the city's legislature—Doris Ward, Ella Hutch, Willie Kennedy, Sophie Maxwell—than we have had black males. (There have been only two of those, Terry François and the Reverend Amos Brown.)

Additionally some women have achieved support by reaching out to what are still niche constituencies like lesbians. Almost all women candidates, regardless of their appeal, still need the special support of women-focused fund-raising groups and committees.

But for various reasons, women who have special ethnic or niche appeal are rarely able to make their candidacies attractive to the larger population. The very reason why black women appeal to black voters makes them less attractive to Caucasian voters. One of the reasons why black women candidates succeed in the black community is that in our community women have always been the ones in which we've put our trust and confidence. It's the mother-raisin'-the-children syndrome. That's what it is. The mother and the grandmother bring up the children, run the family operations, marshal the family, organize the resources. So we react as a constituency more positively to female leadership than we do to male leadership. Other than the preachers, we tend not to place much confidence in the males who offer themselves to us as leaders.

In the white community, black female candidates have to fight the perception that black women are not competent, and certainly not leaders. When whites look at black women, they see the women as servants, maids, and cooks (just as my mother was). No matter how astute these women are, they've never been viewed as worthy of much beyond domestic-service status. You look on these damn boards of cultural and social organizations in any big American city and you see that there's no conscious effort made to ensure that there's female representation of an ethnic nature on the boards.

Being able to cross over into the white community is essential for any black, female or male, to succeed as a political figure.

I suggest black women lay the groundwork by looking to become active on the boards of social, cultural, and charitable institutions like symphonies, museums, and hospitals. It's the way to get respect from a world that otherwise is content to eschew or label you. You have to demand the opportunities to enter these worlds.

Both as speaker of the assembly and as mayor of San Francisco, I worked hard not only to give women opportunities, but also to provide women with opportunities to grow with each other, learn from each other, and be empowered. As mayor I sponsored five "Women's Summits," held annually from 1998 until I left office. These one-day, twelve-hour-long events at the Moscone Convention Center attracted five thousand women annually. We had great headliners like Oprah Winfrey; the late Ann Richards, who had been governor of Texas; the late Molly Ivins, so notable and iconoclastic a journalist; Tipper Gore, the activist for families who also happens to be Al Gore's wife; Kathleen Brown, the treasurer of California; former surgeon general Joycelyn Elders; TV journalist Soledad O'Brien; and the inspiring educator Dr. Lorraine Monroe, who did so much to lift up urban school students.

All sorts of women came—from corporate executives to women on welfare, from high school students to politicians. We really mixed them together all day long so they could learn from one another, get some candid tips, and get inspired. Women organized the events and ran the show. My long-time fund-raiser (and mother of my darling daughter Sydney), Carolyn Carpeneti, pulled the sponsoring funds together from corporations via the women who worked in them. And women like Susan Mosk, a leading attorney, U.S. Congresswoman Maxine Waters, Anne Gust, another leading woman attorney who also happens to be Jerry Brown's life partner, and successful minority businesswomen like Jackie Besser and Caryl Ito chaired the actual events. I was, of course, thrilled each year to be the only man among five thousand women.

I really wanted women to have the chance to connect and cross over their worlds. We kept the price of tickets down and provided hundreds of scholarships. We even ran training programs before the events for women in public housing projects so that they would feel fully credentialed in their own minds when it came time to participate.

Over the years since then I've heard hundreds of stories from women who attended who then went on to better things: running their own businesses, managing families smartly, running for office. Providing these incubators of power was something I could do that society wasn't doing. It's something we should be doing. Maria Shriver, as California's First Lady, is now, through her Minerva Awards programs, providing women a chance to connect, converse, and grow. I want women to have the chance to see that they can fit into worlds they might not imagine they could. And I encourage all women, but especially those interested in politics, to make the effort to reach the other worlds of society. That's how I grew. It's how everybody grows.

And when in office, make yourself an integral part of the political system. Don't be an outsider. Be an insider. Work on being a reliable part of the system, make yourself effective.

CHAPTER EIGHT

Asking for Money Is Part of the Business

BUILDING CONSENSUS, MAKING YOURSELF helpful to opponents, and building a reputation for reliability are all necessary if you're to have a successful life in politics, but there's one truth that's absolutely basic. It's this: if you don't want to ask people for money then you don't have any business being in the world of politics.

Asking for money is part of the game, as is knowing how to contain the contributors. If you can't ask for money, you should get out of the game unless you're someone like Steve Forbes, who in 1996 and in 2000 ran for the Republican presidential nomination, or Steve Westly, the Silicon Valley entrepreneur who helped found eBay and who ran unsuccessfully in 2006 for the Democratic gubernatorial nomination in California. These two gentlemen, each with a large private fortune, financed their candidacies out of their own pockets. When you've got your own personal pot of cash, you don't have to ask others for it. But if you don't have such a pot, you've got ask for dough. You also must learn how to manage the expectations of the people who give it.

There's nothing shady about fund-raising if you hold yourself and your donors up to the proper standards. In my forty years in politics I've probably done more individual campaign fund-raising than any other person. I've raised about $100 million—more than anyone else in state politics. In that time there's never been an occasion when my fund-raising activities have been held to be crooked.

I've raised more money from the tobacco industry than anyone else. Yet there's no one who can tag me with the charge that Big Tobacco bought me. Hell, I'm the politician who took their money and then raised their taxes. Raising their taxes was good public policy, and they should have supported the tax increase. I certainly didn't feel restrained from doing that because the cigarette industry also happened to be among my biggest donors.

We raised their taxes to fund research into cancer that the reasonable part of the scientific world believed was often due to smoking. We wanted to verify and explore that information, and do more research that would help the afflicted people. I had the political belief, along with many others in the assembly, that the tobacco companies should help pay for that research.

It was dumb of the cigarette industry not to have supported this increase on their taxes. Had they supported the legislation, it would have improved their image.

Anyway, Big Tobacco certainly didn't regard me as one of their boys. At the same time I was raising campaign funds from them, they were also working hard and sneakily to knock me from power. (I shall tell you later the story of how I sustained my speakership despite a win by Republicans that saw them briefly gain a majority in the house in the 1994 elections via tobacco money.)

Why did I even bother taking the money from treacherous Big Tobacco, especially given all the criticism of me that I knew would be made for having taken the money?

The answer is simple: we needed the money. And the best way

to get it, without risking the seats of more vulnerable members, was to have Tobacco give it just to me. I would then spread it around, regifting it through my campaign office. I could take the money because I was not vulnerable to defeat. San Francisco voters were never going to reject slick Willie Brown, their political pride and joy—and the fount of so many good things for San Francisco like extra money for schools and hospitals. So I was content to take the heat. I could stand it. For other members, taking contributions directly from Big Tobacco would have been as politically fatal as lung cancer. Willie Brown, on the other hand, could take the heat about campaign contributions. I could even joke about them.

Once as mayor of San Francisco, I was asked to serve as the celebrity auctioneer of a number of events and prizes. The money from the bids would go to send some deserving San Francisco public high school students on a study trip. On one of the events, the bidding was slow—it was a chance to have a private lunch with me! The bidding was to have started at $1,500, but I was having trouble getting the bids higher. Finally, I said to the well-heeled crowd of movers and shakers who always liked access to the top, "Look, this is a chance to have lunch with me for fifteen hundred. I usually won't even pick up a phone call from someone who has contributed a mere fifteen hundred to my campaign. Now you're getting lunch with me!" The crowd roared and the bidding took off. We sold the lunch for a fine sum, and some kids got to see Paris and speak French with the natives. Was what I said literally impolitic? Probably. But I can't resist a good line.

I was also speaking a home truth of politics. It's a fact that a contributor always expects consideration from the recipient. It would be inaccurate, dishonest, to say otherwise. Big contributors all expect that you'll take their call.

Usually, they're sophisticated enough to know they can't ask for anything. They should understand that a campaign contribution buys the contributor nothing more than an investment in good government. But in forty years, I haven't been able to get past the fact that the calls have to be returned.

CHAPTER NINE

My Solution to the Campaign Finance Mess

WHEN TOM DELAY, the disgraced Republican leader of the House of Representatives, was indicted in September 2005 for money laundering, he was indicted for behavior that was perfectly legal twenty years ago.

What DeLay got caught on was siphoning money donated for federal campaigns into state races. I'm sure he must have been shocked when he heard he was being prosecuted for this—it was not new behavior, it was just now inappropriate behavior. Must have mystified him.

His indictment is not a sign of progress or even of justice. Rather, it's a sign of just what a silly-ass game of hide-and-gotcha the business of fund-raising and regulating fund-raising has become. And that's not good, because fund-raising ought to be transparent and not subject to the manipulation of rules.

It doesn't diminish DeLay's guilt to say that in every state of the union there's at least one Republican and one Democrat who is as guilty as DeLay. It's just that in most states you don't have prosecutors as clever and as vengeful as Ronnie Earle, the Texas DA who figured out how to use the rules to bring DeLay down.

I don't think DeLay should get off for his crimes, but I do think the bigger crime is a climate in which many cheat, and in which the opportunities for corruption, weirdly enough, are enormously enhanced. Here's how it works, here's why it's bad, and here's what should be done.

The old system of fund-raising—before the 2002 enactment of the McCain-Feingold Act—was relatively pure and had enormous deterrents built into it. It certainly was simple. All that was required of a candidate (or a campaign fund-raising committee) was that it report how much money it took in, who gave the money, and on what it was spent.

Now there are limitations on how much money a contributor can donate, how much a candidate or committee can spend, and what they can spend it on. And how they can spend it. But the rules didn't change behavior one bit, nor did they halt the rise in the amount of cash rolling around in politics.

With the new rules, fellows like DeLay didn't change their behavior one bit: they went on raising money, getting cash and commitments wherever they could. They just hired people to fit it all into the new regulations. Expensive people, people who developed all sorts of Rube Goldberg–like mechanisms, elaborate devices to hide the money.

You have to hire specialized consultants, if for no other reason than that they know the regulations. Usually they wrote them. They work in the government to write the regulations, leave government employ, and hire themselves out to candidates to tell them how to beat the very system they designed. What a system! None of the money spent on consultants reaches the campaign, and it raises the cost of campaigns inordinately.

Nor has the new system really cut back the size of contributions. George W. Bush raised $220 million in the last election. You don't seriously believe that came in from a myriad of small contributors, do you? Yet that's what the records show.

But wasn't the old system, under which you took whatever money you could raise and then simply reported it, corrupt? I don't think so. For one, it had a deterrent.

Ironically, what led to this new system of hyperregulation was an example of how the old system, under which you simply reported who gave and how much, actually worked. Charles Keating, the head of a group of savings and loan companies, contributed money to five senators because he wanted them to help get federal bank regulators off his back. One senator, Alan Cranston of California, received $1.3 million, a vast amount, from Keating in the '80s. Cranston properly reported the contribution, which ostensibly was to have been for "voter registration," but when the contribution was publicized, voters and other legislators were scandalized that one man could contribute so much wealth to an individual campaign. Cranston paid for the Keating contribution with his reputation and his job. The U.S. Senate reprimanded him in 1991, and, under that cloud, he chose not to seek reelection. He retired. His career was done.

Today, ironically enough, a big contributor aided by a campaign's consultants could find many ways to hide so large a contribution so that the public would never learn its true source. The campaign financing reforms, frankly, have backfired and made things worse than they were before.

The best answer is complete revelation and let that be the deterrent. Let the model be (and I'm serious) the income tax return in which individuals report the money that comes in to them, where it came from, and what they spent it on. Income tax–type reporting, with jail penalties for fraud, would be an effective and easy solution to the problem of nontransparency in campaign fund reporting. Right now the system just defeats itself, hiding funds and providing golden opportunities for corruption.

Right now everybody knows that people are paying big money for access and for favors. We just don't know who's paying the really big money, hidden as it is under all the regulations.

Under an income tax–type model, you'd have an idea. You'd know who was contributing, how much they were contributing, and on what the candidates were spending the money. You'd be able to see who was paying for ambassadorships and access. Right now, you just can't tell.

And don't tell me that the public financing of campaigns would mean more equity and honesty. The public financing of campaigns just introduces more regulations. Regulations that will be gamed, just as today's campaign finance laws are being played for all they're worth.

Keep it simple.

CHAPTER TEN

Should One Politician Call the Cops on Another?

PEOPLE HAVE CRITICIZED ME as speaker of the assembly and as mayor for not calling the district attorney or U.S. attorney or other ethical or legal authority when I have suspected skull-duggery among the membership or the staffers.

It's true. Rarely have I done such a thing. That's because I take my responsibility to protect the institutions very seriously.

Notice, I didn't say, "cover up" or "hide." I don't believe in that. For one, it's suicidal. You help cover up a crime, and you're on your way to jail. But I do believe that the institutions have to be protected against venality, and I think that you also have to protect your power and value as a real political figure. I have never countenanced corruption in the statehouse or City Hall, and have done much to stop it—but I haven't resorted to whistle-blowing. It hurts the image of the institution and its members. It's counter-productive.

Whistle-blowing takes you out of the loop. You'll be cut out of all information banks. Develop a reputation for turning in your colleagues willy-nilly, you're going to be one isolated figure, and you and your institution are going to be in grave danger.

You cannot be the guy who does the prosecuting and think at the same time you're going to be the confidant of people. You will not have the confidence of people who want to ask you for your judgment on things that may serve them well along with serving you well. You won't be an effective leader unless you have complete, free-flowing information from inside as well as outside. And those who provide information have got to know that you are not going to turn them in for a photo op. Not that you let them get away with a single dirty thing.

It's also counterproductive to your office as a leader or a mayor to be a baby prosecutor. Because many times if you were to develop a piece of information into something by which you could prosecute, you'd be in the business of having to develop additional evidence. That would automatically place you at odds with whoever is giving you the original information. And it's not always necessary to prosecute people to stop them from doing bad things. For instance, I know of a guy. I hear all sorts of stories about him. Once I heard he had been soliciting a bribe for a vote. Obviously he should not have been doing that. Well, in this case I quietly removed the guy from the decision-making process. I didn't need proof; I didn't have to develop evidence. I just told him he was out and he couldn't vote. He got all indignant and wanted to know why he couldn't participate.

I didn't tell him the truth, which was that I had heard that he was trying to take a bribe. I told him instead that someone was looking to set him up by offering him a bribe. Thus, for his own safety he was being moved out of the process. He went away sheepishly. My little story, which suggested that what I was doing was saving him from the kinds of perfidious enemies who prey upon a naïve and honorable gentleman, gave him some sort of out and got him out of the way. But he knew that I knew the truth, which was that he was playing around with nasty people and that it had to stop.

Most individuals like this one didn't realize they were bordering on illegal conduct. It didn't look bad to them. It didn't fit their idea of evil. They thought they were just being sharp. Even if they did think they were edging beyond the law, they would never acknowledge that to you. You'd get nowhere trying to get them to see that. But if you can get them to see the facts of life and do so without calling in prosecutors, then you save a life and do no harm to the system. The system is never damaged if you do preemptive strikes. That's far more effective than grabbing somebody after the fact. You will also maintain your place in the information loop. None of your sources will feel you'll snitch. And believe me, you need sources and snitches. Next to money, information is the most valuable commodity in politics.

PART TWO

Willie Brown Rises in the World of Politics

Willie Brown recalls his arrival in San Francisco as a wide-eyed teenager, his political mentors, his rise in the world of politics, his family, and his ascent into political power—with various tribulations along the way.

CHAPTER ELEVEN

A Black Teenager Arrives in San Francisco

WHEN I FIRST ARRIVED in San Francisco in 1951 as a teenager wanting to go to a decent college, I had no intention of going into politics. The idea that I would one day be sitting in the White House negotiating with the president of the United States was not a thought I ever would have entertained. I never even imagined being elected to office, let alone to the mayoralty of San Francisco or the speakership of the California legislature. At seventeen, I'm not sure I even knew what politics was.

As a kid in Mineola, I followed current events and politics mostly through the weekly black newspapers sent down from Kansas City and Chicago. So I knew of people like Adam Clayton Powell Jr., the dapper, powerful congressman from Harlem, but he was an influence in the way that musicians like Duke Ellington were—a stylistic and general inspiration. Black politicians were from a distant world. There was no politics for black people in Mineola back then. I might just as easily have thought of a career in the movies or on the football field. A political career just never entered my mind.

I had ambitions, of course. What I wanted to be when I arrived in San Francisco at age seventeen was a math teacher. If you had asked me then what I would like to have become at age fifty or sixty, I probably would have told you that if I had become a math teacher in a public high school with a weekend job selling goods at Sears, Roebuck, I would have regarded myself as a success. That would have been the fulfillment of my American Dream.

My mother, Minnie, wasn't even sure that she should let me go to San Francisco. Uncle Itsie, her brother, wanted me to come. But while Itsie was a glamorous guy with fine cars, clothes, and women, mother wasn't sure he was the best influence. "Itsie doesn't have a job," she pointed out to me, "he doesn't go to church." But he always had plenty of money, and he had standing in the community. Uncle Itsie, whose formal name was Rembert Collins, had come to San Francisco during the Second World War when good-paying jobs in the military and in shipbuilding were plentiful for black people. Itsie worked in the Bethlehem Steel shipyard, but he really rose in the world by meeting the needs and wants of busy people with cash looking for action and excitement. Starting in 1943 when he became thirty-eight and was beyond draft age, he left the war industries and started running card games. A smart fellow was Itsie. He took what opportunities the world presented to him. He thought I was smart and was a kid who deserved something more than what Mineola had to offer.

Minnie wanted me to have opportunities too, but she also wanted me to have some straighter influences. So she offered a compromise: I could come to San Francisco under Uncle Itsie's sponsorship, but I also had to get a job, join a church, and go to school. I had already heard of one school up in the San Francisco area called Stanford University. I didn't know much about it. But I heard it was the best. I told her about that.

So she let me go in Uncle Itsie's care. He certainly knew his way around many worlds, not just the gambling milieu. I was soon on my way to meet one Dr. Duncan Gillies, a professor at San Francisco State College. I told Dr. Gillies about my ambition to study math at Stanford University. He listened attentively and put me through some math problems. He gave me the news: I was indeed very bright and mathematically inclined, but the schooling I had received in Mineola in the segregated schools left me way behind my white peers. I was shocked. Of course, I knew that we black kids were receiving a separate schooling, but I had no idea how deficient and inferior it was.

But Dr. Gillies said that his own school, San Francisco State College, might be willing to take a chance on me. I had to agree to a ten-week trial as a probationary student. In those ten weeks, I crammed. I used a dictionary like I never had before. I had to look up everything. All I did was study. But I did well and they accepted me. Eventually I began to do well enough to pay attention to other campus activities, like fraternities and dating. And I encountered political campaigning and clubs, which then as now were a big part of campus life.

I quickly joined Jones Memorial United Methodist Church, a church with a strong civil rights commitment even in the early 1950s. Eventually, I became so active that I would become youth director.

In the first weeks before I enrolled in school, though, I had time on my hands. Uncle Itsie did his own teaching, which was as influential as any formal schooling would prove to be. He instructed me to learn the city. Each morning in those early days he put his pocket change on my bureau. My instructions were to take the money and go each day to a different part of the city, walk as much as I could, and talk to as many people as I could. I was fascinated by this Baghdad by the Bay, by all the different kinds of people, and their various cultures. They never seemed to tire of talking. They still don't. And I have never tired of the habit Uncle Itsie started in me. To this day, I walk some portion of the city every day. Today, I repeat the process with my five-year-old daughter, Sydney. She, like me, delights in the sounds, sights, and smells of the city. She particularly likes Chinatown and can sound out a few Chinese (as well as Spanish) words. When I first started roaming the streets of San Francisco, I knew no one and never expected to be anyone. Now Sydney accepts as normal that her father's photo adorns the walls of many shops in town.

As soon as I was enrolled in San Francisco State, I looked for odd jobs. Trying to earn money to go to school and to survive, I was desperate for any job. At the outset Uncle Itsie was helping by providing a place to live, but that was just short term. He was generous, but that occasional pile of pocket change was all that he could afford. I got no money from home. Nobody in the family had a nickel to send. So I registered at State College's job service for any and all jobs. Most were odd jobs; some were very odd jobs. One of the oddest had a lasting impact on me.

It was listed at State College this way: "clean out the attic of Westminster Presbyterian Church." I knew where that was, not far from where I was living. So I went over there to clean out this attic. When I arrived I realized that this attic probably had not been touched since the church was built about eighty years earlier. The dust and dirt were thick. If I had had any clue about the health hazards associated with dust and dirt back then, I probably would have walked out. But I did the job. It took two days. By the finish, I was darker than I am now. And then I had to help the janitor clean the floors.

All this was noticed by a man named Allen Sparks, who was director of social services for the church, along with his wife, Beryl. They were a young couple who had gotten their jobs with the church right out of college. What impressed me was that they were not preachers. They were social workers. More importantly, they were something I had not yet encountered in this world: they were socialists, Christian socialists. I thought they were Quakers or something. They did all sorts of things for people that I didn't know church people did. If somebody got arrested, got in trouble for domestic violence, got in trouble for drinking, lost his job, had a kid in trouble—they would help. They were like ward heelers.

I was impressed by their willingness to help people and also by the array of needs that people in a big city had. Back in Mineola, people got in trouble, but it was all taken care of by the family unit or maybe by my grandmother putting in a word with the sheriff. The Sparks really impressed me, because they worked hard for people just to help them.

They were very depressed, though. This was their first time working in the ghetto. They were having a hard time building trust and getting through to the people who needed them. After they saw how hard I worked on the cleaning project and knew that I was in school and thus presumably bright, they offered me the job of janitor of the church. I think they also wanted someone around who could translate, as it were, and someone who was also interested in them and in people. They taught me to be proactive on behalf of anyone in need. And of course, I began to learn a lot about social conditions and the way in which society burdened people. From the Sparkses I learned something about public service.

At the same time, academically, I began to move away from my interest in math. One day a classmate of mine, who would later become a judge in Alameda County, Benjamin Travis, told me he was going to apply to law school. He suggested I accompany him to the admissions interview. I had no interest in law school then; I didn't even know what it was. But I went with Ben downtown to the

Hastings College of the Law, a branch of the University of California. I sat with him while he answered some questions about the law, current events, politics, and judicial topics. As he answered, I realized I could answer the same questions just as well if not better. At the time at San Francisco State, we students had a lot of bull sessions going on in the cafés and classrooms, in which I participated often and well. But I thought they were just bull sessions. I had no idea that I had any special aptitude, interest, or insight. Certainly I didn't think it was anything I could capitalize on. But it was apparent from this session at Hastings that I had some capacity and talent for a profession that I had known nothing about. I applied to Hastings and got in. At the time, frankly, it was easy to get in to law school. You didn't have to take the kind of exams you do now. Nowadays, I doubt I could get in to law school.

I stayed at Westminster Presbyterian Church. While I was working as the janitor, the church gave me a small room next to its gym. It probably had been designed as a dressing room for a coach. It had just a daybed, a tiny bath with a shower, and that was it, but I took it. And I lived there for years, learning from the Sparkses and from school. Some sort of future, quite different from any that I might have envisaged back in Mineola, was beginning to shape itself, but I still wasn't thinking of politics.

I had so little money, I had to make it stretch out. One day a week, I would buy a loaf of day-old white bread, a can of tuna, and a jar of sandwich spread. I'd open the tuna, drain off the water, and mix it into the jar of sandwich spread. I'd place that jar of tuna spread and that loaf of bread outside on the windowsill of my room—that was my refrigeration. That practice was not uncommon at the time and is still common today in San Francisco's crowded Chinatown. Every morning I made a sandwich for lunch. The whole jar of tuna and sandwich spread would last me for a week. That's really what I survived on.

As students at San Francisco State and at Hastings, we didn't have the kind of student centers that campuses have today to provide hangouts. We hung out in cafeterias; they abounded in San Francisco then. Now they're all gone. I guess they've all become Starbuckses.

At the corner of Van Ness and Market, there was a branch of a chain called Gene Compton's restaurants. When I could afford it, I'd go there for breakfast and gossip. For nineteen cents you'd get a piece of toast with butter and dried prunes with syrup. That would be breakfast. Then that tuna sandwich would be lunch. For dinner, when I had money, I went to a place called the LaSalle, up the street from Hastings. You could get a burger, french fries, and a salad for about $1.50. We had no money for beer or wine, so we didn't develop any drinking habits.

For a date you might go to Moar's on Powell, the leading cafeteria in the city. Or you might go up the street to a steak place, Tad's, where they cooked a steak in front of you and served it with a potato and salad for $1.09. (I've known women who weren't as tough as those steaks.) But that was a treat.

Then you'd walk down to Woolworth's at the cable car turnaround. Woolworth's had a great lunch counter, pricey by our standards, but popular with people who had steady jobs in the stores and offices downtown. It was too expensive for me, but I liked the peanut clusters there. They were an old Southern treat. In the San Francisco of that day you had food and treat items that were popular with working people all across the country. Today we've lost a lot of that blue-collar cosmopolitanism. But then, seared ahi with a freshly made sauce beats a tuna sandwich on stale bread any old day.

San Francisco was a relatively progressive city even then, so at most of the cafeterias black people were welcome. But there were some restaurants where you wouldn't try to go in. And there were plenty of places where you wouldn't try to get a job or even shop. You just didn't.

Some stores downtown discouraged black shoppers, but some clothing stores were open. The first suit I bought on my own was from Howard's on Market and Fifth, in the heart of the downtown shopping district. Ben Friend and his son Gene owned the shop. They later went on to own other, better stores, but Howard's was hip. I still remember that first suit I bought: a double-breasted blue serge suit that came with a light blue shirt and yellow tie.

Buying clothes at Howard's was quite a change from what I was used to in Mineola. In Mineola, blacks bought from the Sears, Roebuck, catalogue. But it took forever. I'd order a pair of shoes and by the time they arrived, I'd have outgrown them. Sometimes you wouldn't even get what you ordered. They'd just ship you what they had. I remember wanting ankle boots—I was going to be the first kid in Mineola with ankle boots! And the ankle boots I wanted had a gold chain as an adornment. But by the time those ankle boots got to me, the gold chain looked unfashionable. Even worse, I had grown a full size. But I wore those boots anyway. To try to return anything to Sears and get a replacement was so complicated and time-consuming that you just put up with what they sent you in the first place. So I wore those ankle boots. They ruined my feet. But I wore them anyway. I wore them for three years.

So I was glad to get to San Francisco where at least the choice was better. Up in the Fillmore, in the black shopping district, we had stores like Pressler's and Uptown Clothiers. They had clothes with outrageous bright colors that black people wore. Eventually white people began to wear the same colors—but only on the golf course! Yellows, reds, greens, and oranges—and cut in exotic styles. Great stuff.

On every corner there was a shoe store: a Johnston & Murphy on one, a Stacy Adams on another, a Florsheim on a third, and a

Thom McAn on a fourth. The poor people went to Thom McAn, so you couldn't, if you were a dude, be seen coming out of Thom McAn. If you shopped in Thom McAn, you made sure you carried your purchases out of the store in a brown paper bag brought along for the occasion. You didn't want anyone seeing you buying in there.

Anyway, by the time you got something home, it was probably out of fashion or at least out of season. The reason is that at most stores, blacks couldn't get credit. You couldn't even pay for things in installments. The best you could do, which is what we all did, was buy on the layaway plan. That meant you could pick out an item and start paying for it, but you couldn't pick it up until you had paid in full for it! That could take several months. You'd lay away something in March or April that you wanted to wear in the summer, but by the time you finished paying off your layaway, well, it was October or November.

It was a terrible world, when I think back on it, just a terrible world. But you tolerated it.

San Francisco's Western Addition, an old neighborhood of Victorian houses, had become San Francisco's Harlem and was in full flourish when I arrived. Fillmore Street was its 125th Street. It's been justly celebrated as a center of jazz and nightlife, but it was also a community center. That's where the churches, associations, and doctors were. As I grew familiar with the town and began to be seen around as a bright young fellow, people in the Western Addition and in politics began to take an interest in me.

Scores of people encouraged me to get into politics and helped me when I did. Two people were crucial, though. One was a black physician named Dr. Carlton B. Goodlett. The other was a political genius, a white fellow named Phillip Burton.

Dr. Goodlett was not only a black physician, he was also an entrepreneur, community leader, newspaper publisher, and generally a cantankerous old party. He meant so much to me and to San Francisco's blacks that when I was mayor I happily signed Supervisor Michael Yaki's legislation to rename the street on which City Hall sits in his honor. (That was also when we named a portion of the Embarcadero, the roadway on San Francisco's waterfront, for the celebrated columnist who also had done a lot for me, Herb Caen. Dr. Goodlett and Herb Caen couldn't have come from more different worlds, but they both became good friends to me and frankly invested a lot in my success.)

Dr. Goodlett was different from many physicians I knew in the Western Addition. Many physicians subsisted off referring patients to attorneys who would then pursue injury cases for the patients. The physician would get a cut for the referral. Dr. Goodlett refused to do that, much to the consternation of many patients who were looking for a payday from an accident. You had an injury, Dr. Goodlett would treat you, but you had to find a lawyer on your own. He was a man of principle.

He'd had quite an education. Originally from Florida, he received a bachelor's degree from Howard University in Washington, DC, and then earned a PhD in psychology from the University of California, Berkeley. He taught for a while but then went back to school, earning an MD from Meharry Medical College in Nashville in 1944. He started practicing medicine in San Francisco in 1945 and was soon involved in everything.

With money earned from his practice, he bought a weekly newspaper, the *Reporter*, and then merged it with a rival black paper, the *Sun*. By the time he retired, he was running nine weekly papers. He also developed a savings and loan bank, and he was constantly involved in real estate development. He developed projects here and there, sizable ones, but he was so cantankerous that he was never allowed to become a truly significant developer. But he also had balls enough to bid for the airport parking con- tract. And he got it. I admired his energy and his catholicity—he believed in being involved in everything.

Dr. Goodlett once even ran for governor: in 1966 he was mad at the Democrats for something and though unsuccessful, managed to cause them headaches. He was trouble, but principled. Once Mayor John F. Shelley tried to throw him out of his office. Goodlett began shouting, "It's not yo' office. It's the people's office. And I represent the people." He took up the cudgels easily and fiercely. Goodlett was a man of seeming contradictions. He was an ab- solutely committed political radical who was also a hardworking capitalist. He was an astute politician who was also a shrewd busi- nessman. His newspaper, the *Sun-Reporter*, was decidedly progres- sive in its political views. But—and I used to kid him a lot about this—he paid minimum wage. He was also a talent spotter.

He not only was the leading physician for blacks in San Fran- cisco, he was the leading physician for political radicals, white rad- icals. He himself was tough as nails, but he was also involved in progressive peace causes all over the world. In part because of him, I became involved in the antiwar movement against Vietnam as early as 1962.

He was very close to Phil Burton, the white politician who be- came the leading congressman from San Francisco, serving from 1964 to his death at fifty-six in 1983. Goodlett dined at least once a week with Burton and his wife, Sala. Today, Speaker Nancy Pelosi holds Burton's seat. She was their political daughter.

Back then in the early '60s, Phil was representing San Francisco in the California assembly. Even then he was a leading political force in San Francisco, fighting the old machine and turning the town upside down. Until Burton came along, politics in San Fran- cisco consisted of a comfy arrangement between Republicans and old-line Democrats. Both groups were rather conservative. The Democratic cadres were Irish with a heavy involvement of the civil service and the less radical elements of labor. Burton was considerably more radical and politically much smarter.

My introduction to Phil Burton was via Dr. Goodlett and Phil's younger brother, John. John and I met when we both were enrolling in Air Force ROTC at San Francisco State. This was during the Korean conflict, so we were looking, like everyone else, for deferments from the draft. ROTC sounded like a better deal than a lottery ticket that might land me in a combat foxhole. So one day I was standing in line. We were arranged alphabetically. The guy next to me was John Burton.

At the time, I wouldn't have guessed that John would end up in politics. At San Francisco State he spent most of his time selling football betting cards. He was all frivolity. Sometimes it seems that it was entirely accidental that we both ended up in politics.

That began a long, storied, and often tested friendship. John was in the assembly with me and later became a congressman himself, serving with his brother, and despite battles with cocaine and booze, recovered himself to become a prime leader in the state senate. It's hard to believe that the John of today, an abstemious vegetarian, is the same wild boy I knew back then.

His brother, Phil, was the most brilliant and gifted politician I have ever met. Phil had a commitment to civil rights, civil liberties, and the needs of the poor that made him an ideological radical. But he also had a gift for acquiring and institutionalizing power, especially through his genius for reapportioning seats in the assembly and in the California congressional delegation, that marked him as a master politician, a super politician.

CHAPTER TWELVE

Phil Burton, Herb Caen, Jesse Unruh, and Me

PHIL BURTON WAS AN INNOVATOR. He invented a tool of campaigning that is now so commonplace that it seems as if it's been around forever. And versions of it are so varied and ubiquitous that the device itself may no longer be as useful as it was when Phil first came up with it. It is called the "slate card."

It's a small document you could take with you to the polls, similar to one issued by the elections department back in the days of one-language ballots and simple districts. The election department would send you this little card summarizing the ballot when it sent you all the ballot information. You could check off the squares and take it into the voting booth with you as your own personal guide to the ballot.

What Phil did was to issue a document that looked exactly the same as the official card—but he would have filled it in for you. He would have showed you how you were supposed to vote. You didn't have to bother reading a proposition or studying a question. If you were with Burton, you took his card into the voting booth and marked the Xs just as his slate card showed. It was enormously effective.

On Election Day, as we went around to see how we were doing, we would inspect the wastebaskets at the polling places. We'd just count up the discarded Burton slate cards and have a rather accurate sense of how our candidates were doing.

Today almost every political club, almost every campaign, almost every political consultant issues a slate card. As a candidate you even can buy space on a card. It's like being a Google sponsor—your name comes up first. Indeed, slate cards are a lucrative business for campaign consultants and an expensive one for candidates buying space on them. But so widespread today is the use of slate cards that I think they now have lost their effectiveness. But Phil Burton started it.

Slate cards and reapportioning districts—he was a genius at those things.

When I was coming up, I wanted to be just like Phil Burton: ideologically committed and superskillful at the game of acquiring and securing power. I was awestruck by everything he did: just breathtaking, often subtle maneuvers. Every good San Francisco politician wanted to be just like Phil Burton. We thought, quite correctly, that was the nonpareil of politics.

He defended his turf, San Francisco. In 1960, as a member of the California assembly, he stage-managed a reapportionment of the assembly that left San Francisco, with a population of about 750,000 but declining in numbers, with five assembly seats, while it was arguably entitled to four seats at best. Meanwhile, Orange County, the fastest-growing county in the state with a population of 650,000 in 1960 that was certain to burst, got only three seats. The difference, of course, was that San Francisco was Democratic, while Orange County was not only Republican, it was the stronghold of the nutty right-wing John Birch Society. Burton wasn't going to give conservatives a chance.

The fifth seat for San Francisco had its own peculiar history. When the reapportionment was being done, the reapportioners mistakenly or stupidly divided the state up into seventy-nine assembly districts. But the assembly, by law, has eighty seats! So Phil Burton, in front of his colleagues, took a map of San Francisco and drew some lines on it and came up with a fifth seat. What became the fifth San Francisco assembly district was an area of town already represented by a longtime incumbent, an old-timer named Ed Gaffney. Ed was not much of a parliamentarian—he spoke only once a year in the assembly and that was to endorse Mother's Day.

Phil, like Dr. Goodlett, was also a talent spotter. He liked what I was doing in the early days in civil rights, and he liked my personality. He also thought I could win Ed Gaffney's seat in the assembly.

Other blacks had run for the assembly before in San Francisco but didn't do so well. But the times were changing and I was getting to be a prominent person because of my work in civil rights. There was no question but that I had the bona fides.

For example, I conducted the first sit-in demonstration in San Francisco. This took place in 1961 at a new housing development called Forest Knolls and eventually resulted in a fair-housing ordinance being enacted in San Francisco.

It was just one of those strange, spur-of-the-moment things. One day while some friends and I were at a baseball game, my wife and some of her girlfriends decided to go see a model home at an open house in this Forest Knolls. The minute Blanche and her friends, who were also black, showed up, the real estate people showing the model house just up and disappeared. They wouldn't show the home to Blanche and left her and her friends standing there.

Eventually they went home. From the ballpark, I called home as usual to see what was happening and Blanche told me about it. I told my ball-game buddies, John Dearman (who is now a judge in San Francisco) and Everett Brandon. They said, "Well, if that's the case, let's go see what they'll do with us." So instead of going home from the ball game, we went to Forest Knolls.

We went to the model home, and the same thing happened: the real estate people showing the house just disappeared. They bailed. But John and Everett and I didn't bail.

We had looked around and found that the telephone worked, the television worked, the refrigerator even had some beer in it. So we decided to stay. And the first sit-in in San Francisco began.

At the scheduled closing time, the real estate people hadn't come back. They sent a guard to close up. We said, "Fine. We'll be back tomorrow." Everett, an enterprising guy, said, "Why don't we call the newspapers and let them know these people won't deal with you about the house, and that we are going to sit in."

Sure enough, we called. The next day—a Sunday—we decided to up the ante a bit. I got my wife and kids and we all went by as a family after church. The television cameras and the newspapers were all there.

We started a demonstration that lasted about two weeks. Dianne Feinstein, now California's senior U.S. senator and then a neophyte in politics, showed up to demonstrate along with us. The mayor finally stepped in and convinced the developer that he should show us the house. I was interviewed, of course, on national television. One friend from back east called and said, "Listen, I've always known you to be far more definitive than you are in this interview. Is there something you're not saying about this deal?" I said, "Yes, they keep saying I want to buy this house. But I actually don't want to buy it—I just want to be shown it. I don't have the money to buy that house!"

A couple of friends said if the developer offers to sell you the house, you have to buy it—otherwise you'll embarrass black America. So all of us will chip in. Go ahead; say you want to buy the house.

By the time we had been shown the house, my wife didn't want to buy it either. It wasn't up to her standards. But as a result of that demonstration, we did the get the housing ordinance passed.

I was engaged in a variety of civil rights struggles over those early years, organizing them, representing people who had been arrested. I was very active. And so in 1962, I embarked on my first election. I would run against Ed Gaffney for the seat that had been reconfigured by Phil Burton as San Francisco's "fifth seat" in the assembly. The decision to run was reached jointly by me, Phil Burton, Dr. Goodlett, and other members of the black community, along with more leftish labor unions, including those that represented janitors, laborers, service workers, and by Jewish civic groups that had been active in the civil rights struggle.

My opponent, Gaffney, had been in the assembly since 1940, except for one term in the early '50s when he had been defeated. Although the district had been reconfigured by Phil Burton to include the Western Addition, it was hardly a black district. In fact, I have never run for an assembly seat in a district that was more than 15 percent black. When I ran in '62, it was still largely an old-fashioned San Francisco district with a heavily working-class, heavily Irish population.

It was a marvelous campaign. It was done on pennies. I spent only $4,900, a pittance compared to today's multimillion-dollar campaigns. And I ran the campaign out of a bar, the Playpen, owned by one of the few black Republicans in San Francisco, Bunny Simon. Even back then, I got along with Republicans. Bunny's son Tim is now a member of the California Public Utilities Commission, having previously served as Governor Schwarzenegger's judicial appointments secretary—a post for which I endorsed him. Political friendships go back a long way in San Francisco.

That '62 campaign was a great amalgam of black, Jewish, and labor support. We had an awful lot of fun, hitting the doorsteps, targeting voters with mail, and ending up each evening drinking at the Playpen. I would lose to Gaffney, but only by 900 votes out of 31,000 cast.

Two years later, having learned a lot and having become more famous around San Francisco, I would run again.

After the '62 election, I did not stop campaigning or reaching out to San Franciscans who were not in the district but who were prominent and had the interests of the whole city at heart. Some of them, seeing a politician of note in the making, sought me out. One was Marian Conrad, a hardworking lady laboring in public relations who was also well connected with San Francisco's society, journalistic, and arts worlds. She was related by marriage to Barnaby Conrad, a famous San Francisco bon vivant, novelist, painter-sculptor, matador, and bar owner. Barnaby's bar, El Matador, was a celebrated international hangout. All sorts of celebs gathered there, along with the society, media, and political types. I began dropping by.

Marian invited me to lunch, and she was impressed. She suggested I meet with a man named Herb Caen, who even then was San Francisco's most celebrated columnist, the chronicler and conscience of the city.

At that first lunch with Herb, we talked for hours about politics, San Francisco, journalism, sports, clothes, women—everything. At the conclusion of the meal, he said, "I think we ought to have lunch every week." For the next thirty-five years, until his death, we did.

He had decided early on that I was, first, his kind of person, and second, his kind of elected official. That never varied. He began to quote my quips in his column. In his breezy style, he reported on my doings and carryings-on. But he wasn't a constant Willie Brown cheerleader. He criticized me. He took me on when he thought I was wrong on an issue, or personally too arrogant, or bullheaded. If he thought there was something for which I should take a shot, he shot me—and he was so incisive a writer and wit that it made me wince. But he always treated me with friendship.

We became famous for our weekly lunches on Fridays at Le Central, which also included a coterie of other friends. People used to gather at the window to watch us and look for an excuse to come in and talk with us. Many people thought we divided up and controlled the city from those lunches, but they were mostly laugh fests and bull sessions. I still miss Herb to this day, but his picture hangs over our table at Le Central, where the gang still gathers on Fridays.

Herb and I did lots of things together. We went to ball games, charity events. We always spent New Year's Eve in Paris, and we roamed San Francisco together in search of the best of everything from haute couture to hot dogs. When I met Herb, the friends of his from his generation were tiring of the ramble. But I was ready for it. Plus I shared his curiosity about everything. He was ready to go anywhere, and did. That's what I think made him so preeminent a reporter: he was always going out, going in search of the city. Today's reporters rarely leave the office. Herb loved roaming the streets. He had curiosity.

Through his column, readers began to discover that I was a San Franciscan who loved the place and its spirit. This helped me enormously in my second race in 1964.

Of course, we had help from some new issues and from some astute polling conducted by Phil Burton. The big new issue was a plan by the state to run a freeway directly through sacred Golden Gate Park and adjacent neighborhoods. From a highway engineer's point of view, the freeway through the park made perfect sense: it would connect the Golden Gate Bridge with freeways to the south, making an easy route from the southern suburbs to the northern. It had the support of incumbent Ed Gaffney. But it was anathema to San Franciscans.

In those days, California's burgeoning growth was made possible by its expanding freeway system. But unlike Southern California, where the new freeways cut through what was often open pasturage, San Francisco was already a built-up city, with proud neighborhoods, some of which had just been ravaged by urban renewal. So there was a lot of opposition to the plan for a freeway through Golden Gate Park and to any further sundering of neighborhoods. But this was before the age of community protest. The feelings of the citizenship needed articulation and the issue needed leadership. In my 1964 campaign we managed to do just that. People loved it when I held a press conference in the park under a beautiful sheltering tree that I promised to protect against the ravaging highway engineers. No one even seemed to notice that this particular tree wasn't in the path of the proposed freeway! It was a marvelous issue for us, and in an early triumph of political activization, the freeway was never built.

We did more than empower and energize neighbors, we enrolled them as voters. In 1962 we didn't even think of trying to register new voters, of trying to activate the previously uncommitted. You can't win without expanding the base. The principle behind this—involve the excited but uninvolved—has animated my thinking in every political battle since.

There's a corollary too: once new people are involved, you have to make room for them at the table. Scores of political leaders have lost votes and clout because they have failed to make room for new blocs. You've got to make room. Sometimes in the legislature, as speaker, I would notice that an incumbent was no longer the real representative of his community. I would not want to lose that seat, so I would find a new, more attractive candidate. And I would always take care of the displaced politician by finding some other office for them to seek or finding some perch for them somewhere.

On Election Day 1964, I handily beat Ed Gaffney. I would never lose another election in my life.

When I went to Sacramento to take my seat as a legislator, my first move, though, was a lulu. I got on the bad side of the most powerful man in the house. This was Jesse Unruh, speaker of the assembly. In my first action I voted against Speaker Unruh when he was being reelected speaker.

I voted against him because he supported Ed Gaffney. I didn't even know I was going to oppose Unruh until my name was called on the roll. I hadn't even thought about it. I had just reacted to Unruh's name and I knew I couldn't vote for him. I hadn't planned anything. When I voted against Unruh, John Burton, who had just been elected to succeed his brother, Phil, in the assembly, blindly followed. Then a third guy named Stanton, who absolutely hated Unruh and who just assumed that the two of us must have something going on, voted against Jesse when his name was called on the roll. At the end of the roll call, Unruh had all the votes but our three. I gained a lot of attention by having cast a vote against Jesse Unruh.

Of course, the speaker punished me. On the floor of the assembly, he seated me with a racist. At the time, members were not seated with members of their own party, so Jesse put me next to a conservative Republican from San Mateo County named Carl "Ike" Britschgi. I straightened Ike out, though. His real problem was that he had never before met a black man; I introduced him to the real world. We became friends.

And Jesse assigned me to a tiny office, next to the cafeteria, with a very conservative Democrat, who was out of favor. This was Jack Fenton from Los Angeles. He too had beaten one of Unruh's candidates. But Jack and I became great friends.

Over the years, Speaker Unruh and I also became friends. One day, a few years later, after I pulled off some parliamentary maneuver that impressed him and gained his respect, Unruh said to me, "It's a good thing you're not white." I asked him why. "Because," he answered, "if you were white, you'd own the capitol." He eventually decided the best way to handle me was to turn me into an ally. Unruh taught me quite a lot. He was the first speaker to think creatively about the role money, unprecedentedly large sums of money, would have on the legislature and its members. His creativity lay in the ways he began to think about to corral this money and keep it from corrupting the house. Other speakers previously had just dealt with the circumstances of politics in which they found themselves, but Unruh worked to shape those circumstances. He really was imaginative about using the gears and levers of power. He believed in remachining things, not in just operating the levers. So he taught me not only how to attain power but also how to think about it imaginatively.

That's something most politicians never do. Most just want to do deals. I learned from Unruh that you could shape the game itself. He was like a football or basketball coach who cooks up amazing new offenses that no one ever thought of before, but which were just waiting for someone to seize the day and invent them.

CHAPTER THIRTEEN

My Own Family Life

OFFICIATING SEVERAL MONTHS AGO at the wedding of one of my nephews and his bride in the San Francisco suburb of Walnut Creek brought back to mind another part of my life that began back in the early days and which, like my political life, has gone through a lot of changes. At my nephew's wedding, I pointed out that in September 2007 my wife, Blanche, and I would mark fifty years of marriage. It's just that we hadn't lived together in twenty-five years. "I don't know," I said, "whether the marriage failed and the relationship survived or vice versa, but something very valuable lasted."

Blanche and I, obviously, have had our ups and downs over the years, but we have three terrific children, we talk to each other every week, and it's been my pleasure to support Blanche and our family financially all through the years. I would never allow any member of my family, close or estranged, to fall into want or need. We still share many things, though there are a few secrets.

At the close of my nephew's wedding, where I had remarked that Blanche and I were still married, Blanche came up to me and said, "Willie, when we hit that fiftieth anniversary, I'm going to hold a big party in my new Oakland apartment—for myself!" That was enough of a hint for me. I spent hours over the next weeks searching for just the right piece of jewelry for her and gave it to her at a lovely tête-à-tête to celebrate our anniversary. She showed it off to her friends at her party.

As you know, I've led quite an active and varied social life over the years. Blanche maintained her cool about my life. But every once in a while she made it clear who was boss. One day just before I was to be inaugurated as mayor of San Francisco, Blanche—along with thousands of other people—read an item in Herb Caen's column that implied a girlfriend of mine and I were going to get married. One of Blanche's friends asked her about the story. Declared Blanche, "Listen, she may have him at the moment, but come inauguration day and he's up there on the platform being sworn in, I'll be the bitch holding the Bible." Blanche has always kept our family together.

With my wife I have had three children, now all adults. They are my two older daughters, Susan and Robin, and my son, Michael. With Carolyn Carpeneti, yet another girlfriend and an attractive blonde from San Francisco, whom I had the good sense to train in the fund-raising business, I had a baby five years ago. This is my daughter Sydney. I love hanging out with my little girl. Sydney and I spend Sundays together. That continues a family tradition: no matter how busy I was with my politicking, Sunday was to be spent with my children. That's Dad's day. Sydney and I often walk together through San Francisco's Chinatown or one of the other great exotic districts of the city. I try to go to her school events.

Sydney seems to have the same gene and love that I do for "working a room." Several months ago she performed in a dance recital. I went as her date. We parents all brought flowers to give to our children after they danced. In the lobby after the show I gave my little daughter her bouquet. She smiled sweetly, handed me back the flowers, and said, "Daddy, wait right here. I have to go say hello to people." Off she went to say hi to her little friends. Every once in a while, she brought over a parent who wanted to say hello to me. Then Sydney would say, "Stay put, Daddy," and she'd go off on her rounds. I wish all the women I go with to events were Sydneys.

Sydney also likes pro football and loves to slam the leather dice cups with me as we play the old San Francisco game of Boss Dice while watching the games on Sunday afternoons. I taught all my kids a love of football, basketball, and dice. But no one is as fast at the mental arithmetic that makes a good dice player—or fund-raiser or state budget maker—as my little daughter Sydney.

My firstborn, Susan, was born eleven months after Blanche and I were married. She was just a delightful child. She ended up being the only one who hung out in the bars of San Francisco with me when she was a kid. As a little bitty kid she sat on the bar stools and ordered Shirley Temples. She loves baseball and picked it up, I imagine, watching me pitch in the softball leagues. I pitched for Herman Warren's Half-Note Bar. As a five- and six-year-old she was hanging with us older folk. Even then, she had a lot of poise, moving from world to world easily.

Surprisingly, her teachers thought at first she wasn't bright. I knew better, just from her social interactions. But we did discover when she was about ten that she had a learning disability, dyslexia. She transposed words and letters, inhibiting the speed with which she could learn. It was actually discovered by a teacher who knew Susan was smart. At the time, very few understood dyslexia. The public schools weren't paying attention to it, so we took Susan to the private Kittredge School where they helped her. Later she attended the Urban School of San Francisco, an excellent private high school. Thence she went to College of Marin and on to New York University. From there she went to film school at the University of Southern California.

Susan has always been a filmmaker. From the time she was

eleven or twelve she was making movies. Her first was called *The Mean Man's Christmas*. It was about me! Her little brother, Michael, played me. Robin, our middle child, played Blanche. Susan continues to work as a documentary filmmaker, often focusing on the lives of San Francisco school children. With the help of San Francisco philanthropist Maurice Kanbar and the Bayview Opera House she recently did a film about San Francisco children visiting Africa and France. She also teaches filmmaking at the African American Art & Culture Complex in San Francisco. And under the inspiration of U.S. District Court Judge Marilyn Patel, Susan has helped recruit children of color to sing in the San Francisco Boys Chorus. More than forty boys, under Susan's guidance, have begun voice training under the Willie L. Brown Jr. Music Scholarship program at the Boys Chorus. And Susan has taken on the work of organizing the photo and video archives of my own Willie L. Brown Jr. Institute on Politics and Public Service.

Our Robin was more like Blanche. She's left-handed; Blanche is left-handed. She's athletic and Blanche is every way athletic, artistic. Robin works for *Newsweek* as an art director, having graduated from the Parsons School of Design in New York. Robin married a photographer, a white guy, Bobby Friedel, and they now have two little girls, Besia Rose Friedel and Matea Rae Friedel. Robin and Bobby were married in San Francisco at the City Club where my old friend the Reverend Cecil Williams of Glide Memorial Church performed the ceremony.

Robin is the ultimate New Yorker. She loves working in the media world. She worked for *LIFE* magazine and is especially proud of the issues she collaborated on commemorating civil rights anniversaries. She's also worked on the launches of new magazines at Time Warner and is always excited about the next issue of *Newsweek* she's working on. Robin has the vibrant style and excited interest that New Yorkers seem to have in all things. For a while, she tried living in Los Angeles, where she worked for the *Los Angeles Times*, but while she enjoyed her work, L.A. seemed like an outpost to her. She was soon back in the center of the world: New York City. I like to think I'm on top of news and trends, but when I visit or talk with Robin and her family, I feel as if I'm being happily thrust into the middle of next week's news.

My son, Michael, never wanted to be anything but a business-man. He dropped out of San Francisco State University and started his quest by renting out skates in Golden Gate Park on Sunday afternoons. He graduated from the skate rental business to managing the coffee department at the Cost Plus store down on the waterfront. He saved his Cost Plus money and opened a shoe store, selling new, fashionable shoes from London, on Post Street near Hyde. Michael anticipated the expansion of the hip Polk Street traffic up Post Street but he was a little ahead of the times. The store did not do well. But like his father, he learns from every-thing—misses as well as hits.

He started a second store on Grant Avenue between Vallejo and Union in North Beach. Then he found himself a small space, five or six hundred square feet on Haight Street, and he opened a shop called Solo, and then another store on Haight called True. These he has parlayed into additional stores and businesses, in-cluding a bar on Haight Street and a shop in Walnut Creek.

He lived with a woman, put her through law school, and then when she graduated and became a lawyer, he broke up with her and started dating the woman he ultimately married. They were married in Hawaii about four or five years ago. I performed the marriage. His wife, Isabelle, already had one daughter, Tyler, and since then they have had a son, Mateo Brown, and a daughter, Lourdes Brown. The five of them live in Oakland. Michael's branching out from retailing into housing development. All my kids are solid citizens.

None of my kids has ever been involved in drugs or any negative thing that would create an issue for the family or for a political campaign. The worse stunt Michael ever pulled was to build a skate ramp in the backyard, creating terror with the neighborhood parents because their kids spent all their time in our backyard on that rickety handmade facility.

Michael also graduated from that into skateboarding throughout all of Northern California. I helped bring the X Games to San Francisco as mayor, in part because I saw how enthusiastic kids like Michael were about extreme sports. The Games added a lot of energy and joie de vivre to the old city.

Blanche would clue me in on what events to attend as the kids were growing up. I always showed up, no matter what I was doing, as requested by Blanche. But Blanche had the primary responsibility to provide caregiving while I pursued my politicking. That liberated me. But for anything of any significance she determined that I was to be there. It was never at the request of the kid. She always did that. In exchange for all her care, she always got Sundays off. Blanche could disappear. She could do anything she wanted; she didn't have to have anything to do with us on Sunday.

I got the kids up in the morning. I cooked their breakfast for them. I got them dressed for church and drove them to church. After church, I always took them to lunch at some place like Compton's Cafeteria or Moar's Cafeteria. They were the simple places I had haunted as a starving student, but the kids considered them to be quite an elegant outing. And then on Sunday afternoons, if I had to pitch softball they went with me, particularly Susan. Every Sunday evening I cooked dinner for them. The menu was always the same: rack of lamb with glazed carrots. I don't think any of the kids eat lamb to this day. I never knew how much they detested my cooking until much later.

At dinnertime, I insisted that we listen to some tape reflecting black history and then talk about it. I played an awful lot of speeches by Dr. Martin Luther King, Jr., during Sunday dinner so they'd know something of where they came from and the struggles their people went through. The kids never objected. They were always attentive, well mannered, and never gave me one ounce of trouble. It was a tough discipline for three lively kids, but they listened, and if our conversations were any measure, I think they learned. I do regret they didn't like my rack of lamb, though.

Not all my efforts at their education were successful. I had wanted them all to play the piano, something I always wanted to do but never could do. So I bought them a piano, one of the first investments we ever made. Not one of them ever touched the instrument. When I finally got rid of it, it was as good as new.

Their relationship with their mother is a marvel. They tell her and discuss with her everything under the sun, most of which never reaches me unless Blanche needs any help giving them advice. If she needs help, she will ask me, but I don't intrude on their relationships with their mother. Blanche does share with me, however, about what the kids are going through. But the boundaries there are something that I respect.

I've tried to give my kids a lot in life, including help with cars and homes. Shortly after graduating from high school, every one of them got a car. Michael has destroyed maybe two or three. Robin destroyed one. Susan is the only one who never destroyed a car.

More importantly, every one of the children had my commitment for her or his education anywhere in the world if they wanted it. Full price.

Occasionally politics intruded on family life—often in a happy way. When Robin was about to deliver her first child, my first grandchild, I was hosting a meeting at the White House with Bill Clinton. I interrupted the president to tell him I had to go for the birth of my first grandchild.

He announced that to the whole crowd. The president had his driver take me to the airport and I flew to New York to see my first granddaughter.

David Dinkins, the mayor of New York then, had a car and siren meet me at the airport to whisk me from LaGuardia to the hospital. I was there within hours.

That's how it's been for most of our lives. I've never missed any child's birthday—wherever they are. I also have taken the entire family to Paris; I have taken each one of the kids on a trip to Europe. Robin, Michael, and Blanche are avid football fans, so I include them in my box seats. Susan loves baseball, so she always enjoys the baseball tickets. She controlled the mayoral tickets behind home plate! She was very sorry to lose those when I left office.

My kids may not have had a conventional upbringing, whatever that is, but I was absolutely determined that, unlike my growing up, there would be a male presence in those kids' lives. I used to always be there and I used to drag my political friends and their children into the house, whether it was George Moscone, John Dearman, John and Phil Burton—they came into my life, my house, and added a male presence. It was good for the kids to know other kids and dads whose families were in politics. I particularly remember John Burton's daughter, Kimiko. She was a good friend of Michael's. It was a pleasure to have all these kids and grown-ups forming a kind of tribal circle.

Although Blanche and I led very different lives, there was never a breakup. The two of us kept the family circle going. We've always been in each other's lives. We're friends.

Blanche, who is part Filipino, and I met at San Francisco State. I was in the black fraternity Alpha Phi Alpha. Every year we had a college female we designated as the sweetheart of Alpha Phi Alpha. Blanche was the sweetheart. I was the social chair and convinced the membership that they ought to set aside a small amount of money each month for flowers, candy, and gifts for the sweetheart. I told the boys we should show all the other fraternities how you really charm the girls. Of course, I intended to take personal credit for all of this with Blanche. Uncle Itsie would have been proud of me, using that kind of political thinking to steal Blanche away from a little football player who was paying her court as well. Two years younger than me, Blanche was a first-class dancer. Later, she taught at both San Francisco State and Hayward State University. She is now a retired college professor from the state system. She also had a dance troupe, the Wajumbe Performance Ensemble, that has traveled all over the world, including Africa and Europe. Her emphasis on folk art wasn't just aesthetic. She really was and is into folk religion. She has gone from having a float in the annual Carnaval parade in San Francisco to being a respected elder in the Yoruba religion. She is a full priestess of Oshun and is a hounsi in the Haitian Voudou religion.

I used to kid her, asking when she would break the neck of a chicken, but she is very serious and is much respected in the spiritual field. But one thing—I made sure I kept the family assets in my name. I trust Blanche, but I didn't want any property ending up in the hands of a group that might even remotely be a cult. That could have led to headlines.

CHAPTER FOURTEEN

Gay Rights: How Some Historic Legislation Was Really Made

IN THE SUMMER OF 1968, running for reelection, I was looking for endorsements by groups in San Francisco, and scores of organizations were looking for candidates to back. So one night I attended the endorsement evening sponsored by an early gay group called SIR, or the Society for Individual Rights, which was meeting in a donated room over a storefront in San Francisco's seedy Tenderloin neighborhood. That was all the group could get. Gays weren't very popular then.

As a matter of fact, the word *gay* hadn't even then come into wide usage. SIR indeed was less a precursor of gay groups like ACT UP than it was modeled on intellectual and ideological groups from the civil rights era. SIR focused on changing laws and ending police harassment, though it also published early community bulletins and ran health campaigns. It tried to work through mainstream political channels and it made its arguments intellectually and ideologically.

But you didn't find mainstream people in the membership of

SIR. Teachers, police officers, firefighters, nurses, lawyers who were gay couldn't afford to join groups like SIR. The social cost was way too high. Identify yourself as a gay person back then and you could lose your job. People were in the closet out of total necessity.

Needless to say, many politicians shunned groups like SIR. But I wanted endorsements and believed in people being able to live unhindered lives. I had been a leading activist in the civil rights movement in San Francisco and wasn't going to stop now.

So I went to the SIR endorsement meeting. It was the last of about six such meetings I attended that evening, so I arrived late. The meeting was under way. I put my name on the sign-up sheet. I would be the last speaker, after John Burton, my friend and ally, who was running for another San Francisco assembly seat.

The room was crowded, all seats were taken. So I stood in the back next to Burton and listened. I noticed that after making their general pitch, everybody closed by saying, "And I will vote to enact the model penal code." Each time, the place would go ripshit crazy with applause. Well, by the third time I heard that, I asked Burton, "I'm not familiar with this model penal code they're talking about. What is the real story?"

John said, "Well, it's a revision of the general penal code being carried by Al Song [a Democratic state senator from Los Angeles]. One of its modifications is that it removes criminal penalties for certain sex acts [like oral copulation or anal intercourse] between consenting adults." Burton told me that Song's model penal code would involve making more than four hundred changes to then current California law.

Well, I instantly thought that the politicians who were garnering applause by saying they would vote to reform the code were getting away with something. The sheer political fact was that no bill that contained four hundred changes in the law was going to pass—not for years. So the pols who were up there promising weren't telling the whole truth, and they weren't really intent on helping solve the problem. They could say, "I'm for it," but given the reality that such a bill would not pass, they didn't have to really deliver.

When I rose to speak, I said exactly that. I said, "You've been applauding wildly for anyone who says they're for the revision of the code. But the replacement of the whole code isn't going to happen. Anyway, you are interested in one section of the code, and one section only.

"And that's the section having to do with sexual acts between consenting adults. So why don't we do this: Why don't we concentrate on a bill dealing with this one single section you're interested in? Why don't we just move to eliminate the criminal penalties for sex acts between consenting adults?" And now the place really went crazy. They were yelling, applauding, approving!

John Burton got up, having already made his pitch, and said, "If Willie Brown introduces the bill, then I'm coauthoring it." The place went wild again. And that's how it started.

There was no big meeting, no conference of professors, lawyers, and judges that started the move to legislate an end to criminal penalties for sexual acts. It was strictly a seize-the-moment opportunity. Gay rights in California began with a moment of opportunism. Sometimes that's how the committed make progress.

And when decriminalization finally became law eight years later, it wasn't because there was then a grand consensus behind the legislation. No, passing the bill required one of the most daring—and fun—political capers I ever was involved in. We used helicopters, jets, parliamentary maneuvers, and a disappearing state official (who then suddenly reappeared) to get the bill passed. Again, even for ideas you believe in, you have to sometimes resort to tough, hard-nosed ball.

But it wasn't all political opportunism and skill. The legislation also emerged from a sense of outrage. My outrage. As a criminal lawyer in San Francisco in the 1960s, I represented scores of people whose lives were being ruined by the fact that certain sexual acts entailed criminal penalties. The penalties didn't affect just gays; they affected everyone. Straight or gay, you couldn't hold a teacher's license, be a member of the bar, or hold a nurse's license if you had run afoul of this law and were convicted of a felony. Your professional license would be revoked upon conviction.

Bad things were really happening to people. Big-time. This was a real problem, not an imagined one. The cases were outrageous and humiliating for the people involved.

In one case, I represented a woman who was a passenger in a car being driven across the Golden Gate Bridge by her boyfriend. As they went through the tollbooth, she was performing a sex act on her boyfriend. The toll taker noticed and called the police. The woman passenger lost her license as a teacher. What they were doing in that car that night may not have been discreet, or even safe driving, but she didn't deserve to lose her profession because of a busybody toll taker.

In another case, a San Francisco man lost his professional license and livelihood because of a neighbor. This fellow was making out in his apartment one night with his boyfriend when a neighbor observed. She called the police. The guys were busted for crimes against nature. What struck me was how nosy the elderly neighbor was. To witness the scene, she had had to climb up on the toilet seat in her loo, stretch to peer out a window, and then down into the window below. Now that's nosy.

The nosiest snoops of all were the police. They regularly sent officers to loiter in public restrooms looking for people committing sex acts.

By the time we were ready to introduce the bill in 1968, I knew of hundreds of examples of people having been arrested for acts where there was total and complete consent between the parties. There was no commercial transaction either. Yet these people were being busted, charged with felonies, and prosecuted. Often with good lawyering and an intelligent judge, we could get the charges reduced to misdemeanor level, but even so, people lost their jobs and found themselves having to put all kinds of injurious and humiliating data on job applications.

When I first introduced decriminalizing legislation and presented examples of the injustices at a press conference, I received lots of press coverage. But the coverage was slighting. It regarded the bill as an oddity, a naughty. The legislators were even worse. Conservatives called it "the cocksuckers' bill." The bill died after only one hearing before a committee. It was just allowed to expire. I would go on to introduce it again, and again, and again.

The churches, of course, were opposed. My own denomination, the Methodists, held prayer services to save my soul. One minister got up in the pulpit to say, "We know he's not one of those people; he has a wife and children. And he's doing this out of an effort to help these people. But it's not in the way the Lord would want it."

They didn't confine themselves to pressuring me through the sweet hour of prayer. The Methodists, along with some other churches, employed a lobbyist in Sacramento. They sent the lobbyist down to my pastor to talk to him about my carrying the bill. The pastor knew there was no stopping me and left me alone. This was before the right-wing evangelicals became such a power, so the religious opposition in the legislature was not as intense as it might have been later. The born-agains hadn't yet been born politically.

So every year, we kept introducing the bill, and each time, through those fascinating times in American history in the early '70s when social attitudes were changing, we developed a little more traction, we attracted a few more coauthors. As gays and lesbians developed political power in the '70s, they made this bill an anchor tenet of their movement. Over time, our bill developed amazing political equity and credits for those of us involved.

By 1975, I could envisage a good result. I counted the numbers and saw we could get forty-one votes in the assembly—a bare majority—and twenty votes in the senate, which was one short of passage. If we could somehow get the bill through the senate, the bill might become law because Jerry Brown had become governor. I wasn't sure that Jerry would actually sign the bill; I knew he wouldn't veto it.

So we went for it in 1975. George Moscone, presiding in the senate, figured out a daring way to get the bill through that house, where we figured we could get a vote of twenty for and twenty against. Weirdly enough, our plan to succeed depended on a lot of senators believing that the tie would never be broken. Like the early candidates who promised to support the reform of the entire model penal code while realizing that the promise was an empty gesture, many senators who were voting for the bill were actually hoping it would die in a tie.

The bill would only pass if Lieutenant Governor Mervyn Dymally broke the tie. We had to get a lot of senators to believe that would never happen.

So Moscone, Dymally, and I arranged for the lieutenant governor to be on a well-publicized trip out of state to Colorado around May 1. We didn't tell anyone we planned to sneak Dymally back into the state to break the tie. On that day, with Dymally out of

California, we brought the bill up for a vote in the senate. By 1:00 p.m. we had the tie vote in the senate. It was tough getting there. To get to the twenty pro votes, I had to convince another black, a senator from Los Angeles named Nate Holden, to give me a commitment that if I needed his vote I could count on it. Blacks generally did not support this bill. It was unpopular with the churches and with the black community. But Nate said that if I really, really needed his vote, I could have it. But I couldn't tell even Nate what the real deal was until the vote was twenty to nineteen. Nate was no more gossipy than anyone else, but if I had told him early on how we set up this ploy to lull the Republicans into thinking that the bill would fail on a tie, unbroken because the tie breaker was out of state, he would have marveled and had to tell someone.

Nate's vote came after a ferocious morning of debate. People were frothing! When the vote came to twenty and twenty, members were eager to get out of the senate and get home, letting the bill die. Then George Moscone, the presiding officer and my co-conspirator, did what no one expected: he locked the senators in their chamber. No one could leave. And he instituted some parliamentary maneuvers to make it almost impossible for senators to change their votes. That kept the tie at twenty to twenty. The senators had no clue at that point that George and I had no intention of letting the senate adjourn. To preserve the vote, we put them in lockdown. Just like prison. None of the senators, including our own, liked being locked up—they were balky and cranky. One senator's wife told him to resign rather than put up with this. He did not.

Dymally was summoned from Colorado. In those days, there were no private jets available to us. So we had to get Dymally on a commercial flight from Denver to San Francisco. Then the Highway Patrol would helicopter him into Sacramento. It took five hours to bring him back to Sacramento.

At 7:30 p.m. Dymally entered the chamber, voted yea, and broke the tie. Sexual acts between consenting adults were decriminalized after eight years of effort and some hard-edged politicking. The bill became law.

In the same month, Moscone and I passed legislation to decriminalize the possession of small amounts of marijuana. Then we improved welfare benefits. We San Franciscans did a lot of progressive work in a few months' time—with the help of liberals from Los Angeles.

At the time I remember thinking that the world had really grown up a lot between 1968 and 1975. It had. But I also remember that none of these great social improvements would have come about unless some of us were also willing to use old-fashioned skill and political daring to make change. No progress ever takes place unless you're also willing to be tough and canny.

CHAPTER FIFTEEN

Starting On My Rise to Power

BY THE MID-'70S I was also becoming a figure on the national political scene, sought after not only by national politicians eager for support and for my growing expertise about California politics, but I was also being pursued by the national media. Like so many things in my life, this emergence was sudden and seemed accidental. The lesson, which is a tough one for politicians who spend most of their time just trying to keep the lid on the day's crises, is in knowing when to recognize that a crucial happy accident has occurred and that it can be made to be beneficial.

This particular happy accident occurred when I was working on George McGovern's presidential campaign. I had worked on presidential efforts before, especially with Jesse Unruh on Bobby Kennedy's 1968 presidential campaign where I had risen to become one of Kennedy's California cochairmen. In 1972, McGovern, who was the natural heir to Bobby Kennedy's campaign and spirit, was my man. We won the California primary, defeating Hubert Humphrey, George Wallace, and Congresswoman Shirley Chisholm of New York. Although we won with a plurality, not a majority, of the vote, under California law we were entitled to all the delegates the state could send. Off we went to the 1972 Miami Democratic Convention with a 271-member delegation that happened to be one of the most diverse ever elected to a national convention. About half were women, more than fifty were only college age, and fifty-one were black. We had all sorts of people, from farmworkers to stars like Shirley MacLaine. Some of them were so poor that I had to ask my old friend Adolph Schuman, one of those people who could so reliably be called upon to provide cash in a political crisis that I called them the "Green Caucus," to pay the fares and living expenses in Miami of the needy delegates.

The only thing we were short of in our delegation were the people who usually made up state delegations: party organization regulars. We were a model of the type of truly representative delegation that the Democratic Party, in a set of recommendations made by a commission that happened to have been chaired by George McGovern, voted to encourage following the debacle of the notorious 1968 Chicago convention. We truly represented the population of the party, not the needs of party bosses. Ironically, the credentials of our delegation would be challenged on the floor of the Miami convention by Hubert Humphrey's people, who would claim that the California delegation didn't represent the makeup of the Democratic Party of California.

All they were trying to do was to derail McGovern's then almost certain nomination. But I was astonished at their chutzpah. Here were Humphrey's people, an organization of old-line, old-time, machine Democrats claiming that the most diverse delegation in history wasn't truly representative. They contended that the delegation also should have included delegates committed to Humphrey, Wallace, and Chisholm—the very people who lost to McGovern on Primary Day in California. They had the effrontery to contend that our delegation was in violation of the reforms George McGovern's commission had put in place following the

1968 convention. Pure sophistry. Although we had right and California law on our side, an intense, convoluted, passionate fight tussled for days in Miami, and got wrapped up in arguments over the seating of other delegations. It was a mess and touch and go for days. Managing the fight took every bit of generalship and ingenuity I and other leaders of our cause could muster. I was exhausted and preoccupied when the happy accident took place that would propel me forward as a national figure in Democratic politics. It was a speech on the floor of the convention.

I had decided to try to break through the backroom arm twisting, deal-making efforts, rumors, and genuine passionate confusion by making an appeal to the convention at large. I would have to make the appeal simple, personal, and persuasive to cut through the fog of mixed feelings and perplexity that plagued the delegates. I did.

I moved through the issues raised by the specifics of the question before the convention. I mentioned the numbers of women, blacks, Hispanics, and young people who would be displaced if the delegation, of which I was chairman, was not seated.

I pointed out that our delegation had won Primary Day fair and square. "We ran," I told the delegates, "and won in fifty of the fifty-eight counties [in California]. We didn't try to violate the law. We obeyed the law and we beat them. . . ."

Then, speaking as a black man with a sterling record on civil rights, I made it clear that this was a fight about right and that a defeat would be an insult to every Democrat who had ever fought for progress in voting.

"Seat my delegation," I said as I wound up the finish. "I did it for you in Mississippi in '64, in Georgia in '68. It's now California in '72. I desire no less. Give me back my delegation."

The speech lasted less than three minutes. Of course, it carried the day. My delegation was seated, and I became a hero to the convention. When I concluded my speech, some delegates began shouting, "Willie Brown! Willie Brown! Willie Brown!" Their milder fellows merely erupted into cheers and applause, drowning the few Humphrey delegates who tried to boo. It was the emotional high point of the convention.

When I tell you I hadn't realized the whole performance would be on prime-time national television, you won't believe me. But it's true—I wasn't thinking of TV exposure when I got up to make my speech. If I had been thinking ahead of TV, I would have blown the whole thing; I would have made it a much longer, much more florid speech. As it happens, my three-minute speech made perfect TV. My pithiness in making a complex case simple, followed by the drama of the floor demonstration brought me to the attention and respect of top journalists, especially those in TV like Mike Wallace and Sander Vanocur. I became much sought after as a commentator and explainer. I was a national figure. And it was an accident.

CHAPTER SIXTEEN

Stabbed in the Back on the Way Up

BACK IN THE ASSEMBLY, I would be learning that just as happy accidents such as my prime-time speech to the Democratic Convention can help one's career, sometimes the best-laid career plans can go awry. In 1974, I would run for speaker of the assembly—an apparent shoo-in—and I would lose. I would lose by one vote.

Through the early '70s under Speaker Unruh and his successor, Speaker Bob Moretti, I had risen in the assembly. By 1974, I was chairman of the Ways and Means Committee under Moretti.

I had not wanted to be chairman of Ways and Means; I had wanted to be Moretti's main man on the floor of the house, his majority leader, running debates. That was a colorful, glamorous job and would have given my talents and skills as an orator, debater, and manager of legislation an outlet. To me the chairmanship of Ways and Means was a job that was wrapped in detail. But it was a considerably more powerful job than majority leader, as I would learn.

For one reason, Ways and Means ruled the entire California budget, every dime had to be approved by the committee. For another, almost every piece of legislation to be considered by the assembly first had to come through the Ways and Means Committee. So if you took the job of chairman seriously, you could have enormous influence over the budget and you also could learn about every idea that was current in thinking about politics and in public policy.

Moretti thought that I was smart enough to handle all the varied subject matter and that I should learn how to handle a budget. Frankly, he thought I needed this nuts-and-bolts experience if ever I were to become, as he hoped, speaker. So I became his Ways and Means chairman. As majority leader, Moretti appointed Walter Karabian, a brilliant legislator from Los Angeles who also was influential with Latino members although he himself was proudly Armenian. Moretti also appointed John Burton to run his Rules Committee. It was a quality leadership team—something quite new in the politics of the California assembly.

The Ways and Means Committee was both my college and postgraduate school for learning what would make good public policy, and also for learning the ins and outs of old-fashioned, hard-hammering inside politics. I loved every minute of being there.

To make sure that we were getting the best ideas on public policy, I appointed a brilliant collection of people to the committee's working staff. I hired some whizzes. Among them was Phillip Isenberg, who went on to become a member of the assembly and later mayor of Sacramento. Steve Thompson handled health issues, and John Mockler dealt with education. They and other staffers went on to have brilliant careers in public policy after they left. I also relied heavily on a man named Alan Post, who knew more about California government than anyone else. He was then the legislative analyst for the assembly, a man charged with scrutinizing all legislation. He also had an institutional memory that guided me through the hidden meanings and import of legislation. I also prided myself on learning every bill until I knew the legislation better than the members sponsoring the bills. This "superknowledge" of mine sometimes led to resentment by sponsoring members who didn't like my taking over the examination of witnesses on bills. But I was fascinated by it all and couldn't help myself. We really introduced a quality, knowledge-based approach to legislation. This was itself a kind of new politics.

And on the budget side, I learned how to do things the old-fashioned horse-trading way. It was the practice then for each of the two houses annually to draw up and pass a budget. The two differing budgets were sent to a conference committee where they'd be reconciled into one bill. Often those conferences consisted of a meeting between just two men: the chairman of the Senate Budget Committee and myself.

In those days, the chairman of the Senate Budget Committee was white-haired senator Randolph Collier, the "Silver Fox of the Siskiyous," a classic legislator of a long-ago era. He had been first elected to the legislature in 1939 as a Republican. In 1962 he became a Democrat. We had nothing in common. My great-grandfather had been a slave in the South. His grandfather and his father had owned slaves back in Alabama. But in those budget conferences, closed to the public, without even a staff member present, we hammered out budgets. We could do anything. We penciled in a hospital there, deleted a park here, and changed outlays all around. Collier, who represented the sparsely populated North Coast of California but who salted it with public works, taught me his tricks. Without so much as a public hearing, I learned how to do favors for my San Francisco, for legislators who needed a boost, and for programs that needed help. It wasn't a freebooting party; there was a lot of trading back and forth. But I learned how to do it with Collier, who became a close friend and supporter, an early example of my winning over a Republican.

Just another great day as mayor of San Francisco.

As an infant on the front porch rocker in Mineola, Texas, held by my grandmother, Anna Collins.

2

As a sixteen-year-old in Mineola Colored High School, dreaming of being a quarterback or a point guard, but never a politician. Say, what is a politician anyway?

3

4

The scrawniest quarterback you ever saw. Outside the home at Mineola when I was about fifteen.

Uncle Itsie arrives in Mineola from San Francisco in his brand new Buick Roadmaster. He made the trip annually, always in a new car, but never stayed very long. Either the law was after him or one of his women friends was, or else he just missed San Francisco.

With a girlfriend posing at the Texas state fair in Dallas. Notice my buckle shoes. I saved up for months to buy them from Sears Roebuck. They took so long to arrive, I had outgrown them when they got to me. I wore them anyway. They were my dress shoes.

Blanche Vitero and I, out on a sorority formal at San Francisco State College. We later married in September 1957, and have three beautiful children and our own special relationship; we haven't lived together in twenty-five years, though we remain married and are friends.

7

8

Campaigning against racism in San Francisco in the mid-1960s.

9

That's the political genius congressman Phil Burton on my right, and his equally talented brother, John, on my left. This was at the height of my dashiki-Nehru jacket phase. My, how those duds frightened the farmer dudes in the assembly.

Angela Davis, in the late '60s, shows off a charming side, while I show off some unbelievable threads.

10

11

The leadership brotherhood: With Rev. Cecil Williams of San Francisco's Glide Memorial Church and Rev. Jesse Jackson, getting ready to kick off a civil rights protest.

12

In 1972, by dint of some impassioned remarks I made at the Democratic Convention, I became a national political figure and a part of George McGovern's presidential campaign. He was the smartest man who never became president.

The Brown family in the mid-1970s. That's Blanche, Susan, Robin, and Michael. I'm immensely proud of them all.

In San Francisco in the early days, campaigning in the Western Addition. San Francisco may be cosmopolitan, but politicians are expected to show horsemanship still.

15

The three musketeers: My two oldest friends, Wilkes Bashford and the late Herb Caen, and I at one of my parties. We three had lunch together almost every Friday for thirty-five years.

My mother, Minnie, and I at one of my great parties.

16

17

My daughter Susan, son, Michael, youngest daughter Sydney, and daughter Robin at the dedication of the Willie L. Brown Jr. Academy as part of the San Francisco public school system in 2005.

18

With my brother, James Walton, and sisters Gwendolyn Hill and Baby Dalle Hancock at the dedication of the Willie L. Brown Jr. Academy.

Presiding over the California assembly as speaker on our first day in our restored chambers, January 8, 1982.

19

With my mother, when I was Speaker of the California Assembly, outside my new Sacramento home. I would soon pay her back for all her love and support by taking her to Paris.

20

21

Two speakers: Former speaker Jesse Unruh, my mentor and friend, and I are surrounded by lobbyists whose liquor we are no doubt drinking and whose wishes we are defying.

22

Jay Leno was one of the top comics who came to Sacramento to entertain the assembly. I ran the place like a Vegas showroom. There was nothing dull about Sacto when I was in town. The members loved it.

23

Sammy Davis, Jr., was a loyal friend who came out to entertain whenever I needed him. He also entertained the assembly in Sacramento. One night the members dragged him to a karaoke bar and sang to him. He advised them to stick to deal making, not lyric wrangling.

24

Archbishop Desmond Tutu spoke to the assembly about South Africa. I arranged for serious visitors as well as entertainers to inform and illuminate the legislators' minds.

25

The great Rosa Parks, far right, addressed the assembly. I wanted the members to meet real historic figures. That's assemblywoman Gwen Moore in the middle.

26

On May 1, 1991, President Ronald Reagan and Nancy Reagan visited me in my offices as speaker. The only time he returned to the capitol after being elected president was at my invitation. We had a fine relationship. Notice Mrs. Reagan checking out the décor. She had a designer's eye.

27

I visited Washington frequently while Bill Clinton was president, often staying at the White House. The president invariably pulled me aside from whatever conference was going on to discuss politics privately in the hallways while the great actors and schemers whirled around.

28

Stepping from the Amtrak train in Mineola. Restoration of rail service to Mineola was one of the early high points of my tenure as mayor of San Francisco. Thanks to Bill Clinton.

Oprah Winfrey and I laughing it up at one of the Women's Summits I organized as mayor. Oprah was a gracious participant and supporter.

29

Larry King and I exchanging the lowdown at some country hoedown. Odd setting for a couple of urbanites.

30

In November 1996, *Newsweek* proclaimed Rudy Giuliani and myself as America's most effective mayors. That's because Mayor Giuliani and I were both results-oriented. We didn't make decisions on the basis of political survival. We wanted things to happen, not favors from the system.

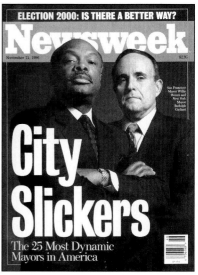

3

32

Senator Hillary Rodham Clinton listens to a few points I was making about politics in a hall of the U.S. Senate.

33

Governor Arnold Schwarzenegger and I are close pals. Here I am presiding at his second inaugural—much to the consternation of more partisan Republicans and Democrats.

Listening as mayor to San Francisco schoolboys. As mayor my door was always open. You have to listen to everybody—not just the contributors. You never know where the next bright idea might come from. Besides, I love kids, especially the kids of San Francisco.

Today, of course, the managing of the budget takes place in a much more open atmosphere, but I wouldn't trade any of the lessons I learned in those conferences for all the "sunshine acts" passed in all the states.

A side effect of my successful managing of the Ways and Means Committee was that I became the heir apparent to Bob Moretti as speaker, a fact that led to that politically instructive plan which was to go oddly awry. When things did go wrong, though, I was to discover a crucial fact about politics that later would prove key to my rise as a real political power. The point is that even in defeat you can unearth a powerful tool or two for the future. It went like this:

By 1974, I had become the obvious successor to Bob Moretti because, as chairman of Ways and Means, I was largely running the assembly for him. Bob had never been much interested in the tedium of the budget process, crucial as it was, and he wasn't much more interested in the general legislation that came before the house. He much preferred looking after the members, their political problems and prospects. He loved keeping track of who needed rewarding, who needed a favor, who needed punishing. He liked the social and political aspects of the job more than anything else. And by 1974, when Ronald Reagan was stepping down from the governorship, he even lost interest in those. He had decided to run for governor. That took up most of his attention. So with Walter Karabian running the floor of the house as majority leader, I was running the budget and the legislation. It was naturally assumed that I would succeed Moretti in the next term when Moretti would step aside either to become governor or just leave.

The 1974 Democratic primary that Bob ran in was a bruising affair. Jerry Brown, then California secretary of state, was a candidate, as were San Francisco Mayor Joseph Alioto; George Moscone, then a San Francisco state senator; Congressman Jerome Waldie from the East Bay suburbs of Oakland; and

William Matson Roth, scion of an old San Francisco shipping family. Jerry Brown won the primary in June 1974. Moretti came in third.

A few days later, Moretti, more dispirited than I would have imagined by his defeat, did something I advised against: he resigned as speaker. The speakership was open and suddenly there was a fight on in the caucus of Democratic members to succeed him.

My main opponent was the late Leo McCarthy, another assemblyman from San Francisco. McCarthy and I had been on opposite sides of the local Democratic political wars in San Francisco over the years. We supported different candidates and our groups fought over the control of the local Democratic County Committee. I was allied with more liberal Democrats: Congressman Phil Burton, Assemblyman John Burton, and George Moscone. McCarthy, a very decent man if a dull politician, was part of a then weakening older machine that for decades had controlled the Democratic Party in San Francisco.

In the assembly, though, Leo had been allied with some liberal members. One of his allies was Howard Berman of Los Angeles, who happened to be tight with Jerry Brown, winner of the Democratic gubernatorial primary. This would have an impact on the fight for caucus votes for speaker as members sought to show themselves allied to the man who probably would be the next governor of California. The desire to be part of this nexus brought McCarthy a few votes.

Politicians always like to ally themselves with a winner or the candidate who looks like the winner. Thus, the Brown-Berman connection brought McCarthy votes even though few assemblymen were in love then with Jerry Brown. As secretary of state, Brown had instituted changes that affected legislators. He limited the campaign contributions they could receive and subjected fund-raising to scrutiny by an ethics board. More viscerally, he

116

changed the way they ate, at least in Sacramento. Until Brown's reforms, legislators mostly dined out on the wallets of lobbyists and
their clients. Indeed, we used to say around the legislature after the
day's work, "Let's go find a pigeon and eat." A pigeon was a lobbyist. All you had to do was to go into one of the restaurants or bars
favored by politicians and lobbyists; catch the eye of a lobbyist and
your meal was paid for. You didn't even have to eat with the lobbyist or listen to a pitch, you just had to make your presence known.
A lobbyist would pick up your tab. When Jerry Brown limited the
amount of money a lobbyist could spend on a meal for a legislator
to ten dollars, he changed the dining habits of legislators utterly.
The pigeons were limited to providing bird feed. Nonetheless,
people wanted to be connected to Jerry Brown, so Leo McCarthy's
candidacy for speaker was enhanced.

But I was still the front-runner—until the McCarthy camp
bought a vote. This was the vote of my roommate! Leon Ralph, a
black member from Los Angeles, and I shared an apartment in
Sacramento. Indeed, I asked him to nominate me for speaker at
the Democratic caucus.

When I first asked Leon for his support, he had wanted me to
make him chairman of the Rules Committee. That would have
made him the majordomo of the assembly with control over
everything from office space to parking spots to the number of
staffers members could have. (One Rules Committee chairman
was fond of telling lovely and ambitious young women he'd meet
in the capitol that he could and would get them jobs in the assembly. He did. They'd have dreams of policy jobs and would soon
show up at an appointed office for work. Meanwhile, he would
have phoned his chief of staff and said, "Make way for another elevator operator." Yet he did surprisingly well personally with these
young ladies.)

I told Ralph that I couldn't and wouldn't make him Rules chairman in a Willie Brown speakership. Frankly, he wasn't competent enough to handle the job and I was determined that my speakership reflect the Moretti model, which was based on quality leadership. Nonetheless, Ralph agreed to support me and to nominate me, and I counted on Ralph and a few of the other brothers in the assembly to put me over the top.

On June 18, 1974, we held the caucus to choose a speaker. What a surprise. Other candidates' backers rose to nominate their guys, and I kept waiting for Ralph to stand up and nominate me. But he just sat there. When all the other nominations had been made, I looked across the room at him and caught his eye. He gave me a sad shrug.

One of my other supporters, also getting the picture, quickly rose and nominated me. Then the election was held. I lost—by one vote.

Ralph had stabbed me in the back, and in the front. It's only then that we discovered that the McCarthy-Berman camp had made a deal with Ralph. In return for his double-crossing me, he was named chairman of the Rules Committee.

And I was punished. The new speaker ousted me from the chairmanship of the Ways and Means Committee. Indeed, I was stripped of everything. I was given the smallest office in the capitol. My desk occupied the entire room. The office was so tiny that the chairs for people waiting to see me were out in the hall.

This chastisement was not something about which I had any regret. I deserved being put in a fucking small office because when I got the chance I'd do the same thing to those who crossed me. I believe in the spoils system.

That would be the end of the story but for a curious thing that happened shortly before the pro forma vote of the whole assembly that would see McCarthy installed as speaker. It would give me the tool to change the dynamics of politics in the assembly and to become speaker.

Some of the members of the Democratic caucus who had not voted for McCarthy were still uneasy about having him as their speaker. But by the tradition of the house and the caucus, they would be expected to vote for McCarthy once the election for speaker moved to the floor of the house. That was just how things were done: the winner of the caucus got the votes of all the caucus. After the caucus fight was over, you backed the winner unanimously on the floor. Party discipline ruled. And thus through the unanimous vote of its membership the majority party would get to choose the speaker. Of course, there might always be one or two strayers or abstainers (remember, I had voted against Jesse Unruh as speaker in my first vote in the assembly), but by and large as a member you went along with your caucus's choice. And time and clever dealing usually healed wounds that may have been opened during the caucus fight.

But long after the wounds should have healed, there were still a lot of Democrats who didn't like the idea of McCarthy as speaker. But what could they do? Align with Republicans?

The thought occurred to some of them that somehow a coalition of anti-McCarthy Democrats and Republicans might be formed to elect Willie Brown as speaker. Weirdly enough, these conversations started in Russia, where members had gone on a junket during a house break. Walter Karabian, a Democrat, led the talks. Two liberal Republicans from Southern California, Paul Priolo, who represented Malibu, and Bob Beverly, who was the member for Manhattan Beach, joined in. (Beverly, by the way, had the perfect answer for reporters who would ask him if he had been on a junket. "No," he would say. "I did not go and I paid for it myself.")

I had had nothing to do with these talks and wasn't even on the trip (although I had planned to go; I still have my elaborate visa entitling me to enter the USSR). Obviously, I was informed by telephone. The junket moved on to Israel, and at the King David Hotel more conversations were held with members back home. A King David Hotel Accord had been reached—then suddenly, it all fell apart. A few of the rump Democrats got cold feet at the prospect of making a deal with Republicans. McCarthy was not their choice for speaker, but dealing with Republicans was an ever-greater anathema. The junket rolled on, and the idea was quickly forgotten.

Except by me. What was wrong with a speaker chosen by bipartisan vote? Why not elect a speaker with a coalition of Democratic *and* Republican members? I wasn't sure that this was an idea that might ever prove useful. But I didn't forget it either.

As the new speaker, McCarthy not surprisingly appointed Howard Berman to be his majority leader. He made Julian Dixon, a black member from Los Angeles, the chairman of the Democratic caucus. Dixon and Berman would eventually make their way to higher office as United States congressmen. I helped them get to those posts. I just wanted them out of Sacramento.

McCarthy also made some terrible appointments. He appointed a dreadful little guy from down in San Bernardino County to be chair of the Transportation Committee. That was a storm center of a post because Governor Jerry Brown appointed a very aggressive person, Adriana Gianturco, as his transportation czar. The two were always feuding, a mess that wasn't helped by the fact that McCarthy's Transportation chairman, who is now dead, was also a nasty guy. Eventually he was busted for soliciting sex acts in public parks. His career was soon over, but not without embarrassment to the staid McCarthy. McCarthy's leadership team was certainly motley.

Within a year McCarthy was in trouble. He was obviously having difficulty governing the house because he had so many untalented and unscrupulous people on his leadership team. Almost all the talented Democratic members of the assembly had voted for Willie Brown as speaker, which meant that McCarthy was reduced to running the place with losers and people like Leon Ralph, whose vote he had bought.

Leo soon realized that not only could he not run the assembly with that gang, but also the potential for scandal in the house was very great. Some of his people were, as we used to say of schemers in the house, "highly entrepreneurial." Leo was terrified that scandal would erupt.

He didn't know how to get a handle on the assembly. So he came to me one day and said, "Willie, I really need your help." I was still in the exile he had placed me: ostracized to the smallest office in the capitol. Now he wanted to bring me into his leadership team. "You know your way around the house," he said. "I need your expertise." But he had no intention of restoring me to the suddenly vacant chairmanship of the Ways and Means Committee, the powerful post I had held under his predecessor, Speaker Moretti.

McCarthy's departing chairman of Ways and Means was John Francis Foran, one of the few very good guys he had on his team. Foran, also a member from San Francisco, was McCarthy's best friend and highly competent. John also knew how talented I was and had objected from the outset to McCarthy's exiling me. Foran had told McCarthy that it was a mistake to lose me, humiliate me, and run the risk of alienating me. Indeed, early in McCarthy's speakership, Foran came to me and apologized for McCarthy's behavior towards me. Foran also asked me for help in learning how to run the Ways and Means Committee. I was always happy to help him. Foran and Brown always had a good working relationship. Now Foran was leaving the assembly to go to the state senate. I knew that McCarthy would not offer me back that powerful post. It was just impossible for him to put the man who had nearly defeated him so close to the top.

So I wondered what he had in mind. "Well, Speaker," I said, "tell me what you need."

What he needed was a watchdog and a bulwark against corruption. Certain subjects, handled by varying committees in the legislature, attracted sleazy lobbying and the possibility of payoffs. These were things like horseracing and the regulation of liquor sales.

McCarthy had in mind to put the scandal-prone subjects under the purview of one committee and to make me the chairman of the committee. "I'm counting on you," McCarthy told me, "to keep the house from blowing up with scandal. They won't pull anything if they know you're watching."

I agreed to take this watchdog's post and became chairman of the Revenue and Taxation Committee, or "Rev and Tax." It didn't seem like such a major deal. I didn't expect it would cut into my work at the time, which was building my private law practice.

Indeed, one condition I imposed on McCarthy as part of the deal was that the committee would meet on Mondays. To give me the time to work on my law practice, I only came to Sacramento then on Mondays and Thursdays, when the whole house was in session and when you had to sign the roll to get paid. I needed the other days of the week for my private work, and I wasn't going to come to committees that met on other days. McCarthy agreed.

That I wasn't interested in getting fully involved in the life of the legislature also eased the politically paranoid among McCarthy's camp who might have seen me growing as a threat if I were day to day in the assembly, building relationships, involving myself in all the deals and intrigues. They figured that with my insistence on coming to the capitol as infrequently as possible that my real ambition still lay outside the house and with my law practice. Frankly, that was true. But if they thought that the fact that I spent most of my time in San Francisco meant that I wasn't in contact with members of the assembly, they were very wrong. During that time, an awful lot of members came to San Francisco for some R & R. Invariably they spent time with me. I made sure they had a good time. I treated them—out of my own pocket—to tickets for 49ers games, Giants games, Warriors games, afternoons at the racetracks, and I took them with me as I made my nightly rounds of the restaurants, clubs, and hangouts of my golden San Francisco.

Sacramento was a dull town for members in the McCarthy years. Even he went home for dinner with his family every night, driving all the way to San Francisco. When I later became speaker, I turned Sacramento into a lively spot, bringing in name talent from Ray Charles to Desmond Tutu to Richard Pryor and the U.S. Women's Olympic Soccer Team to speak with and entertain the members. When I became speaker I made Sacramento as attractive as Las Vegas to the members: there was always something flashy going on. It was fun to be there, fun to be part of the crowd.

But in McCarthy's day, the assembly was a very workaday world with just legislation and intrigue over deals to fill the hours. That was one of his problems: there was too much time for intrigue and too much temptation.

So I decided to give McCarthy a hand and became his watchdog, running the Rev and Tax Committee. To my surprise, this B-level committee would become both a workhorse committee and a marquee committee.

California's tax system had been a fairly equitable and progressive system. But in the early '70s, as taxes and revenues rose, the system, especially the property tax system, came under increasing attack. At first it seemed as if just a few gadflies opposed to taxes in general were proposing changes in the tax structure to cut back on the property taxes. But as inflation increased property values and thus taxes, and as the increasing revenues swelled the size of cash reserves in the state treasury, the system came under widespread attack. I tried to behave responsibly and spent hundreds of hours on legislation and legislative deals that would have relieved the taxes that home owners were paying but would not destroy public services. Scores of bills, by varying interests, were proposed in both houses and the goings-on back and forth were exhaustive. But no measure of relief and reform that we proposed and could pass would assuage the spirit of tax cutting abroad in the land. On June 13, the voters passed that stupid-ass Proposition 13, which did indeed cut taxes. It also vitiated public services. California, once the gold standard in public services, has thirty years later yet to recover. And there were huge inequities in Prop 13.

Following its passage, we tried to correct some of the unfairness especially towards people like renters, and we came up with new forms of revenue. We did manage to develop a unitary tax to ensure that foreign companies making money in California paid a fair share of taxes. In my time as chair of Rev and Tax, I devoted endless hours to the subject matter at hand—frankly, I was fascinated by it, if also frustrated. But it sure turned out to be more work than I had intended.

Meanwhile, Leo McCarthy was looking at a new kind of trouble on the political front. This was a challenge that I would help him beat back. Ultimately, it led to my becoming speaker, though. Goes to show: you have to be ready for accidents of history. But they can sometimes be devastating.

CHAPTER SEVENTEEN

The Assassinations of George Moscone and Harvey Milk

ALTHOUGH I HAD MOVED to a powerful and consuming post when I took the chairmanship of the Revenue and Taxation Committee in 1976, I was still not part of the leadership team in the assembly and saw no prospects with the McCarthy people. So while I kept my assembly posts, I also continued to work on growing my private law practice and maintained an interest in San Francisco city politics, which would be profoundly affected by what happened in the city in the last weeks of 1978.

On Monday, November 27, 1978, I was making final arguments in a criminal case being heard on the third floor of San Francisco City Hall, which then housed county courtrooms. I was defending a man who was the head of the San Francisco office of the Internal Revenue Service. He had been arrested for drunk driving and asked for a jury trial.

It was a good case. When stopped on the freeway, he was subjected to a sobriety test by a California Highway Patrol officer. The officer had the driver close his eyes and attempt to touch the tip of his nose with his finger. The driver missed his nose.

Earlier in the trial, I put the officer on the stand and asked him to demonstrate the test. In seconds, I was shouting out to the jury, "He missed his nose!" The judge told me to be quiet. "But the officer did miss his nose! He did! And he's sober." The jury got the message. I was sure of acquittal, and eventually it came.

That morning, after I finished my closing arguments, Superior Court Judge Charles Goff gave his instructions to the jury, which retired to deliberate shortly after 10:30 a.m. I exchanged a few pleasant words with Judge Goff, and then with time on my hands, went downstairs to see my old friend George Moscone, then in his third year as mayor of San Francisco. He was forty-nine years old.

I walked into the mayor's suite through a plain, unmarked back door. Mayor Moscone's friends and top staffers knew it was usually unlocked. The door opened onto a narrow hallway that connected the mayor's offices. I walked to a back room adjacent to his formal office. This small hideaway was used as a quiet retreat, a place for intimate and informal conversation. George called it "the coffee room," though he'd often offer you liquor as well as coffee. The mayor used the space often, preferring it to the adjacent wood-paneled cavernous chamber that was his formal office. As I entered, George was, indeed, in his coffee room. He was talking on the phone, scrutinizing some papers. I took a seat there as I had dozens of times.

He hung up the phone and we began talking about what was going on that day. We also made plans for a fun event that we both liked to indulge in: Christmas shopping at the Wolf's Den. The Wolf's Den was a corner, for men only, in the posh department store of Joseph Magnin Co. on Union Square. You could sit and have a drink in its clubby confines while models displayed the latest fashions. They wore intriguing negligees and brought along jewelry and trinkets galore that you could buy for your wife or girl-friends.

George and I seldom bought anything, but hitting the Wolf's Den during Christmas season was a regular, jolly custom. It made for a fine festive San Francisco holiday afternoon.

I would be the last person to see the mayor before Dan White, a former San Francisco policeman, shot him dead a few minutes later. Then, White, after killing the mayor, raced across the spacious corridors of City Hall and assassinated Supervisor Harvey Milk, forty-eight years old.

During the few minutes that George and I talked, Dan White sat in the office of Cyr Copertini, George's confidential secretary. It was a little holding pen of a room on the other side of Mayor Moscone's office where visitors waited until he could see them.

Dan had followed a mail clerk through the unmarked door that led into the private hallway connecting all the mayor's offices. He went directly to Cyr Copertini's little room. He asked for a minute with the mayor. She went in and told George. He told her to ask Dan to wait for a few minutes.

Dan sat down and chatted. He was armed, carrying a fully loaded handgun and ten extra bullets hidden in his pocket.

By coming in the back way, Dan had avoided the mayor's reception room, where bodyguards sized up visitors. He'd already evaded the metal detectors at the City Hall main doors by sneaking in through a basement window. And though he didn't seem nervous to people who saw him that morning, White, who was an ex-cop, probably wanted to avoid scrutiny by and conversation with the police on duty in the reception room.

Dan White, thirty-two, had been a member of the board of supervisors, San Francisco's city council. Elected a year earlier, he seemed a model politician for the working-class Excelsior district in southeastern San Francisco. After all, he was not only a former San Francisco police officer, he was also a former San Francisco firefighter.

But San Francisco had been in turmoil in recent years. The customs, manners, and prejudices of the old, conservative working-class city were, the old-timers felt, under assault by an influx of gays and alternate-lifestyle practitioners. One of the old Irish strongholds, the Eureka Valley neighborhood, had already become the gay mecca. It is now known as The Castro, named after its landmarked cinema. A lot of people in politics, like Dan White and his fellow supervisors Quentin Kopp and John Barbagelata, acted as if Armageddon were at hand. They were popular. Indeed, Barbagelata had narrowly lost to George Moscone in the 1975 mayor's race.

The motto of politicians like Barbagelata, Kopp, and White towards gays was "Tolerance—yes; but acceptance—no." Kopp was particularly good at exciting animosity and hostility, and White, I think, truly felt that Western Civilization was collapsing all around him. He wasn't equal to the times. He also had personal problems—financial ones. He had a lovely young family but was going broke trying to support them on a supervisor's $9,600 salary. He also owned a food stand, Hot Potato, down at Pier 39, the development of tourist shops and attractions near Fisherman's Wharf. He had wrangled that out of the developers, but the potato stand wasn't bringing in much money.

On November 10, 1978, Dan White suddenly resigned from his seat on the board of supervisors. I had advised George to fill the seat immediately and not to bother with interviewing people. I told George, "Don't go in for all this dithering and showing consideration. It does nothing but ruffle feathers and rile people." But politicians like to make a play and a show about filling vacancies. I wish George hadn't, but he and his advisors wanted to show they were being thorough in their search.

One of the reasons I counsel political leaders to fill vacancies immediately—indeed, my appointees, all reliable and trustworthy people, often didn't know it until they heard it on the news—was that otherwise you run into some strange emotional situations. You have to be thinking of how people respond emotionally.

Four days after Dan resigned, his seat was still unfilled. Suddenly, he decided he wanted his old job back. If George had immediately filled the post, Dan wouldn't have had a chance to stew over this. But with the post unfilled, he did. Dan argued that he merely had changed his mind. Having inexplicably found a way out of his money troubles, he said, he could resume his duties as supervisor. He wanted to withdraw his resignation letter. But, alas, the city clerk had already officially recorded the resignation. That seemed to make him angrier.

Some insiders were telling Dan that Supervisor Harvey Milk was counseling George against reappointing him. When Moscone finally told Dan that he would not be reappointed, some people think that Dan blamed Milk for the decision. Delusional, Dan envisaged a conspiracy of establishment politicians and gays working against him.

Harvey Milk was one of the first modern gay politicians in San Francisco. There had been others in the past, but they were closeted and/or not very militant. Harvey was a product of the gay lib years, with their demonstrations, verve, and vigor. Elected to the board of supervisors, he was the first openly gay elected officeholder in San Francisco history. And he had a brilliant political mind for tactics and strategy. Though he was no fan of Dan White, he didn't have a decisive word on the matter of reappointing him.

People have mistakenly assumed that Dan got the word that he would not be reappointed from George that morning in the coffee room and that's why Dan killed George. In fact, days earlier the mayor had called Dan and all the others who had wanted the job to tell them that he had decided on someone else. Indeed, George and his staffers told them who the new supervisor from the Excelsior district would be. That man, Don Horanzy, was sitting three rooms away in the mayoral reception room with his family in both Hungarian and Philippine ceremonial garb just as Dan White was sitting in the anteroom and as George and I were talking in the coffee room. The mayor had planned on swearing in Horanzy at 11:30 a.m.

I finished my coffee and went back upstairs to Judge Goff's courtroom to await the jury's decision in the drunk driving case. I hadn't been at my table for more than five minutes when Rudy Nothenberg, the deputy mayor who also had been one of my top staffers in Sacramento, came in and grabbed me. He said, "Hey, man, I think they've killed George."

I said, "What are you talking about?"

He said, "George is dead . . . in his back room."

I screeched, "You gotta be kidding me!"

At that moment alarms began sounding throughout the massive City Hall. Panicked, people began running. I went back downstairs. I think I went down with Rudy.

We went into the mayor's coffee room. We saw the awful scene and blocked the doors to keep people out. Police inspectors were already standing over George's dead body. The cigarette he had been smoking still smoldered in his hand. Police Inspector Gary Wommack, the head of the mayor's security detail, who had been at his usual post in the reception room, picked up the cigarette and stubbed it out.

Dan White had shot George Moscone twice in the back while

George was making him a drink. Then White shot him twice more in the back of the head.

At the moment I didn't know who had done it and wondered if it was an aftermath of Jonestown. On November 18, 1978, nine hundred followers of Jim Jones, an obscure but charismatic San Francisco religious cult figure, had committed mass suicide in Guyana, where they had moved from San Francisco.

It's worth taking a moment to consider Jones because the enormity of the tragedy involving his followers makes one wonder how politicians and police failed to notice his sinister hold on people.

Hours before the mass suicide in Jonestown, Jim Jones's people there had shot and killed visiting San Francisco Bay Area congressman Leo Ryan and four reporters. Ryan had gone to Guyana at the request of constituents to investigate complaints from family members who believed that Jones had brainwashed their loved ones. Ryan was killed for his trouble. Jones's henchmen also wounded Ryan's aide Jackie Speier, who survived and went on to a distinguished career in the California legislature.

But who was Jones? He was indeed a strange person. Olive-complected, he wore sunglasses all the time—you could never see his eyes. Though he had a congregation of thousands, he was a marginal figure in San Francisco church circles. And though he didn't have much in the way of financial support to offer politicians, he had become a political figure. George Moscone had appointed him to the Public Housing Authority, which essentially made him one of the largest landlords in San Francisco. He was good to politicians, showing up at rallies and meetings with hundreds of supporters, but he never got too close to politicians. Not close enough so that we really knew him.

His congregation was made up of really lost souls. Many of these people had no one else in the world; few had family members who might complain or notice what was happening to them.

And for a long time, Jones seemed to have been doing good. He provided people with food, shelter, a sense of belonging. His operation seemed not unlike others that took in the broke, broken, and bereft and helped them along. Indeed, at first his operation in Guyana seemed like the typical out-of-town extension that many groups had: a rural, removed place where intensive rehab could occur. We all should have noticed more, particularly since he was forcing congregants to turn over their incomes and meager assets to his operation. His main San Francisco locus was an auditorium out in the Fillmore district that was the scene of (seemingly) vitalizing religious worship. Other groups were doing the same and were doing well by their people. We just didn't see how thoroughly bad things were. That's really what happened with Jim Jones and San Francisco.

When George Moscone was shot, it was natural to wonder: could the shooting be part of some massacre planned by the Jones people? We also did not know in the moments following George's shooting—and would not know for another thirty-five minutes, because of the confusion—that just one hundred feet away on the other side of City Hall Supervisor Harvey Milk also lay dead.

No one in the mayor's office knew Dan White had gone to Milk's office. No one knew where he was. In fact, he had exited by the same back door I had used just ten minutes earlier. Off he went, through the marble passages to the supervisors' offices. He had passed Supervisor Dianne Feinstein's office. She had called out to him, and he said, "I'll be back in a minute. I have something to do." Seconds later, she heard gunshots and went into Milk's office and discovered his body. White had fired two bullets into the brain of Supervisor Milk.

He then escaped through another open window and made his way to the Doggie Diner, a coffee shop farther up on Van Ness Avenue, beyond City Hall. From there he called a friend on the police force, Inspector Frank Falzon. Falzon went and sat with him for nearly two hours while Dan talked and calmed down. Then the police inspector took the former police officer to jail. At the diner, Falzon learned that in addition to killing Moscone and Milk, White had a list of people whom he had also intended to assassinate that morning. My name was at the top of the list. White had told Falzon that he believed Moscone, Milk, former supervisor Carol Ruth Silver, and I had conspired to keep him from being reappointed to the board of supervisors. White told Falzon that he believed I was the mastermind behind the conspiracy. I would not learn of this, or that I was on White's hit list, until many years later when the information was released in a documentary film.

Meanwhile, the police and medical people were swarming over the mayor's and the supervisor's offices. Early in the crisis, the police put a bodyguard on me. I wasn't sure why, but at that point we didn't know if the killings were the work of a group or a single shooter. I don't think the police in City Hall knew that either when they placed the guard around me. For a while that morning, they also assigned an assistant district attorney to stay with me as an additional protector.

But we had work to do. Rudy Nothenberg and I grabbed "the Book," which was what City Hall hands called the city charter, to see who legally succeeded a dead mayor, and, frankly, to see how that would affect things politically. The legacy of George Moscone was at stake.

The charter, as we had expected, called for the president of the board of supervisors, in this case Dianne Feinstein, who was just about to leave politics after having lost two mayoral races, to become the acting mayor. The charter then called for the board, at the earliest opportunity, to choose an interim mayor to serve until the next election, which was already scheduled for 1979.

Oh, it was a terrible day. The other task we had to handle immediately was notifying Gina Moscone, George's wife. She was in the family station wagon crossing the Golden Gate Bridge on her way to a cousin's funeral. We reached her by radiophone and told her to turn around and come to City Hall. We didn't tell her why. When she reached City Hall, it was my job to tell her that her husband, the father of her four children, had been assassinated.

I also was giving my friend Herb Caen at the *San Francisco Chronicle* a kind of running account by telephone of what had happened; but I was not sure of anything. None of us were. The authorities were doing their job. And though we knew that George was dead, it was a sign of how shell-shocked we were that we were still hoping that somehow George was still alive.

Around 1:00 p.m. on the day of the shooting, when we finally knew that White was the sole killer, and after Dianne Feinstein, now the acting mayor, made her announcement of the horrifying events, I left the chaos and confusion of City Hall. Rudy Nothenberg asked me where I was going. I said, "To Le Central. I need a drink or something." With the facts of the shooting established and Dan White under arrest, the police lifted my bodyguard. But not everyone in the city knew what actually had happened.

As I left City Hall, a group of brothers from the Bayview, San Francisco's black neighborhood, greeted me. I knew many of them, rough-and-ready guys. They asked me where I was going; they told me they'd give me a lift. I drove downtown with them. When we reached Bush Street near Le Central, we couldn't find a parking space. So they left me out about fifteen yards up the street from the restaurant. Some also got out of the car and began walking down the street behind me.

Near the restaurant, I passed a parked white delivery van. Just as I got adjacent to the van, the sliding door opened with a bang. It was one of the loudest noises I've ever heard. A man stood in the open doorway of the van.

I felt the bruthas drop behind me.

The deliveryman looked like he was about to shit. He saw five or six guns aimed at him. I hadn't known the bruthas had guns. They hadn't come along to comfort me, as I assumed, but to protect me.

Frankly, I'm surprised they hadn't opened fire.

I looked at those guns and I said, "What are you doing? It's just a delivery guy." By now, the deliveryman had fallen back into the van in shock. They put their guns away.

The deliveryman was still in shock. I asked him to come and get a drink. He declined. We stayed with him a few minutes until he felt better. Then I went into Le Central and had a drink. I talked to Herb Caen on the phone.

He was on his way over to join us for lunch. But for once I didn't stay to meet with my old friend. I went out to walk by myself. All I could think of were those guns aimed at the deliveryman on Bush Street. I'll never forget that.

The killings turned me away from city politics. I had wanted to run for mayor in the future, in 1985, when George would have finished what we hoped would have been his second term. It was something George and I had discussed. But my interest went right out the window with his death. It was the horrible sign of just how sick San Francisco politics had become.

I went back to my law practice and continued my membership in the assembly, even though I didn't seem to have much of a future there either. Things would change. In another two years I would become the speaker.

CHAPTER EIGHTEEN

Loyalty and Betrayal on the Way to the Top

THE MID-'70S WERE INDEED a giddy time for California Democrats. We were the glamor unit of national Democratic politics. Jerry Brown, the governor, was a fab figure who started running for president the moment he became governor. When he wasn't going all over the country giving speeches and raising money, he was hanging out in Los Angeles with Linda Ronstadt, Warren Beatty, Shirley MacLaine, Jack Nicholson, and that whole Hollywood crowd. They became part of our Democratic show. Indeed, our Democratic delegation to the 1976 convention was fully populated with liberal, left-wing Democrats from Hollywood. To the public, weary of Gerald Ford and Jimmy Carter, California Democratic politicians seemed like rock stars, and the future seemed limitless. It was a wonderful, intoxicating thing. Even Speaker Leo McCarthy got caught up in it.

He started thinking of running for the U.S. Senate. So he ceased to focus on the assembly, concentrating instead on putting together the resources to become the next U.S. Senator from California. Well, that was a lightning bolt for his overly ambitious lieutenant, Howard Berman, and his cohorts who, in their opinion, had been responsible for Leo's rise to the speakership. They thought that Leo was growing selfish. He certainly let the glamor go to his head. On December 1, 1979, Leo held a major fund-raising event with Ted Kennedy as the speaker at the massive Los Angeles Convention Center. It was a howling success. It was huge.

Leo, though, was so ungracious that he did not even introduce his members to the crowd. He took and kept all the glory to himself. And instead of having the campaign contributors make their checks payable to an account to elect *all* Democratic legislative candidates in California, he had them make them out to his own senatorial campaign fund. Oh, Leo's backers like Howard Berman were furious, slighted, and ornery at having been totally ignored at the evening and in the fund-raising.

Berman and his guys met at the end of that evening and decided they were going stage a coup. They were going to replace McCarthy as speaker with Howard Berman. And they plotted whatever way they could.

The only nonparticipant in all of this was one Willie Lewis Brown. I did not even know about the plot. I didn't know of any of this unhappiness or what have you. There was no evidence of it in the few hours each week that I spent at the capitol. I was in the dark despite the fact that many of the troops who had been on my side in the '74 fight against McCarthy were once again active. Of course, they were signing up with Berman because he was going to take out McCarthy, the man who humiliated them after he became speaker.

As speaker, Leo was always insulting my people. That was a terrible mistake. He and his top aide, Art Agnos, had dumped on my people full-time. They'd go out of their way to kick the shit out of them. One of my people could be sponsoring something as simple as a pro–Mother's Day resolution, and they'd get screwed over by Leo and Art—just because they had been with me. So when the time came, a lot of my people walked over to Berman's side. Not that they were all that in love with Howard, but Berman made them the offer of full membership in his army, so they joined his cadre.

In December 1979, Berman and his guys decided to try a courteous route first. Berman and a delegation met with McCarthy and told the speaker they wanted him out before the 1980 elections. They were being polite, but they issued an ultimatum: either Leo would give them an exit date or they would give him one. The meeting ended with only an agreement to keep meeting on the subject.

I first learned of all this moments after Berman and his delegation first met with McCarthy. Berman telephoned me to say he wanted to come down to San Francisco and see me.

"Well, what do you want to see me about?" I asked.

"I want to talk to you about the speakership."

"What about the speakership?"

"Well, let me just come down and see you."

I said okay and hung up. Five minutes later, Leo McCarthy called and told me the story about the visit from Berman to announce war.

I told Leo, "Well, that's interesting because Howard Berman just called me and I assume he wants to talk with me about maybe hooking up with him."

"What's your reaction?" Leo said.

"I'm not interested in being involved in any fight against you," I told him, "and the proof of that is in the fact that I am not resigning the chairmanship of Rev and Tax. Anyone who wants to move against you should have the courtesy to quit any honors you have given him. I don't take a title from a man and then try to oust him."

"That's great," said Leo.

Howard Berman came down and we had dinner in a little

French restaurant in San Francisco's Pacific Heights district. It was a three-hour get-together in which Howard told me why he was angry with Leo and why he thought it was in the best interest of the assembly that he take over as speaker.

At the end of the meal, I said, "You know, Howard, you guys—you and Leo—teamed up and dumped my ass in the '74 speaker's fight. But I've been loyal to Leo and you as part of his leadership ever since. Now you're trying to talk about enlisting my support to dump Leo. It seems to me you really don't understand loyalty. I don't think I'm a player in this."

He said, "Well, keep an open mind."

"Fine," I said. "You always have to keep an open mind. But I'm not a player. You can't count on me."

You know, I suppose you can carry belief in the concept of loyalty too far. But I believe in it, and I really was shocked at Berman's disloyalty. When I later said publicly, "Howard Berman wrote the book on loyalty," he didn't even get the sarcasm.

"What about your other friends?" Berman asked when I said he couldn't count on me. He was unstoppable.

"I don't know," I said. "I haven't even spoken to any of them. I haven't told them that you called me. But I did tell McCarthy that you called me, because he called me too. And I told him I agreed to meet with you."

Then, within a day, I believe, Leo met with me and said, "I'm gonna do exactly what you said: I'm dumping Berman."

"That's a good thing," I said. I also told Leo that I believed Berman's next move would be to oust Leo's lieutenant, Art Agnos, as chairman of the Democratic caucus in the house. The caucus chair was not appointed by the speaker but was elected by the membership. And I believed that by then Berman had more votes in the caucus than Leo did. Sure enough, Agnos was ousted.

Berman elected himself as chairman of the caucus! In effect, he was telling McCarthy in deafening tones: "I have more votes than you do, Leo."

With Howard Berman now running the caucus, Speaker McCarthy felt he had been cut off at the knees. Actually he felt as if some things a little higher than his knees had been cut off. He was sure he was finished. He called a meeting of his disheartened supporters at the San Francisco Airport Hilton Hotel in late December 1979. He was certain he had to quit because Berman had more votes in the caucus than he did.

By the time I arrived at the meeting in my black Porsche an hour later—dressed in black leathers, as was my then girlfriend Wendy Linka—the mood in the room was also black, but not cool black the way I was. They were in a crepe-hanging, mournful, black mood.

It was, they were certain, over for all of them.

I stood at the back of the room and listened to them talk about how Howard Berman had done them in by winning control of the caucus and how this was the end of Leo's speakership.

I was the last one to speak.

"I don't understand what the problem is," I said to the room.

"What do you mean?" somebody asked. "Leo's got to quit."

"Why?"

Someone said, "Well, Berman's got the votes."

"You're fulla shit," I said. "There aren't forty-one votes in the house against Leo. There might be twenty-eight, there might be twenty-nine, but in my humble view, that's not forty-one. Sounds to me like you're counting votes, and you're about thirteen votes short. It'll take forty-one votes from the whole house to unseat Leo. So let's take it to the mat. I bet you they can't get forty-one."

Now all of a sudden, a light went on in everybody's head. "Holy shit," said my friend Mike Roos. "Here's a guy who actually knows the rules, and you know what? He's right."

You could see the relief in Leo McCarthy's face. His speakership was saved.

You could also see what was going on in the minds of other members there. They were thinking: Willie Brown is an awfully talented man.

Howard Berman continued, however, to batter away at Leo McCarthy, trying to unnerve him right on the floor of the assembly. He had a colleague rise every day as the first order of business and "move to vacate the chair"—in other words, toss the speaker out. That's a psychologically damaging way for a speaker to start the day: facing a motion to remove him. It was like hearing "I hate you" first thing in the morning at home every day.

But as I told McCarthy, at this point it was just a war of nerves—a skillful and treacherous war, indeed—but Berman didn't have the votes to oust him. The Republicans would never ally with Berman to dump McCarthy.

It's not that the Republicans were loyal to Leo McCarthy. They weren't. But 1980 was an election year, and the Republicans wanted the Democrats to be in complete disarray, killing each other. The Republicans figured they could take advantage of a fractured and disarranged Democratic machine to knock off a few Democrats in the fall elections.

Berman continued his war against his mentor while continuing also to hold the job of McCarthy's majority leader. I thought this was insane, bad politics. You don't tolerate having the people moving against you also holding gift positions from you.

"Berman should resign as your majority leader," I had told McCarthy. "And so should anybody else who holds a title from you who is now working against you. If they're going to be with Berman and against you, they ought to first resign and then start trying to throw your ass out. They ought not to be holding these titles from you."

"You know what," said Leo, "you're right. I'm going to fire that son of a bitch." He had said that before. This time he meant it.

He was going to appoint Art Torres of Los Angeles as majority leader, but he was not the right man for the job of majority leader. I was.

I told Leo, "You're misusing me as chair of Rev and Tax."

"What do you mean?" he asked.

"Well, I can manage and operate the floor better than anybody. And you need someone there who is actually going to focus on legislation. Right now, everybody's focused on the fight between you and Berman. Nobody is focusing on legislative substance: on aid to schools, health care, the tax revolt. You need that while you're in a fight for survival. I can do both things: get some legislation passed and protect your speakership. Put me in as majority leader."

Some have thought that this was the first sortie in a campaign on my part to become speaker. But it wasn't. Politics is actually like football, and that's how I was looking at this situation: if McCarthy was going to survive, he needed the best quarterback. That was me. I really had no further ambition then. I was happy building a law practice, happy with my life, and I would be happy fighting on the floor. Frankly, I like a scrap. And I like a scrap that's about survival.

So Leo put me in as majority leader. Art Torres, annoyed at Leo, promptly crossed lines and joined Berman's people, as did Torre's close friend Richard Alatorre. They weren't annoyed with me. They still remained my people, but in the current game, they joined Berman. Berman may have thought he had made converts, but they were just following convenience.

I made other recommendations to McCarthy, urging him to get rid of others who were reneging on him. Many of his commanders, captains, and lieutenants had defected. I insisted we oust them from their posts. It was ugly, but so far the fighting was all intramural.

Then something unprecedented happened. Berman decided to defeat his enemies in the assembly by running people against them in their home districts. The speakership fight would infect the general election. In the past, no matter how bitterly you hated a guy in the house, you didn't try to defeat him at the polls if he was a member of your party. Until Howard Berman came along.

The resourceful Berman ran well-financed candidates in the Democratic primaries against almost every Democrat who wasn't supporting him in his speakership fight. On Primary Day in June, Berman's candidates did very well. McCarthy suffered severe losses. When the dust cleared, Berman's candidates had won more nominations than Leo's had. When the general election in November at long last came around, after a bitter, tedious summer when the torn-apart assembly got almost no substantial legislative work done, the results of the primary election were confirmed: in the new legislature, Berman would in fact control more Democratic seats than McCarthy.

Two days after the election, McCarthy called a meeting of his supporters. He was a defeated man. He didn't even sit at the head of the table. He was ready to resign as speaker. He suggested that we ought to negotiate a peace treaty with Berman to see what kinds of committee assignments and terms we could get from the Berman people. He furthermore suggested that Willie Brown should lead the peace delegation.

I made a speech, which essentially said: "Yes, we ought to sue for peace, but we ought to make sure that this caucus doesn't divide up and some people get the best deal and some people are severely penalized.

"We ought to continue to act as a unit. To negotiate what our relevance and standing in the house will be."

Everybody agreed to that and went along with it. We stayed as a unit. That was a great exercise of restraint by those veterans who knew how to rush to the phone and cut private deals with the Berman people—which would have been a sharp thing for them to do.

What I didn't know then was that immediately after that meeting, Maxine Waters from Los Angeles said to Elihu Harris of Oakland and Mike Roos of Los Angeles, "Stay behind."

The three caucused and they said, "You know, Willie Brown, not Howard Berman, should be the speaker." They decided to talk with me as soon as possible.

Meanwhile, the peace delegation, of which I was the head, called Howard Berman for a peace conference. Berman set the meeting for my law office at 1515 Vallejo Street in San Francisco. He showed up with democratic assembly members Richie Robinson, Art Torres, Teresa Hughes, and a few other people. Inexplicably, Art Torres brought his toddler son with him. I had my members Mike Roos from Los Angeles, John Vasconcellos from the Silicon Valley , and a few other people. But I knew it was not a serious meeting, what with a four-year-old running around.

I also discovered there wasn't much to negotiate for. There weren't any chairmanships available. Berman had already given away everything that was significant. I'm sitting there with John Vasconcellos who wants to be chair of Ways and Means, but Berman said that he had already given that to Richie Robinson. He had already given away the chairmanship of the Rules Committee—all the big committees.

So all my people are sitting there, saying to Berman, "Why are we even having this meeting? You've already dealt us out. You're just informing us of your plans, not settling down to negotiating a plan with us." Berman wasn't there to do business, just to let us know we were exiled. The meeting was a disaster, a complete disaster. It wasn't acrimonious, just completely nonproductive.

At this point, I was disgusted. I didn't even want to be part of the game, even though Berman told me that he had a role for me. Well, he wasn't going to be stupid the way McCarthy had been in 1974 and exile me. He offered me the chairmanship of the Joint Legislative Audit Committee. He said, "It won't interfere with any of the things you're doing, like your law practice. It doesn't meet regularly, just on your own schedule," and so on.

That was a huge mistake: you don't try to buy off the leader of the peace delegation in the presence of his cohorts.

Berman figured that by refusing to deal with the group gathered against him, he'd essentially busted up the anti-Berman coalition. He figured we'd all break up now, scurry, and then try to make individual deals with him for something.

He was wrong. The group decided that indeed there was nothing for them with Berman, but they weren't going to explode into atoms.

To reinforce that point we asked to meet with him together again as a group in Sacramento in a week. He agreed.

CHAPTER NINETEEN

Elected Speaker

THE NEXT DAY, while I was in my law office, the receptionist came in and said, "There are three people here to see you: Maxine Waters, Elihu Harris, and Mike Roos."

I wasn't sure what they wanted, but obviously things had been happening overnight. I invited them in. Maxine said to me, "We don't want you to do anything. But we want you to give us fifteen or twenty minutes of your time. And we want you to listen to us."

They started to tell me they thought it would be a smart move for me to form a coalition of anti-Berman Democrats and Republicans to elect a speaker.

I, of course, questioned these three young, inexperienced people closely. I told them about all the perils and all the risks. I told them they'd be discredited in Democratic politics—they'd be shunned as lepers by the rest of the Democratic Party if they did anything like that. But they were all committed. They had taken the blood oath to support a Democratic-Republican coalition with me as the coalition's candidate against Berman as speaker. After they told me that, Maxine said to me, "What do you think?" I gave them my answer with these words: "I count to four."

"What do you mean?" Elihu Harris, a black member from Oakland, asked.

"I count to four. Four votes: the three of you and me makes four. That means we need thirty-seven more members to get to forty-one."

"How do we get to forty-one?" Mike Roos asked. They were obviously committed.

"First, I'm calling two other people who I know are just waiting for my call."

"What do you mean?" asked Maxine.

I said, "There's been two guys who for days and years now have been hamming the hell out of me to run."

They laughed, and I called the first of the two, Doug Bosco. Doug represented the wide-open tree counties of the Northern California coast. He later went to Congress. We found him on the road with an early cell phone.

I said to Doug, "I need to talk to you. I need to talk to you about a matter of some importance. I need to see you."

I didn't quite trust cell phones even then. They're not confidential. Bosco wasn't so inhibited.

"Okay," he said. "I don't know what you're planning or what you're doing, but count me in. I'm in."

So now we were five. Then I called Leroy Greene, a member from Sacramento, an older fellow who had been an engineer and had built quite a reputation in the assembly as a specialist on public education. Greene had been one of the members who had been targeted for defeat by Berman in the Democratic primaries. In that race, I used all the resources I could command, financial and otherwise, to run Leroy's campaign. Leroy won, obviously. And Leroy wanted to get at Berman like you wouldn't believe. I called him and said, "The drill is on." My three coconspirators' ears sparked at that phrasing. Did they intuit from my language that maybe I had been moving towards something like this for some time?

Leroy said, "What number am I?"

"Number six," I told him.

"Well, who are the others?" he asked. "How did anybody get ahead of me?"

I told him about the others. "I'm on," he replied.

I made another call. This time, I phoned Curtis Tucker, a black member from Los Angeles. Curtis was one of those who had wandered into the Berman camp but was not in love with them. In fact, as you will learn, Curtis had already been long at work in an effort to make me speaker! He was number seven, but we instructed him to stay quietly with Berman until we told him otherwise. We needed someone in that camp.

Then I placed another call that I knew would bring the eighth and ninth votes. I called Richard Alatorre, one of the Los Angeles members, and told him what was what. He was vote eight. And I told him "to figure out how to make sure Art Torres is in line and comes along. But stay quiet." Art wasn't always focused, so he needed a watcher.

"He'll come," said Richard of Torres. Torres became vote number nine. Torres's allegiance to me surprised some, and his tale was typical of the fast-moving realliances in the house. Most people would have guessed that Torres would have been with Berman, not me. Torres had wanted to be majority leader under McCarthy. Art was so solid a Willie Brown man that he didn't hold it against me that I, and not he, had become majority leader. You don't hold it against the other player who goes into the scrimmage when the coach has benched you. You hold it against the coach. Torres retaliated against McCarthy by joining Berman, but his real loyalty was to me. Once he knew I was a candidate against Berman, he would come home.

I also had Alatorre call Walter Karabian, the Armenian prince who had left the assembly in 1974 but who was still a key influence

148

upon and mentor of Latinos in Los Angeles politics. Karabian was a brilliant guy (he had been majority leader in the assembly under Speaker Moretti when I was chairman of the Ways and Means Committee) and I considered him a close ally on assembly matters, even though he was no longer in the assembly. He had long hated McCarthy passionately and disliked Berman almost as much. A good infighter. I needed his advice and his influence with Latino legislators. They listened to him.

So now we were up to nine. I called Leo McCarthy and asked him to see us right away at his local office in the San Francisco state office building.

At the meeting with Leo the next day, we discussed the idea of a Democratic-Republican coalition to elect a speaker, though we didn't tell him I might be the candidate and already had votes. Leo behaved exactly as I thought he would—hemming and hawing, full of Hamletlike indecision about Democrats acting in alliance with Republicans. Leo and his lieutenant, Art Agnos, asked for a meeting with all the remaining McCarthy backers to review the cons and pros of backing a coalition speaker to stop Berman.

So we called such a meeting at the San Francisco Airport. I continued to make sure that McCarthy and Agnos did not think that I would be the candidate. Instead, for speaker, we floated the name of Frankie Vicencia of Los Angeles, an amiable guy who was the most conservative Democrat in the assembly.

I knew McCarthy, Agnos, and their cohorts would be open to Frankie as a candidate because they thought the Republicans would want a conservative, malleable guy like Frankie. They also figured they could control Frankie. They knew they could not control me.

Ironically, Frankie was the man McCarthy was not comfortable having in charge of liquor and horse racing interests and lobbyists.

He had made Frankie the chair of the committee that dealt with racing, but then had moved horse racing regulation to me when I took over the Rev and Tax committee.

For me, floating Frankie's name was obviously a risk. But if Frankie were to end up being the candidate, I'd say nothing about any of this and I'd just go back to practicing law. I'm smart enough to know you don't always benefit personally from your own efforts. When you open the door for yourself, you have to be prepared for the possibility that it might be someone else who walks through it.

My fellow conspirators like Maxine, Mike, Elihu, and the rest weren't comfortable with Frankie. They didn't think Frankie was up to the job. But if it were a question of saving the speakership from Berman, I knew I could sell them.

So the big meeting took place November 10, 1980. A lot of the members I could count on to vote for me weren't present. Because they were nominally in the Berman camp, they hadn't been invited. My full strength thus was not present. It was Frankie's show. But what did happen, which is what I suspected would happen, proved to be as valuable as a floor demonstration for Willie Brown.

At the meeting, Frankie surfaced his own name as a candidate for speaker and said that he had already called some Republicans who had said they'd be comfortable with him.

Then one caucus member, Sally Tanner, a great, tough lady, began grilling Frankie on his leadership skills. Maxine Waters was scowling as Frankie attempted to answer Tanner's questions. Maxine's face was twisted in unhappiness, but she didn't say a word. Eventually, though, Maxine walked over to me and said, "Come outside."

In the hallway, she said to me, "I can't support that motherfucker. He's too stupid."

I said, "Maxine, just get your ass back in there and sit down. Just listen. Sally is doing the job that needs to be done."

Sally was still walking through questions. She asked Frankie about his preparation for the role of speaker. She asked him about the budget. She asked him about navigating the waters of inter-party fights. He couldn't answer any of those things.

After an hour, Frankie said, "All these questions that you are asking, only one guy can answer those questions: Willie Brown. We ought to be with Willie Brown."

Sally Turner handled the case brilliantly. And although she had told me long before that she thought only two people—Jesse Unruh and Willie Brown—should ever be speaker, she hadn't been programmed to dismantle Frankie Vicencia. But she did.

Soon the members at the meeting were signing up for Willie Brown. Those who came forward included a whole host of McCarthy people, rural conservative Democrats who never in their lives would naturally be for me. But now they were.

Eventually, more than twenty names were on the list. Leo McCarthy and Art Agnos didn't sign until we were well up to twenty names. The deciding vote in this caucus came from Dominic Cortese from Santa Cruz. I had never met him before. "I've been a Democrat all my life," he said. "I've never voted for a Republican or with a Republican. This is quite a thing you're asking me to do: join a coalition with Republicans. Give me ten minutes. Let me walk around the building. My wife's in the coffee shop. Let me talk to my wife and come back and we'll cast my vote."

Of course, he voted for me. That gave me twenty-three votes from the Democratic caucus. Berman had twenty-three. That took care of forty-six out of the forty-seven votes in the Democratic caucus. The forty-seventh vote, the tiebreaker in the caucus, abstained. The sole abstainer was Tom Hannigan from Solano

County. He felt so much pressure that he went skiing and could not be reached.

So now I was even with Berman. It was time to move to the Republicans. But before we took the fateful step of approaching them to form the coalition, we decided to have one last meeting with Berman.

Frankie Vicencia led the meeting. If I had led it, it would have turned into a full-fledged confrontation—Berman would have ignited, and we actually still wanted peace within the caucus. Vicencia laid out a list of eight or nine items that we wanted, including committee chairmanships. If Berman granted those items, we'd vote for Berman.

Berman turned us down on all the items. He wouldn't enter into an acceptable agreement. The war was on.

The next step was to deal with the Republicans. But I was way ahead on this game.

Six years before the 1980 speakership fight, I met a Republican operative in Washington, DC, who was then unknown to most, but who in the Reagan years came to prominence as a political mastermind. His name is Ed Rollins.

I met Rollins at the trial of Ed Reinecke, then the Republican lieutenant governor of California. He was on trial in Washington for having allegedly lied before a U.S. Senate committee investigating Watergate. I had known Reinecke in Sacramento and found him to be a perfectly okay guy. He asked me to testify as a character witness on his behalf before a jury that included black members. I did speak on his behalf based on my knowledge of him when he had been California lieutenant governor. Reinecke was convicted, but his conviction was later overturned. While I was in Washington, I met Rollins, who was helping Reinecke. Rollins was also a talent spotter and a classic behind-the-scenes guy.

Later in the '70s Ed Rollins showed up in Sacramento as the chief strategist for the Republican minority in the assembly. He worked for Republican leader Carol Hallett, a member from the vast agricultural Central Valley. Both she and Rollins were looking for some way to leverage the Republicans' position in the house. Rollins became the crucial backer of the idea of the Republicans supporting Willie Brown as speaker of the house in 1980—though of course he kept mum about this in public.

Truth to tell, there were people in and outside of the assembly who had been working quietly and often unaware of one another to make Willie Brown speaker. These included my mentor, Jesse Unruh, the former speaker, who was California state treasurer in 1980. Rollins and Hallett were the chief Republican backers of a Willie Brown speakership. There were all sorts of relationships, even crossing party lines. One of the Democrats, Curtis Tucker, a lively member from Los Angeles, had grown very close to Republican leader Hallett, a relationship I encouraged.

These were all very loose forces committed to an idea that might never come to pass. But as the Democrats fell into complete division, the forces began to focus. Add in the work of Mike Roos, Maxine Waters, and Elihu Harris, who came up with the same idea on their own part, and you suddenly in the fall of 1980 had a hydra-headed movement to make me speaker. But my actual candidacy seemed a surprise to many.

When on November 21, 1980, the *Los Angeles Times* first reported that Willie Brown was a candidate for speaker, it struck the *Times* as a novel and confusing idea—especially because it challenged the long work of their homeboy, Howard Berman. They seemed to think my candidacy was quixotic, a will-o'-the-wisp, a slightly nutty idea. But they must have known that things were in the works.

The *Times* story was headlined, "Deal with GOP Suddenly Makes [Willie Brown] Threat to Fellow Democrat Berman." The first paragraph of the story read,

> Assemblyman Willie L. Brown Jr., a witty and flamboyant black leader from San Francisco, suddenly and unexpectedly emerged Thursday as the man who could defeat Assemblyman Howard L. Berman's long and carefully planned effort to become Speaker of the Assembly.

In a few weeks, the unexpected became reality. I became speaker, beating Howard Berman.

Working with Rollins and the Republicans to make the deal was a pleasure. It was a straight and sincere deal, though my friend Mike Roos likes to say, "Willie promised them everything they wanted and gave them nothing." It's a good line, but it actually was a sincere deal. It just wasn't the cave-in to Republicans that Bermanites tried to portray it as.

What I did do when dealing with the Republicans was promise them things that should have been in place years earlier. They were logical reforms, not giveaways. That's what they wanted.

I met with Carol Hallett, Ross Johnson, Ed Rollins, and a few other Republicans I didn't even know. "You guys tell me what you need," I said. I already knew—via back-channel discussions—what they wanted. But this is how you should handle a negotiation, anyway. First, find out privately what they need, then deal with it at the formal meeting.

I agreed to give the Republicans five chairmanships of their own. That was new, and fair. I agreed that every committee with a Democratic chairman would have a Republican vice chairman, and vice versa.

I agreed to proportionate memberships for the committees: the number of Republicans on a committee should reflect the number in the house. That's the way it should be. It was always unfair that in a house with, say, thirty-three Republicans and forty-seven Democrats, you had a committee of two Republicans and eight Democrats.

And I agreed that on the floor of the house, the Republicans should be able to sit together. A symbolic move to some, but an important one.

I also agreed that when it came to redistricting the house, we would provide the Republicans with adequate resources to do their own studies and propose their own competitive map. I allowed them their own staffs and computers for reapportionment. That was new. But I wasn't going to give away the store: the maps had to be competitive with ours.

I also had to show Democrats who were reluctant to deal with Republicans that the partisan Berman camp itself had also gone to treat with the Republicans. There was plenty of quiet evidence of that, but we needed something showy. Jesse Unruh pulled a marvelous ploy. At a cocktail party in Los Angeles, sure to be attended by *Los Angeles Times* reporters, Jesse arranged for the otherwise partisan Berman to be observed in an intense and intimate conversation with a Republican—the lieutenant governor of California, Mike Curb. I don't know how Jesse pulled it off, but the publicly observed scene showed Berman wasn't so simon-pure. That's politics.

And then we had to make sure the Republicans who had committed to us would stay with us, because we knew they'd be catching hell for treating with Willie Brown. So we arranged a press conference at which each Republican declared his vote and backed it up by sending a telegram guaranteeing his vote. We had it in writing.

But the battle wasn't over yet. The California Democratic congressional caucus stepped in to the fight: eighteen of the twenty-two members signed a letter saying a deal with the Republicans would be a disaster. Only Ron Dellums, John Burton, Phil Burton, and Los Angeles congressman Augustus Hawkins refused to sign.

Nonetheless, it looked like victory was ours. I took our gang of conspirators to New York for a blowout celebration at the Helmsley Palace Hotel. We made quite a weekend out of it: shows, shopping, games, dinners. It was a blast. But on our Sunday night in New York, César Chávez organized a candlelight march in front of the home of Art Torres in Los Angeles demanding that he vote for Berman. César was concerned that farm legislation would be vitiated under a speaker who was elected with Republican support. He needn't have worried. Anyway, his march was for naught: Torres stayed with me.

As soon as the Republicans signed the telegrams of support, it really was over. The rest was last-minute fussing. Then finally on December 1 the vote came. I was elected speaker with fifty-one votes, twenty-three Democratic votes and twenty-eight Republican. I needed only forty-one to win. Berman received a total of twenty-four votes, twenty-three Democratic and one Republican.

Some patronizing sort said that I had been elected speaker in 1980, after having been defeated in 1974, because I had grown more humble in the meantime. Nonsense. I hadn't grown more humble. I had just grown more nimble.

I would go on to serve as speaker for fourteen and a half years, a record. Many said I wouldn't last six months.

I knew what to do to ensure my tenure. First, I had to chase Howard Berman out of the house. I didn't want him around.

The answer was simple. During the reapportionment process that year, we drew some attractive congressional districts. My old nemesis in the assembly took the bait; Howard Berman went to Washington. At least he was out of Sacramento.

PART THREE

"An Offer Like That Could Land Us Both in Jail"

Willie Brown discourses on money games in the capitol, the FBI's attempt to get him, and how he kept his speakership even after the Republicans won the majority in the house.

CHAPTER TWENTY

Old-Time Money Scams

NEXT TO REQUESTS FOR stories of coups and deals, the subject I'm most asked about concerning my assembly years is the use of cash to buy influence. In the early days, when I was first in the assembly from the mid-'60s to the late '70s, there was a lot of it. Mostly penny-ante stuff, but a lot of it. As I rose to power, I stopped most of it by changing the ways in which funds were raised for campaigns.

A little history: until the mid-1970s, American political campaigns, even for statewide office, were relatively inexpensive. For well-liked incumbents they could be really cheap. As recently as 1982, the late U.S. Senator William Proxmire of Wisconsin, a truly parsimonious fellow, managed to win reelection to the U.S. Senate having spent only two hundred dollars on his campaign, mostly for postage used in returning proffered campaign contributions! Compare that to 2006, when it took from three million dollars to ten million dollars to run a campaign for the U.S. Senate.

Back then unscrupulous candidates were simply taking what money there was, doing what they wanted with it, and thinking up bizarre scams to procure more. I did not want this freewheeling boodling to continue when it became obvious that gargantuan sums of money would be coming into politics. The scams were already unbelievable.

One day in the early '70s, when I was a member of the assembly's Ways and Means Committee, Bob Moretti, the speaker, telephoned me from a golf course. "You won't believe this," he said.

He had just been playing golf with a Los Angeles businessman who asked Moretti during the round, "Is the legislature really going to outlaw goose feathers in California?"

Moretti stopped. "What are you talking about?" he asked.

The businessman, who was the head of the association of California pillow makers or something like that, said he had been approached by a member of the assembly, whom I'll call "X." Assemblyman X told the trade group that there was a move in the assembly to ban the use of goose feathers in the manufacture of pillows in California, because the goose feathers were seen as a health hazard. Naturally, the group was horrified and worried. As it happened, this was during a period when the state of California was banning the use of all sorts of things.

But then this assemblyman told the pillow maker he could help. He personally could keep the legislature from banning bird feathers. All it would take would be a little cash, a little feathering of his personal nest via contributions to his campaign chest. Of course, there was no such legislation. The assembly had not been the least bit interested in goose feathers. The only interest in geese the California legislature has taken that I know of has been to order, per a bill in 2004 by my old friend John Burton, to ban the production of foie gras in the state starting in 2012.

Back then, I immediately took the assembly member who was intent on shaking the pillow makers down out to the proverbial woodshed and shook some sense into him before he could get himself, the house, and these constituents in trouble. And we in the leadership removed him from any committees where he was in a position to hit up citizens.

From the golf course, Speaker Moretti had said to me, wonderingly, "How do these guys think up these things?" But in the old days they did.

On another day back then, a lobbyist came to see me. He represented recent immigrants who had medical credentials from their old country, credentials that were not recognized in California. He had been lobbying the chair of the committee on licenses for help with legislation that would enable these professionals to get at least some credit for their professional training overseas when they went through the complex, demanding process of testing and vetting that was part of applying for a California license.

He was having a hard time. The committee on licenses, which was called a "juice committee" because so much lobbying money flowed to its members, wasn't inclined to help. The lobbyists for the established health care professionals didn't want any new practitioners with non-U.S. credentials getting licenses. They said it was to maintain standards, but they really just wanted to keep the professions closed. They didn't want any new members in the guild. The committee, beholden to these lobbyists, followed the restrictive line.

The lobbyist for the new arrivals decided to appeal directly to the committee chairman, who, in turn, seemed sympathetic to the plight of the immigrants. Indeed, the chairman offered to introduce a helpful bill. That twist should have been a warning. But the naïve lobbyist began working with and contributing to the chairman's campaign coffers. When two years had passed without any sign of progress in the assembly, the lobbyist came to see me.

"Is there any way," the lobbyist asked, "that you can get this bill out of the 'ledge council'? The chairman says he can't get the votes to get the bill released from the ledge council. Is there any way you know of that you could help us get this bill out of ledge council?"

I said, "What are you talking about? Getting a bill out of the ledge council? Are you sure you have the name right?" His story made no sense.

While there is an office of lawyers attached to the assembly called "the legislative counsel" and known to insiders as "the legi counsel's office," it's an advisory office to help individual legislators properly draft bills. A member goes in and says to the legi counsel, "I want a bill that will do thus-and-so," and the legi counsel drafts it for the member. Then the member introduces it to the assembly for legislative consideration.

But the legi counsel has no votes. It has no parliamentary function. A bill could not possibly be stuck there. I asked the lobbyist if he meant the legi counsel He said, "That's it. That's the group."

I explained to the lobbyist that the legi counsel isn't a committee or legislative body and told him its real function.

He shrugged and said, "Well, for the last two years or so, we've given campaign contributions to Chairman X of the licensing committee for the purpose of getting this bill introduced. Every year he comes back to tell me that he's been unable to get the votes to get it out of legi counsel, but he'll try again next year."

I figured that this must be one bad bill if Chairman X kept coming back with an explanation like that. Still, we in the leadership had a little meeting and decided to send a memo to the legi counsel to find out why the member's bill had not been sent to the assembly.

The information we got back was even more startling: there was no bill. Never had been. Chairman X had never even sent a memo to the legi counsel asking them to draft a bill.

In two years, the chairman had never done anything—but take

money from the lobbyist. And unless this lobbyist had come forward to me, there would have been no way you could ever check to see how a scam like this was operating. Because the attorney-client privilege governs activities between the legislative counsel and the individual members, there's no freedom of information act governing those consultations, or lack thereof. It's all confidential. Chairman X was running a scam—a perfectly legal scam.

To remedy the situation the lobbyist and his clients were in, we in the leadership got their bill drafted and introduced, and I believe it eventually passed. We took the entrepreneurial assembly member out of temptation's way. He never bothered anyone again.

You have no idea how many schemes and scams I saw in the early days. And that's why by the time I arrived at the speakership in 1980, I knew the repertoire of scams. I knew who the scam artists were. When I became speaker, I removed them from their chairs and from positions where they could do harm.

When I was speaker, if I had any suspicion that a member had done something improper to introduce a bill, I'd kill the bill outright—even if it was something I was philosophically in favor of. I did that quite often. And then the member would receive an invitation "to come sit with the speaker for a few minutes." And I'd lay down my suspicions to him or her. And if you were that member, I'd tell you that I killed the bill because I didn't want the house embarrassed by your chicanery. You, of course, would deny having done any skullduggery. But I would know what you had actually done, and you would know that I knew. You'd be removed from any position of power, and you'd be under my constant surveillance.

Some have said I should have outed such members, gotten up on a soapbox and denounced them. I favored a more pragmatic approach—and I saved the institution of the house from suffering a black eye. I believe that's the best way to handle things. But you need an alert, learned, and sage speaker to do that. You need some-one of long experience who also is going to be around a long time. In today's world, where term limits mean members have to depart the house after three short two-year terms, no member, no speaker gets to develop the skills and the tenure to discern trouble and then to enforce sanctions against members who are playing it risky.

There's greed everywhere. And as an elected type with the re-sponsibility for the integrity and the reputation of the house and of the legislative process, you have to assume that the potential for greed is there. That assumption has to be part of your everyday thinking. And you've got to operate on the theory that you have to find the greed first. You've got to find the guy who is starting to get into thieving—whether it's the member thief, the corporate thief, the lobbying thief, the staffer thief—and make him back out of it before he gets caught. You've got to get the entrepreneurial types out of the way.

CHAPTER TWENTY-ONE

"An Offer Like That Could Land Us Both in Jail"

OF COURSE, I'VE ALSO HEARD the stories in which I supposedly have shaken down people for money, agreed to a quid pro quo. One of the most upsetting ones concerned a meeting I supposedly had with a major California land developer down in Los Angeles when I was speaker.

The mega-developer supposedly had a piece of legislation that he wanted passed. It reportedly dealt with some technical bits of financing. So he purportedly called for a meeting with me! At this supposed meeting in L.A., they allegedly outlined the bill to me.

Then I purportedly asked some questions about the bill—questions that dealt with the intricacies of the legislation. They were impressed with my mastery of the subject matter.

Then—reportedly—there was silence and the developer supposedly said, "Is there some contribution we can make to a campaign fund that will help you and help us?" I supposedly named an entity they could contribute to. Then, as the story goes, they made the contribution, and the bill passed.

Well, I've never attended a private meeting with this gentleman, nor have I ever met privately with any of his people. This is a complete misrepresentation. The teller of this tale, a well-respected Los Angeles lawyer, should have known better. He should be horsewhipped.

The only way I would have met this mega-developer when legislation was likely to have come under discussion would have been like this: Once a year or so, people in various industries would separately have meetings with legislators to discuss problems, concerns, and proposals for upcoming legislation. To such conferences I would bring my staff expert on housing, my expert on environment, my expert on any issue impinging on these guys' concerns. These experts would include both legislators and heavyweight staff policy guys. And when it came to policy guys, I had only the brightest and the best.

At such a conference, you let them all talk. You let them all respond to one another. And although you, Willie Brown, know you're going to make the final decision, you ain't gonna make it in that room. You ain't gonna make a decision in the conference.

And you certainly aren't going to discuss money. You aren't going to do any fund-raising there, or anywhere, while bills are pending before the legislature.

It's not even remotely possible that I would have gone to a private meeting to discuss legislation with someone who was not part of the legislature. I certainly would not discuss money. Only an idiot, a real stone idiot, would have a meeting like that.

It's ludicrous, it's stupid to imagine a meeting wherein someone essentially says, "Mr. Speaker, I've got a bill I want passed. What can I do in return for you?" and then the politician is supposed to say, "Mr. Developer, here's what it's going to cost you, and here's where you send the money." Just ludicrous. No successful businessman would be that stupid. No intelligent politician would be so idiotic.

If such a meeting did occur, the first thing I would have said is, "Whoa, whoa—you're here to see me about a piece of legislation? Do you want to get us both in jail?" Indeed, I would assume that any guy who would say something like that has gotta be wearing a wire! He has got to be part of a sting.

In this business of politics, if you're gonna survive, you've got to operate on the theory that anybody who is so stupid as to put you in a position where your judgment could be compromised, or appear to be compromised, is wearing a wire. You sure as hell don't help them. You instruct your people to have nothing to do with them. You get rid of them.

Even groups supposedly committed to good government bought some of the myths about me. Even though they should have known better.

My greatest critic in the mid-'80s was Common Cause, a group whose members were firm foes of any politician who raised money. Since I was the leading fund-raiser of my own time—nobody in either house, in either party, in any state office could raise as much money as I could—they were always after me. They were absolutely certain that contributors were buying access by virtue of all this money. Except my critics never could trace or tag a piece of legislation because, generally, I, not the members, received the contributions and then distributed the money. Common Cause was always looking for the questionable vote: the pro-choice member suddenly voting against pro-choice. But they could never find telltale votes because there weren't any.

When I put together coalitions on votes, I put them together in such a way that a member never had to vote against a belief. I would never solicit an individual to do that. I had ways of putting together majorities that precluded a member's having to vote in a manner offensive to him or her. I always tried to make sure that when you cast your vote, it was a vote you could defend.

This had the advantage also of meaning that groups like Common Cause could never lay a glove on any of my folk. They scrutinized me personally, of course. But all their efforts went for naught because there was not a soul around, from member to lobbyist, who could say anything other than that I would give you a fair hearing. Nonetheless, Common Cause persisted in believing in their myths. Then, for some incredible reason, they invited me to be the star speaker at one of their own fund-raising events! The guy they deplored as the king of evil fund-raisers was the guy they picked to be the top draw at their fund-raising dinner! Unbelievable, and an occasion for teaching a home truth via a little humor.

They filled up the place, a sizable hall in a Sacramento convention center. They were charging twenty-five dollars a head to get in. Cheap.

So when I was introduced, I stood up and said, "I'm really in confusion here. You're charging twenty-five dollars to meet me, hear me, talk to me. I don't know of anything in the halls of the legislature, or in the governmental decision-making process, where we sell our services for twenty-five dollars." Now they were confused. Did they think I was going to mock them for not charging a high enough access fee?

I went through a list of bills, serious and silly, that were before the house. I said, "How in the name of goodness do you think you could buy any part of those bills for twenty-five dollars? You've got to be out of your minds." Then I made my point: "You couldn't do it for any amount of money. Money just doesn't buy consensus and you need consensus to put these bills together." I ended up getting a standing ovation.

CHAPTER TWENTY-TWO

My Money-Raising Principles

ALL THROUGH MY POLITICAL CAREER I've been thinking about money, that is to say I've been trying to understand the dynamics of how money works in politics in order to maximize its possibilities in politics and minimize its pitfalls. By the time I became speaker of the assembly in 1980, I had developed a few key insights about the raising of political money which informed all our fund-raising during my years as speaker. They hold true today and can apply in most political arenas. But like most principles about money, I found as speaker and fund-raiser-in-chief of the Democrats in Sacramento I had to every day drum them into the heads of assembly members, lobbyists, and contributors.

The first was this: that a contribution buys the contributor nothing. There can never be a quid pro quo. There can never be a situation in which people might think they had created a quid pro quo. This I learned from Jesse Unruh, the legendary speaker of the California assembly when I first came into office.

The second was that the only contributions for which you won't be criticized—and, perhaps, investigated—are those that come from the people who either are your philosophical soul

169

mates (whatever your political philosophy may be) or who love you personally. This was something I learned from Phil Burton, the San Francisco congressman who, like Unruh, was also my political mentor.

The third insight was my own: all campaign contributions should come directly to the top. In other words, assembly members (including me) would raise money, but it would all go to a central fund where I, Willie Brown, speaker of the Assembly, would dole it to races where cash was really needed.

We exploited these insights in all our fund-raising. We solicited campaign money from the friends and soul mates of each member, regardless of where the member stood in the political spectrum. You might be a raging San Francisco liberal or a conservative "Ag-Democrat" from the huge, agricultural Central Valley, but you had people who believed in you. You raised money from them and we pooled it at the top and reassigned it to where it was needed. And all we promised the contributors was a fair hearing and a commitment to good public policy making. When Jesse Unruh famously said to legislators, "If you can't take the lobbyists' money, eat their food, drink their booze, sleep with their women, and then vote against them, you don't belong here," he said it right.

All that a contribution buys you is an investment in good government. That's it. Money is, as Unruh also said, "the mother's milk of politics." But he didn't mean the money was there to nourish the lives of the members. He meant that politics itself, not the members, requires the big money. So as a politician you'd better make sure you're getting the money—but you're not selling anything in return. It's just to make the election cycles go round.

Of course, contributors and the public are fickle, though, about what good public policy making means. As a politician you'd best accept that this is just a fact of life. It's as simple as this: if a piece of legislation passes that they like, then in the public's mind that's good public policy making. If it's something they don't like, then they say somebody was bought off.

The largest single contribution I ever received was a check for $250,000. César Chávez of the United Farm Workers gave me the check one day at Perry's, a tin-ceilinged, checkered-tablecloth saloon still popular with politicians, professional athletes, journalists, and lawyers on Union Street in San Francisco's Cow Hollow district. If you need a politically smart lawyer, I tell people, just hurry down to Perry's. The bar there is a kind of bar association of its own.

Now, if I had taken a sum like the farmworkers' $250,000 from the oil industry I certainly would have been criticized. That wouldn't have bothered me, but a contribution that large from Big Oil probably would have been investigated, which would have been a headache.

But because César, the United Farm Workers, and I, despite some ups and downs (César Chávez led that candlelight vigil in Los Angeles to oppose me when I was running for speaker in 1980), were soul mates and had been forever, no one raised an eyebrow. Nor should they have.

At that time a Republican, George Deukmejian, governed California. The farmworkers were worried about potential erosions, under Deukmejian, of the farmworkers' act passed under Democrat Jerry Brown, the previous governor.

In giving the money to me, César was giving to all the Democrats in the assembly who had supported the farmworkers over the years. He clearly appreciated what we had done and what he hoped we would do in the future.

There was no quid pro quo in that. If he had given money to Democratic assemblyman Jimmy Costa, who opposed the farmworkers, you might think he was hoping to buy a vote. Of course, César would never have given money to enemies.

People will give to you willingly, if you ask, if they know what you are doing and are pleased by your efforts on behalf of something they believe in. Let's say you are at the Sierra Club and you know I've been busting my ass to get an alternative fuel measure passed. You really like the fact that I am trying to do something to get alternative fuel going, so you donate to my campaign. You're motivated by my work.

Or let's say you're a member of the various gay, lesbian, bisexual, and transgender organizations. You really like the idea that I'm trying to decriminalize sexual acts between consenting adults. So you want to make sure that I get elected. And you also want to make sure that I get the financial help that will allow me to help others like myself get elected. So you donate.

That's a normal part of the system. Teachers donate a lot of money to candidates, but it is to candidates who are committed to money for schools, to good governance policy for schools, to higher standards in education. So you donate to the people who are running for office on the basis of things that you both believe in. And needless to say, you restrict your donations to people who you anticipate will be good performers on the issues you believe in.

The point of this story is that, indeed, your friends and soul mates are your best sources of money. They believe in you and want you strong. Now, sometimes if you're a donor, you're going to be pleased with the decisions your members make. But sometimes you won't be. But generally, if the member is making decisions that are based on what is good public policy, people will understand, even if they are not totally pleased. Frankly, I've found that people respect you more if you can explain why a decision against their interest is in the service of good public policy. Intelligent people really don't want pawns. They want politicians who are attentive but who, in the end, vote for what's in the public interest. In an age when we needed vast amounts of money to finance a lot of races in the assembly to hold on to our majority, this dynamic struck me as being exploitable, the source of mutual aid for members. I asked our members to squeeze every nickel out of their friends, even if they held safe, unbeatable seats. They themselves wouldn't need much money. But I could spread that money around where it was needed.

Anyone who had a good relationship with a group that contributed—even if it were, say, with the oil companies or with the insurance industry—went to work raising money from their allies. As a result, we got money from lawyers, physicians, prison guards, developers, restaurant owners, hotel owners, limo drivers, transportation people, concrete makers, road builders, whoever.

I also got organized labor, under Jack Henning at the California Labor Federation, which often gave more than a million dollars in an election year, to change the way they contributed. They had been giving in small dabs to a great number of members, but I asked Jack to change that.

I said to him, "Jack, the interests of organized labor would be better served if you didn't fritter away your money in drips and drabs. You'd be a much bigger player by pooling your money, donating it to the leadership to spread around where needed, and then lobbying the leadership, instead of going to individual members. That's how the teachers association got to be such a big player. That's how the prison guards got to be such big players."

We did the same on the business side. Assemblyman Chuck Calderon was a favorite of the banking industry. If the industry gave Calderon one hundred thousand dollars, Calderon under my direction would then redistribute it.

We also pooled a lot of the money into a central campaign fund, run by me, which provided campaign services to members. All the printing, mailing, media could be done out of the central pool.

I was *not* going to put temptation in the way of members by letting them handle vast amounts of cash. And I certainly wasn't going to allow an array of campaign consultants to control campaign spending—the consultants pocketed commissions on everything, sometimes even on postage stamps. They swallowed up cash.

Of course, we also pursued donations from sources that weren't soul mates of anyone. Their money was good and it was better that the money went to us than to our enemies.

Did the donors whose beliefs seemed inimical to my philosophy expect that their donations would suddenly buy them votes?

No, there was never any discussion about "With this contribution, you're buying thus-and-so." No, they knew they were investing in my leadership, which allowed plenty of room for conflicting views. And they knew they were investing in a leadership that believed in giving them a fair hearing.

But they knew their campaign contributions were not purchasing any favors. I set up this system to avoid that. Only the FBI, apparently, did not seem to notice that this is the way we were doing things on the Democratic side of the assembly. The FBI would harass us, and me especially, for years.

CHAPTER TWENTY-THREE

Tricks the FBI Played to Try to Get Me

THE SUITE OF OFFICES IN the California capitol allocated to the speaker of the assembly is a group of opulent rooms painstakingly restored to their Victorian splendor—by me. The anteroom, just outside my private office, was, in my reign, also a very modern clubroom. I filled it with video games, pinball machines, TVs, comfortable chairs, refreshments. I set it up as a refuge for all the members, Republican as well as Democrat.

I wanted them to feel free to hang with me and to see me at any time. Indeed, I had a steadfast rule that I was available to any member at any time, no matter what I was doing—unless I was speaking to another member. So Her Majesty the Queen of England could be there talking with me in my office, but if a member wanted to speak to me, my staff would buzz me, I'd pick up the phone, and my assistant would say, "Mr. So-and-so from the Forty-second district would like to speak with you." I'd turn to Her Majesty and say, "Excuse me, Madame Queen, but a member is calling," and I'd take your call, figure out your problem. That was a hallmark of my deal as speaker: every member, Democrat or Republican, could disrupt anything that I was doing, unless I was meeting with another member. That went for members of the state senate, the other house of the legislature, as well. State senators didn't come around in the frequency that assembly members did, but they were always welcome.

So I wasn't surprised one day in the summer of 1991 to see a senator from Los Angeles's San Fernando Valley lurking out there among the video games with the other members. My assistant buzzed me to say that he wished to speak with me. His name was Alan Robbins.

Among his peers, Alan Robbins was probably the least-liked member of the entire legislature. He had a terrible personality. His offbeat legislation on morals matters made him seem almost like an evangelical Christian—but he was also regarded as a whitened sepulcher himself when it came to morals. In 1981, he had been acquitted of charges that he had had sex in 1978 and 1979 with two different sixteen-year-old girls.

And in the capitol he was one of the most annoyingly dogged representatives when it came to his own bills. He was always trying to horse-trade on bills, offering amendments about this if you'd do that. On the floor you'd see him sitting right on a member's desk trying to jawbone the other member into a deal. What made it worse was that his bills were usually of low quality: special-interest legislation for land developers. Oh, he was truly disliked.

However, I treated him the way I treated every member: with respect and cordiality. I didn't trust him at all, but I felt that every member was entitled to the deference and courtesy that membership brought them. He was really an underdog. I didn't want to be close to him, but I tried to be respectful and friendly to him. He in turn appreciated that.

So I told my assistant to invite him from the clubroom into my office.

He approached the open door to my inner office, but he didn't step in. Instead he stood on the threshold, with his head and shoulders leaning into my office. The rest of him stayed on the other side of the threshold.

From that odd stance, he said very loudly, "Mr. Speaker, I know you don't like this bill." He named one of his awful bills that was on the floor. Then he said, "But I thought I would try just one more time. Would you be willing—"

I said, "Alan, I already told you, this is a terrible bill. I won't have anything to do with it."

Then he surprised me. He said, "I knew you would have that attitude. I won't waste your time." He turned and walked away. His more typical response would have been to come in and badger me.

Not until years later did I find out that at that moment he was wearing a wire—a hidden recording device—for the FBI. Eventually his secretly recorded conversations that summer were crucial to an investigation that led to the indictment and conviction of four other legislators, though none of them were Democrats in the assembly.

The FBI, unbeknownst to the rest of us, had already nailed Robbins on influence-peddling charges. To secure a reduced sentence, he had agreed to wear a wire and try to incriminate people who he said were his accomplices, fellow boodlers, in the senate and in the lobbying fraternity. He had supplied the names to the FBI. And now he was recording the activities and conversations of those people. I was not on his list of compromised legislators, but the FBI insisted that he wear a wire against Willie Brown.

The FBI first started looking for corruption in the assembly long before I became speaker. Their first sorties started in 1975 when Leo McCarthy was speaker. One way or another, sometimes secretly, sometimes openly, they continued over the years. After I became speaker, I became a target. They were desperate, ruthless, to get something on me. To bring down the speaker, who happened also to be a leading national black politician, would have put them in the history books.

It's amazing to me how dedicated they were—and what a waste their work was. They were profoundly ignorant of how the house worked under Willie Brown and were perfectly willing, as the FBI often is, to entrap people right and left. In their investigations of the legislature, they apparently forgot or never knew that just a few years earlier, I had seen their shoddy work up close. And I even got the chief prosecutor, the U.S. Attorney for the Northern District of California, to acknowledge that the FBI investigated an assembly member without cause.

When Leo McCarthy was speaker, a man named Dan Boatwright represented Contra Costa County, a rapidly developing suburban area east of San Francisco. An FBI agent who lived on the same street as Boatwright took a dislike to him and thought he could prove Boatwright was on the take, hauling it in from developers in Contra Costa County.

They went all over the place, expanding the investigation to other members while still pursuing Boatwright. I was serving in the assembly but still working as a criminal attorney. Boatwright hired me to be his lawyer in the proceeding.

Eventually the prosecution dropped the matter. G. William Hunter, the U.S. Attorney, issued a letter saying there never had been any foundation for the investigation into Boatwright. That may be the only case in history where a U.S. attorney essentially apologized for investigating an innocent man.

Boatwright went on to serve in the state senate. It was for the sake of his political career that I had asked Hunter to issue the disavowal. Otherwise, Boatwright's enemies would have hung the investigation over his head for the rest of his political career. Hunter understood you have to play fair.

But the FBI was relentless, ignorant, hateful, or intent on revenge. Because in 1985, with their old nemesis Willie Brown enthroned as speaker of the assembly, they began a secret sting to get me. They asked everyone they talked to the same question: "Tell us what you know about Willie Brown . . . Give us something on Willie Brown."

They had nothing specific they could go after. They were just desperate to cobble something against Willie Brown. One retired FBI agent later told me they had eight file drawers full of notes and interviews compiled and worked up to hammer something against me.

Now Alan Robbins, hoping to keep his sentence as light as possible, had to go along with them. He wore a wire against Willie Brown. What they were after with him, since they had nothing substantial to go on, was any talk about the bill they could twist. They were looking for any small talk about anything that they could misconstrue.

As to the bill he mentioned, what the FBI wanted was for him, first, to say, "Mr. Speaker, suppose I can get these guys who are sponsoring this bill to do something really decent in the form of contributions in the next set of campaigns." And that was the kind of question Alan was quite capable of asking. That's not the kind of question I would have answered. But the FBI was looking for me to make any answer. They would have tried to use it.

But the only dialogue I was going to have with him about the bill was about the fact that I and my leadership were going to kill it. We did kill it. It was terrible legislation. That his legislation was being killed was nothing new. But while his bills were alive, he would not take no for an answer. He'd just keep coming back. So it was no surprise to see him at my door. What was a surprise was that he backed away so quickly, because Alan was persistent and always loved the BS, the small talk that's part of everyday life in the capitol.

Legislators are constantly bullshitting; mixing in small talk, trash talk, with talk about bills. There are so many times when you are dialoguing about legislation that you mix in baseball, you mix in golf, you mix in woman chasin'. You mix in drinking, you mix in movies—all that. And when you do so, you aren't substantively addressing the legislative issues, but such sidebar banter can be misconstrued.

And even when you're talking about legislation, you can be just BSing. For example, you might say to me, "Willie, would you support this bill?" And I'd respond, "Ah, come on, there's no way you could pay me enough to support this bill."

And you might say, "Well, what would be enough?" And I might joke, "The same amount as Bill Gates gets from Microsoft," or something like that. Obviously, you're just bullshittin'. But think how that looks typed out in a transcript. There's no room for humor in an indictment. There's no room for small talk.

And, curiously, just a few days earlier Alan Robbins and I had engaged in some small talk about cars. At the time, I collected cars, bought and sold them. It was my kind of investment. Others in politics and in the law had heavy investments in the stock market. I'm a black guy; I didn't know anything about Wall Street. I bought Jaguars, Porsches, and Ferraris, among others, and I resold them.

That spring I had been looking for a chocolate-colored Corvette. They were hot. I had been talking about this one day with some legislators from Southern California, which has monster car dealerships, and asked them if they had any tips on who to call. This was before the internet. You didn't Google "chocolate Corvette" in those days; you asked your buddies who were from all over California for leads.

Once a guy from around Bakersfield, a conservative farm town, asked me if I knew of anybody in wicked San Francisco who could cook up a naughty cake for a bachelor party. I called a jolly gay baker in San Francisco's Castro district for him. The cake was baked. They had never seen a chocolate cake like that in Bakersfield before. I believe the remainder of the cake was diced up into innocent-looking pieces and donated to a church picnic.

Back when I was looking for a chocolate Corvette, Alan said he knew of a big-time Chevrolet dealer in the San Fernando Valley who specialized in Corvettes. He said he'd call down and see if the dealer had one. He did. I called down and brokered a price, bought the Corvette—with my own money—and had it shipped up to me in San Francisco.

That day when Alan stood in my doorway, I was going to tell him I bought the car and thank him for the introduction. But then he did that duck-out.

Later when I learned that he had been wearing that wire, I realized what he did by keeping the conversation short. He wasn't going to create an opportunity where there might be any small talk on that recording that the FBI would later twist around. I like to think that's because he appreciated the fact that despite his terrible personality, his pariah status, I, unlike many other members, always treated him with respect and cordiality.

And when did I learn that Robbins had been wearing the FBI's wire? Robbins himself told me—when I went on a visit to a federal prison in Dublin, California, not far from San Francisco. I had gone to see Mike Milliken, the junk bond king and a past supporter of mine. While I was visiting Milliken, Robbins, to my surprise, appeared. He was a prisoner in the same jail. There he told me the story of the strange afternoon when he lurked at my office door.

Alan Robbins's sting wasn't the FBI's first attempt to get me. To bring down an important political and governmental leader was the ambition of many FBI agents and U.S. prosecutors then. It was also the ambition of many politicians.

On the FBI and the U.S. Attorney's side, this was all about career building. If as a prosecutor you bag a politician, you know you're going down in history. If you're Kenneth Starr and you bring down Clinton, you're in the history books. If you're Patrick Fitzgerald, the special U.S. Attorney from Chicago investigating George W. Bush's White House, and you bag a White House official, you're in the history books. In Fitzgerald's case, he has an admirably high standard: he doesn't bring indictments unless he knows he really has a case.

Unfortunately for the ambitions of the prosecutors trying to bring me down, there was never any basis for their investigations. When their investigations, indictments, and trials were concluded, not one Democrat in the assembly was convicted. The only assembly member to go to jail was a Republican, Patrick Nolan, who was the very man who had gone to the FBI suggesting that with a ridiculous sting (which they attempted) they could bring down Willie Brown. Nolan was out to get me because he thought with me convicted, he could ride a new Republican majority to the speakership himself. To the FBI, he spelled out a scenario of how he imagined corruption worked on the Democratic side of the house. He said that I used a system of pieces of legislation, which he called "bag bills," as a device to secure campaign contributions from people who might benefit from the legislation.

But what he was doing in outlining this scenario of how legislation supposedly was passed (or killed) in return for money was not a description of how we Democrats handled contributions, but how he did! He ended up being caught in his own trap.

It astonishes me to this day that the FBI did no due diligence before beginning this investigation. They went into the legislature looking for bribes and quid pro quo contributions, simply unaware that, in the assembly on the Democratic side, I had long ago set up many safeguards against the pitfalls of money raising. We long ago had moved to protect the house and its members from the potential for greed.

One of the FBI's efforts to "get Willie Brown" involved some truly reprehensible dealing by a man I liked and respected. That was the Republican governor of California from 1983 to 1991, George Deukmejian. George allowed the FBI to commit fraud and to debase the legislative process in their ill-founded and unsuccessful efforts to bring me down.

The FBI went to him in 1985 and told him that FBI agents, masquerading as small-businessmen, were seeking to surreptitiously introduce a bill to secure state aid for what turned out to be a fictitious shrimp-processing business. Theirs was a classic "bag bill" as Nolan would have said. The FBI's idea was to have undercover agents posing as businessmen place bribes with legislators in return for help with their fake bill. A lot of conscientious and innocent people in the legislature merely trying to do their jobs got black eyes, and huge legal bills, as a result of this prosecutors' chicanery.

The FBI went to Governor Deukmejian to warn him not to sign the bill if it should pass the legislature. What George should have done was throw these fakers out of his office. He should have called the leadership in the legislature and said, "You are being investigated for possible corruption." That's all he needed to have said.

The FBI obviously would have gone bonkers if Deukmejian had done this, but there was no reason why he had to be in bed with scam artists. It wasn't as if he had been called before the grand jury. It wasn't as if he were being asked to testify in a criminal proceeding.

I found out what the FBI was up to when they raided the offices of the house and its members. I immediately sent the FBI a long letter inviting them to call without a subpoena for any records and information they desired. I told them that I would personally ensure that each member would make readily available all the records and material they wished. I told them, and the governor, that I did not want the assembly defiled by terrifying raids that were in fact unrelated to any crime.

You know what? I never heard from the FBI.

Bizarre. Because very few people offer to cooperate fully with the FBI. Why didn't they follow up on my invitation? Had they found me not following up on my offer, they could easily have obtained a subpoena.

The FBI was not being legitimate. Had they any interest in fairness, in maintaining the integrity of the democratic process, and in observing the separation of powers between the executive and the legislative branches of government, they wouldn't have hesitated to say, "Fine, send us over the papers, Mr. Brown. Here's the list of papers we want."

The first inkling that someone was trying to set traps came one day when Gwen Moore, a Democratic assembly member from Los Angeles, visited me. Gwen represented a largely black district and had taken an interest in economic development for small black businesses. If you had such a business and thought you might qualify for economic aid, her office was where you went. She usually was happy to introduce bills that might help these people.

She came in and told me that she was "carrying," or sponsoring, an economic development bill for some people with a shrimp-processing business near Sacramento. Unbeknownst to us, this was the scam bill created by the FBI.

She told me that the people behind the business had come to her staff and offered them a five-thousand-dollar contribution to Gwen's campaign fund.

For a black member, even a five-hundred-dollar contribution was big money, so this five thousand dollars looked awfully good.

The size of the contribution proffered bothered her, as did the fact that she didn't know the people offering it. Typically, her contributors might have included groups of janitors or even black physicians from her district that she knew. She also might have received money from the farmworkers. Because she knew those people, she knew their money was clean.

But a five-thousand-dollar contribution coming all from one entity and you have no idea who these people are? Well, it's an attractive five grand that you can really use. But there's got to be something fishy.

She said, "What do I do?"

"Why would you even ask that question?" I said. "If you take that contribution, my guess is that somewhere up the line you're gonna get prosecuted."

Gwen didn't take the contribution. But two of her staff guys, who were involved in a local school board race, did take the contribution—without telling her! The FBI, which was the true donor of the five thousand dollars, assumed that the staffers took the money and hid it in this school board race at Gwen's direction. Gwen was called by the FBI and had to face a grand jury. We hired a good lawyer, Phil Ryan, my former legal partner in San Francisco. We made it clear to the FBI that she took no contribution, and that these staff guys had to be operating on their own.

Gwen Moore, as it turned out, was never prosecuted—only because she had had the good judgment to ask for my advice. But one of her staffers was later convicted and sentenced to prison for his skullduggery.

Then in August 1988 the FBI raided the California capitol. The assembly was in session and the members were on the floor. The FBI went up to the private offices of about five or six members.

From the members' offices, they called the floor and said, "We're the FBI. We're in your office. We'd like you to come up."

Well, a member can't leave the floor without a pass from the speaker. And you'd better have a good explanation for why you want to have a pass. I'm a stickler for all members being present when the house is in session. I was not going to let the house be criticized for absenteeism or ghost voting, a practice where one member voted for an absent member. That's really all I required on the days when the house was in session: that you be present in the chamber or the immediate precincts. I learned of the FBI when one member sheepishly came up to me for permission to leave.

"I need a pass," he said. "I need to go upstairs. The FBI is in my office."

"What the fuck are they doing in your office?"

"Well, they're investigating—"

And then a second member came up to me and said the same thing. And then a third. I said to them, "You are not going upstairs. You do not have a lawyer, and anything you say to the FBI could be used against you. So you're not going upstairs. We're going at least to get you lawyers."

One member said, "What should we tell them?"

I said, "What do you mean, 'What should we tell them?'? You're going to tell them nothing. I, however, am going to announce on the floor the following: 'The house is in session and because we are doing business on this floor, no member will be given a pass for the next several hours.' "

I made that announcement. As you might imagine, every member's office has a squawk box that plays the sessions and activities of the house. So the FBI heard the announcement that no passes would be issued. They, of course, had no idea that I knew they were up there and that they were trying to get people to leave the floor of the house. They were so ignorant of how the house operated that they didn't know that members needed passes to exit the chambers.

My office quickly got a call: the FBI would like to have a conversation with me. I said, "Fine. They certainly can. They can make an appointment like everybody else."

Man, did those FBI agents get mad at me. They were livid and they remained in some of those offices for three or four hours. Indeed, I didn't adjourn the house until my sergeants had told me that the FBI agents had at last exited the capitol. And by the time I adjourned the house, I'd found a lawyer for every person, Republican and Democrat, they were after. I made phone calls to lawyer friends of mine around Sacramento and said, "You may not ultimately represent Member X. But I need to let the member know he has counsel."

The FBI wanted to frighten these members. The ostensible reason for the raid was to procure documents for which they had subpoena power. I told my members not to go to see the FBI on that score; our members were not the custodians of the documents the FBI was seeking. Actually, the FBI wasn't really interested in these otherwise available documents. They just wanted to frighten people and get them to say stupid stuff. I wanted lawyers there to vet every question and to show that the members had complied with the law in whatever matter they were being questioned about.

The raid on the capitol came after the FBI had held hostage for several hours an employee of assembly member Pat Nolan. She didn't know what was up and had originally consented to the interview. She went in without counsel. And they started squeezing her. But she was tough enough to sweat them out. She just didn't open her mouth.

But it was obvious to her that they had been hard at work for months looking for people to set up. And from their questions, she knew they had failed. They had to have failed—they were after Willie Brown and other people in leadership positions. They were going to get nothing there. But they tipped their hand when they held her.

She walked out, and they recognized that she would be carrying the alarm; she would be the Paul Revere on the legislative side. That's when they thought they'd better move with the raid on the capitol building.

Learning of that session they had with her, plus the raid, confirmed to me that there was an operation going. I just didn't know how perfidious it was and that it involved phony legislation and the acquiescence of a Republican governor in the phony legislation. I wasn't sure what was happening. They sure were busy.

And unbeknownst to me, at about the same time someone in my office had a strange encounter with what, we were to discover months later, was the FBI.

An employee of mine, Karen Sinotto, who worked on world trade economic issues and who helped set up California's World Trade Commission, came home one day to find someone had slid an envelope full of cash under her front door. The money, according to an accompanying note, was to buy tickets to one of my semi-annual fund-raising parties. This was to have been a party where the headliner was Lou Rawls. The money was from a shrimp-processing firm she had never heard of.

Not surprisingly, this smart lady remembered the words I had continuously drummed into the heads of my staffers: "I know all of you think I'm crazy, but I genuinely believe somebody will forever try to discredit this office. And they will do it by way of money. None of you are druggies or otherwise compromised. So they'll only do it by way of money.

"Whatever you do, do not have anything to do with anybody who is trying to give us money. Marlene Bane and Wendy Linka are our fund-raisers. You refer 'em to Marlene Bane or to Wendy Linka. And each of those women is pretty cold-blooded. They'll ask contributors bad questions, tough questions. Even if you were my mother, they'd make you feel suspect—because that is their role. When it comes to money, don't accept any yourself. Turn it away."

Karen, of course, didn't know what was in the envelope. When she picked it up and opened it she saw that it was full of one-hundred-dollar bills and the business card of this unknown business. She didn't even go into her house. She didn't even put away the bag of groceries she had been carrying. She put them down, took the envelope, and closed the door to her house.

She got back in her car and drove to the address printed on the business card. She went up to the office and chastised the man there, "Are you out of your cotton-picking mind? You cannot pay for tickets to an event with cash money. If you want tickets to our event in San Francisco, there is a savings and loan bank across the street. I'll go with you to the S and L and you buy cashier's checks from the S and L. And if there are any tickets left, I'll be happy to see that you get tickets."

They had to cover themselves, so they went with her and they got a cashier's check. She of course turned it in appropriately, filed a contribution report as required by law. She never even mentioned it to me.

And so some undercover FBI agents suddenly found themselves with legitimately purchased and reported tickets to my fund-raiser. They even went to the dinner concert. I hope they had a good time. Everybody else there did. I give wonderful fund-raisers: no windy speeches, just lots of entertainment. Of course, at the time we still didn't know who they actually were.

Six months later Karen saw a news story about an FBI agent who had nailed a member of the legislature. The story reported that the agent had been working under a false name. It gave the false name, and Karen almost died when she read it. It was the same name of the man who had tried to leave a cash contribution under her door. It was the FBI who tried to buy the tickets illegally with cash money. When she realized what they had been trying to do—set us up—she became ill.

She immediately came to see me. She was in tears. "I've failed. I guess I should resign." I told her, "Don't you concern yourself, you filed the proper report. You didn't know he gave you a false name and phony credentials."

We called Eleanor Johns, my chief of staff, in San Francisco and asked her to look up the filing we had made. She found it, and I said, "Prepare an amendment to our filing, listing the FBI as the actual source of the contribution and explain that we didn't know the real source of the donation until this day. So we're filing an amended report to correct an inadvertently inaccurate filing."

Then I held a press conference and outed the FBI.

What I heard next was that the FBI had gone to a lobbyist, virtually a member of the house family, and asked him about how the house operated. The lobbyist, an otherwise good fellow named Chuck Olsen, had talked to them. Naturally, they had gone to Chuck; he was a former FBI agent himself.

I found all this out in the midst of an assembly debate over one of Chuck's bills. Members were telling me they were uneasy about Chuck's bills, because there were rumors that he had been talking with the FBI, and we were quite certain that the FBI was trying to corrupt legislation. Could Chuck be presenting phony legislation on behalf of the FBI in order to try to sting the members? Probably not, because his legislation was on behalf of longtime and respected professional groups, and the legislation he had on the agendas was rather innocent. But Chuck should not have been talking to the FBI. Chuck was also one of us. He shouldn't have been doing this stuff. There had to be a reaction. I had to make it evident to all the lobbyists that if there were any suspicion they were lending their services and goodwill to the FBI, then all their legislation would be suspect. I chose to make an example of Chuck's bill before the assembly. What I did that day was later described by members as the most stunning display of raw power by a speaker. It also makes a good tale of how Speaker Brown could run his house.

Olsen's bill before the house that day was in fact innocuous—something to do with eyeglasses. You couldn't be suspicious of it or of the sponsors, an association of optometrists with a long and decent reputation in the house.

On the floor, assembly member Lou Papan was introducing and presenting Chuck's bill. He was doing what we called "carrying" the bill for Chuck. What made it even more interesting was that Lou Papan was also a former FBI agent. Those ex-FBI types are always doing favors for one other.

I listened to Papan present the bill. And it was obvious that he was semi-in-love with the bill. When the roll was called, the vote had passed by 58 to 22 or numbers very close to that. It was just a normal bill doing just fine. But a principle was at stake.

As the bill had secured a majority, I saw Chuck and his clients sitting up in the gallery waiting for me to announce the bill had passed. That announcement would have made the vote official. But I didn't announce the vote. Instead, I performed a parliamentary maneuver, a standard one. I told the house that I was "putting a call" on the vote. You do that when you want to try to get more votes for your position or when you want members to switch their votes from one side or another. It's a conventional move that happens quite often. At that point, about ten in the morning, it didn't surprise people. Maybe they thought I wanted more members to vote in favor of it.

But Papan guessed right away that something was up. He came to the podium and said to me privately, "Mr. Speaker, what the fuck are you doing?"

I said, "I'm gonna kill the bill." I didn't tell him why. I just repeated, "Papan, I'm killing the bill."

Such is the discipline of the house that all he said to me was, "It's your business." And then he turned and walked up the aisle to his seat.

The house, when in session, is a busy place. Members move about, onto the floor and then off the floor, as items pertinent to them come up for action. Otherwise they're roaming around, in and out, going to lunch, doing everything under the sun. They're not all sitting there in their seats all day long. And since we typically had 150 items to consider in a day, it was hard to keep track of the members.

But as I saw the chairmen of the various house committees— my chairmen of my committees—appear on the floor, I told the sergeant at arms to summon them to come and see me. I did this one at a time. In turn, over the morning and afternoon, each chairman approached me.

I gave each of them the same message: "When I lift the call on this bill, you gotta change your vote from yea to nay." And each of my chairmen said, "Of course, Mr. Speaker, no problem."

And so through the day as I lifted the call for a few minutes at a time—which was the parliamentary maneuver that gave the members the opportunity to switch votes—my chairmen voted nay.

As the day wore on, the majority for the bill slowly declined. Eventually, as my chairmen switched their votes, the majority fell from fifty-eight to forty-one. Forty-one was the bare minimum needed for the bill to pass. I needed to get the vote down to forty.

As the votes fell, the word filtered out to the house that the speaker was doing something to an Olsen bill, but nobody knew why. All the lobbyists started coming in to sit in the back of the house and watch. Then the newspeople came in to watch. The show went on for hours.

But I was being very casual about it. So no one knew what was happening to the Olsen bill or why. Except for one sharp Republican, Gerald Felando, a close observer of the house who sat in the front row.

He came up to me as the chairmen were switching their votes, and said, "You got something going on with this bill?"

I said, "Yeah, let me tell you what that fucking Olsen did." He was a Republican, but he was so angry at this breach of the house code that he said, "I'm ready to switch my vote."

But I said, "No, Felando, no. You stay right where you are on this bill. I'm putting each of my chairmen to the test, including Dick Floyd and Lou Papan. I hate to do this: they have personal relationships with Olsen and his crew [indeed, Floyd was tight with a woman in Olsen's office]. And, gosh, Lou is the author of the bill."

I told Felando I appreciated his being my backstop, but not to vote. Then he wanted to go up to Olsen and tear him apart. "Sit tight," I said. "Don't go up there."

I needed just one more switch. Felando's switch would secure the trick. But I knew just which vote I wanted: Dick Floyd's. Dick was my chairman of the committee that oversaw the liquor industry, liquor licenses, and horse racing. We called it the "Sin Committee."

Dick Floyd embodied that committee. He was a booze-loving, horse-race-lovin', cigar-smoking, potbellied guy who really loved living big. But he was also blindly loyal. He could be trusted to carry out orders, and never once had he crossed me on a vote. But he was very close to Olsen's office.

So to make my point that Olsen had to be punished, I needed his buddy Floyd to abandon his vote on behalf of his pal's bill. I called Floyd to the speaker's rostrum. A moment of surprising drama followed.

I said to him, "Hey, Floyd, I'm going to adjourn the house in another ten minutes, so we have to close this bill up. And I hate to have to do this to you, but you got to come off the bill."

"Whadda you mean?"

I said, "You change your vote on Olsen's bill. It's important to me, man. I need you to come off the bill."

"I'm not gonna come off Olsen's bill," he said.

I said, "Floyd, you're the chairman of the Sin Committee. I made you that chairman. I need you to come off the bill."

It got rough.

And he said, "Well, you just take this fuckin' committee, if that's your attitude."

I said, "Give me the keys to your office, motherfucker."

And he threw the keys right down on my desk in a way so that everybody could see what happened. And then he walked away.

Then Felando popped up from his seat, asking for recognition. I said, "For what purpose does the gentleman rise?"

"Mr. Speaker, I want to change my vote on a measure. I want the courtesy of your lifting the call on a bill so that I might do so."

He had seen Chairman Floyd toss his keys on my desk and knew what it meant. He knew that I had ordered Floyd to change his vote, and that when Floyd refused, I fired him as chairman and demanded the keys to his kingdom. Felando was ready to step up and help: he wanted to provide the one last switch I needed to kill the bill.

I said, "Mr. Felando, trust me, I'm not prepared to lift any more put calls right now."

He lowered his microphone, which meant he had yielded the

floor. But he came right up to me, and said, "Hey, man, I'm ready to give you the fuckin' vote!"

I said, "No, you don't understand. I now have to do the unthinkable: I have to have Lou Papan, the author of the bill, switch from yea to nay and vote to kill his own bill."

Felando returned to his seat.

I called Papan up. "Lou," I said, "I'm about to announce that I'm removing Dick Floyd from his chairmanship, and am giving it to Gary Condit. I'm firing that motherfucker because he won't come off your bill. So I'm sorry to tell you that you have to come off your own bill."

He said, "Just give me a minute." He turned around and he looked up at Olsen. Olsen then came downstairs to the back of the house chamber. Papan met him there and said, "Chuck, your bill's dead, man. I'm switching my vote. I have to. I'm the chairman of the Rules Committee. And you know my accepting that appointment means that my first commitment is to the speaker. And Willie Brown wants this bill dead. So it's dead. I'd suggest you talk to Willie Brown. You've got to talk to Willie Brown."

Lou didn't know why I was killing the bill. He just knew it was important to me. So he walked back into the chamber. He asked to have the call lifted on the bill so he could change his vote. He switched, and the bill fell to forty yeas. Olsen's bill had gone from fifty-eight votes and seemingly assured passage, right down to forty and to defeat.

Then, of course, Felando's microphone went back up, the signal to the chair that he wanted recognition. "I'm following Mr. Papan's leadership," he said. "I want to change my vote." I let him do so. And about five other members quickly changed votes.

The house had never seen anything like that. The author of a bill had voted to kill his own bill.

But it was not over. The lesson had to be explained. Olsen came right up to see me. I asked Papan to come with him.

I said to them, "See, you two guys are FBI guys, right?" They acknowledged that.

I said, "Chuck, why would you ever talk to the FBI about how the house operates? Don't you think that's my job? If they want to know how the fuckin' house operates, don't you think they ought to be required to ask me? How can I protect my membership if I don't establish a line of authority? Do you think the fuckin' U.S. Attorney would let you talk to his deputies? Or do you think any of his deputies would talk to you about the operation of the U.S. Attorney's office? They'd be fired if they did that.

"And you motherfucker, you're a lobbyist! And I'm not coming over there telling the lobbyists how to do their business. I'm not tellin' the lobbying fraternity you don't have any business doin' this or that. But you cannot talk to the FBI."

Olsen said, "Well, it was just a mistake in judgment. They're old friends of mine . . ." Et cetera, et cetera. "Ah, I understand. I understand. I hope I've paid my debt. I hope you won't kill the rest of my bills."

"Nah, I won't kill any more of your bills. But you tell your brothers out there in the lobbyists' fraternity that they will suffer the same fate, if not worse, if I ever hear of any of you motherfuckers when approached by the FBI doin' anything except referrin' them back to me.

"When you cross the leadership of the house, or help someone invade the house, you're taking on the house. And at that stage of the game, I don't give a damn about the merits of your clients' special bills. You just can't mess with the house."

Olsen was a good guy, a sweetheart of a guy. He went everywhere with us—ball games, horse races, even trips to Jamaica. A sweetheart of a guy. But the FBI had to be shown, you don't be fuckin' around in my house.

Chuck died a few years later. I gave the eulogy at his funeral.

And as for the FBI's attempts to get Willie Brown? They petered out. In the end, it was only Patrick Nolan, the Republican member of the assembly who went to the FBI in 1985 and suggested they try to get Willie Brown via an undercover sting involving phony legislation, who went to prison. Nolan served two years in federal prison for taking illegal contributions in the very FBI sting he himself suggested!

CHAPTER TWENTY-FOUR

Gun Control; Nelson Mandela's California Allies; and Saving Kindergartens

SOME HAVE CRITICIZED MY YEARS AS SPEAKER as having been without an agenda because unlike other speakers, I did not usually announce a platform early in the session and then try to impose it on the membership. In fact, I did have agendas, carefully worked out with my team of legislative colleagues and with my staff. But I did believe myself that a speaker could be even more influential by working quietly but firmly in the background. By not announcing a stance early on on some issues that I felt strongly about, I actually increased my ability to negotiate, to work with others who would have to oppose me if I had taken too public a position too early on.

This is the story of three crises—one involving gun control; another about getting the state to divest from South Africa; and the third about a brutal fight to finance public schools—that resulted in historic legislation. They illustrate that a speaker's canniness and courage are often more influential in effecting change than rhetoric from the podium.

Consider what happened in 1989 when I was speaker and facing the fury of the lunatic National Rifle Association. The assembly passed a ban on assault weapons. Ours was the first legislature in the two-hundred-year history of the United States to ban a gun. We banned sixty-five of the worst.

It's not only an important story of an historic event, it also illustrates the power of unforeseen, shocking, tragic events—if quickly manipulated. And the power of allegiance.

In 1989, after years of unsuccessful efforts to ban automatic assault weapons in California, my colleague Mike Roos came up with an idea to throw the National Rifle Association, which furiously opposed bans of any sort, off balance. The NRA was so strong that it had been able, in the past, to prevent weapons-ban bills from even getting to the floor of the assembly. Gun-ban legislation died in committee annually, to my chagrin. The committees were dominated by Democrats who should have been for the bans. But that's how powerful the NRA was—it even cowed Democrats, forcing them to kill ban legislation before it could even get to the full assembly.

Roos then suggested to Senate President David Roberti, who represented the same part of inner-city Los Angeles that Roos did, a new strategy. Gun-ban bills would be introduced simultaneously in both the senate and assembly. That would keep the NRA busy and its attention divided. While both bills were nearly identical, there were some differences and the NRA's resources would be spread thin by having to fight two battles on two different fronts against two different armies.

Mike also got the California attorney general, John Van de Kamp, and various district attorneys, chiefs of police, sheriffs, and police organizations to join them in backing the bills. Police leadership had long opposed assault weapons, but it was only lately that the rank and file of police had joined in. What finally turned the state's street cops against the NRA was the fight over newly invented "cop-killer" bullets. These bullets were highly destructive ammunition that could penetrate even body armor. Of course, the cops wanted them banned. But the NRA was opposed to banning them. That was enough for the cops: they turned on the NRA.

This was an impressive lineup of support, and the Roos-Roberti strategy of starting a war on two fronts was brilliant. But Mike and Dave had a tough road ahead.

I think Mike was disappointed with me at first, though. Early in 1989, before the legislative session started, I had asked him to give me his opinion of various committee assignments that I as speaker was going to make. He was a selfless, objective thinker so he was one of the people I consulted to take a look at my planned committee configurations. He offered bright comments and observations about various assignments, but when he came to the assignments for the Public Safety Committee, which is where the gun bill would start and where previous ones had died, he was upset.

He said to me, "Willie, I've got this very important gun bill coming up this year. An assault weapon ban. I think this is the year we might be able to get something done on this. And here you want to appoint Gary Condit to the committee.

"Gary is a member of the Gang of Five, one of your sworn enemies who has tried to unseat you from the speakership, and he will not cooperate with Willie Brown. And this will be seen as a bill you want passed. He won't vote for it. And I need a Democratic vote I can count on; otherwise the bill will die in committee. The Republicans aren't going to support it."

"Michael," I said to Roos, "you can never construct a committee around one bill or issue."

I'm sure Mike then thought, "Oh my God, I've got this bill and I'm not even going to be able to get it out of the first committee."

But I had confidence in Mike. And while he might have been disappointed that I had resurrected the career of Gary Condit, whom I had stripped of his committee assignments a year earlier when he and the other members of the Gang of Five tried to force me to resign the speakership, I knew what I was doing. For at the same time, I allowed another member of the Gang of Five to return from exile; I appointed Jerry Eaves to a seat on the Governmental Organization Committee. My allies thought I was nuts, giving succor to the enemy. But I was thinking ahead.

Mike and Dave introduced their bills and then, shortly afterward, on January 17, a terrible event occurred in Stockton, California.

A drifter, Patrick Purdy, age twenty-six, dressed in army fatigues and carrying an AK-47 semiautomatic combat rifle, ran into a schoolyard where hundreds of elementary school kids were at recess just before noon. Hiding behind a trailerlike temporary classroom he began spraying the children with his assault weapon. In three minutes, he fired eighty rounds. He killed five children, between six and nine years old, and wounded twenty-eight others, plus a teacher. Then he fired a handgun into his head and killed himself.

The assault weapon that he used to kill the children was easily available. You couldn't buy a toy version of the gun—they were outlawed—but anyone, sane or insane, criminal or noncriminal, violent or nonviolent, could easily buy the real assault weapon.

Governor Deukmejian was on the East Coast headed to the Bush inaugural in Washington. The supporters of the gun bill, while shocked by the shootings, understood they had to act quickly. They got the press to call Deukmejian in New York and ask if he now would support a gun ban.

Deukmejian was a level guy—he spoke what he thought. And fortunately, because he was on this trip by himself, he wasn't surrounded by aides who could insulate him from the press or try to persuade him to say something politic. Deukmejian said, "I see no usefulness in having these guns readily available."

I knew then that for the first time in history, we had a chance of getting a governor to sign a gun ban.

On January 24, I went with Deukmejian, scores of state officials, and 2,800 other people to a memorial service in Stockton for the shooter's victims, who were either of Cambodian or Vietnamese descent. I saw the tears well up in Deukmejian's eyes. He spoke comfortingly and movingly to the congregation. He mentioned the suffering that his own people, Armenians, had gone through at the hands of the Turks in 1915, and he cried again. Many others did as well. I knew that we would have a gubernatorial signature. I knew Deukmejian would come under incredible pressure from the NRA to veto a bill, but he would not waver. Once he took a stand, he stuck to it.

But first we had to pass the bills. A broadening of the coalition after Stockton helped the cause. Now teachers, physicians, and nurses were signing on. But how to get it out of the committee? We needed one Republican vote to get it to pass.

That one vote would come from some ingenious work by Mike Roos on Republican Chuck Quackenbush, a member of the Assembly Public Safety Committee, who represented Saratoga, a wealthy and liberal town just outside Silicon Valley. Chuck was a Vietnam vet who understood the danger of assault weapons, and his liberal constituency was at heart against them. But he was facing the NRA.

Mike Roos and his staff took action. They located the phone numbers of every registered voter who lived within a ten-block radius of Chuck Quackenbush, starting with the people who lived on either side of his home. They wrote a script that said, "Next week the Public Safety Committee of the state assembly is going to meet to consider whether the kind of firearm that was used by Patrick Purdy to kill innocent kids in a Stockton schoolyard should be banned in California or not. Chuck Quackenbush is going to be the swing vote on this matter. If you agree that they should be banned, we are asking you to phone him now and register your support for this bill and your dismay if in fact he abstains or votes against it." Mike's people then gave out Chuck's office, cell phone, and home phone numbers.

On Monday Mike walked into Quackenbush's office. Chuck pulled a white handkerchief from his pocket and waved it in the air. Chuck's staff later reported that from Friday, when the neighbors first were called, through Sunday evening, Chuck could not get in his car or walk into his house or office without the phone ringing with someone saying, "You've got to vote for this bill and here's my name and address," each of which was very close to his home.

The bill passed the committee and went to the floor of the assembly. There, in spite of the horrific intimidation of the NRA, Mike began to build a coalition of members for the bill. He had a solid base of Democratic votes, but to gain the majority of forty-one votes, he needed three Republican members. He already had Quackenbush, who wasn't going to waver. And he had Republican Bill Filante, a physician representing liberal Marin County, who would not give in to the NRA.

He needed one more vote. He thought he had it in a Republican from San Diego, but one day she came to him in tears, saying she could no longer support the bill because of the coercion and threats of the NRA.

On the day of the vote, the bill passed by forty-one to thirty-five. Where had the forty-first vote come from? Not from the Republicans, but from one of the renegade Democrats in the Gang of Five who had tried to topple me from my speakership. The vote came from Jerry Eaves, whom I had resuscitated by appointing him to the Governmental Organization Committee. I had gone to Jerry and said to him, "I know this is a difficult issue for you, given your constituency. And I know this is difficult because of what happened between us. But this is an historic moment. You can make the difference. Regardless of what has gone on in terms of this fight we've had over who ought to be speaker, whether it's me or somebody else, Jerry, if you vote for this bill, I'll support you against attack. I would never let you hang out to dry over being attacked on this issue." And I meant it.

That's allegiance.

Governor Deukmejian signed the bill.

A long struggle that saw California legislation help stop apartheid in South Africa ended in triumph when, in June 1990, Nelson Mandela, just five months after being released from twenty-seven years of imprisonment in South Africa, came to California as part of an eleven-day tour of the United States. He visited New York, Washington, DC, Boston, Miami, Atlanta, Detroit, and Los Angeles. Only in California did he make multiple stops. I met him, along with other political figures including then congressman and now Oakland mayor Ron Dellums, at Oakland Airport and attended a joyous rally in Mandela's honor at the Oakland Coliseum.

During our visit he thanked me for all that we in the assembly had done to put pressure on the South African government, particularly our persevering and successful efforts to get the State of California and the University of California to stop investing in companies doing business in South Africa. He said the divestiture by the giant State of California had put so much pressure on the South African economy that it led directly to his being freed. He later repeated his remarks to the fifty-thousand people in the coliseum, saying, "We salute the State of California for having taken such a powerful, principled stance on behalf of divesting." Indeed, the San Francisco Bay Area had been especially crucial in making divestiture from South Africa public policy and an instrument of change.

Standing there that day with him was an incredible outcome in a battle that often seemed quixotic. For decades blacks and whites in the Bay Area had been struggling to help South Africa, but victory often seemed so far away. Yet there I was shaking hands with the man who was soon to become president of the nation that had consigned him to rot in prison. As I shook his hand, I could only wonder at the work it had taken.

As far back as 1973, my friend the Reverend Amos Brown of San Francisco's Third Baptist Church had been campaigning against South Africa's apartheid laws and its punishment of black leaders like Mandela. San Francisco longshoremen refused, in 1984, to unload goods from South Africa. The cities of San Francisco, Berkeley, and Oakland had made their own early efforts to stop investing public funds in the apartheid regime. Naturally, devising a statewide public policy that could be used as a tool against the regime, there was a major effort of African Americans in the legislature. In 1979, Maxine Waters, then a member of the assembly and now a member of the U.S. House of Representatives from Los Angeles, began calling for the state to pull its money out of South Africa. Her bills met defeat every time through 1985. One focus of her attention had been the pension funds of the University of California, which were worth more than ten billion dollars.

Incredibly, the university, a supposedly enlightened institution, had resisted divesting over the years. This led to protests and demonstrations from students, faculty, and citizens of a scope and intensity not seen since the days of the free speech movement (of which I was part as a lawyer for the protestors) back in the early '60s. Rallies were held, sit-ins took place, and on Sproul Plaza, at the main campus in Berkeley, students built replicas of the shantytowns black South Africans were forced to live in. And the students themselves lived in the shanties.

The protests, of course, extended to the meetings of the university's governing body, the Board of Regents, on which I sat by virtue of being speaker. (Indeed, at one time, I actually held two seats on the board: one as speaker and one to which I had previously been appointed by Governor Jerry Brown. I gave up the personal seat shortly after becoming speaker, but not until I had negotiated the appointment of a replacement acceptable to me.) I put as much pressure as I could on the board, but the members were averse. Their arguments, wishy-washy to my mind, were that divestiture might hurt the pension fund's health and that the regents individually might be liable to lawsuits for failing to invest "prudently." It seemed to me they were listening to lawyers and administrators, not to the public, not to principle.

I was astounded by what I heard at a May 1985 legislative hearing at which UC administrators explained why they were opposed to divesting. When I asked David Gardner, the president of the University of California, if the atrocities of the South African regime bothered him even a bit, he replied that he was familiar with the effects of oppression. He pointed out that he himself was a Mormon and that his Mormon grandfather had been forced to relocate to Utah to escape religious bigotry and prejudice. Then he said, "I abhor oppression, but I don't choose to advertise it." I gather he meant that while he disliked bigotry, he wouldn't take a public stand against it, and neither would the University of California.

I answered him this way: "You can end discrimination against you by changing your religion. Blacks in South Africa cannot change. Willie Brown cannot change his skin as he could change religion. There are no Utahs for Bishop Tutu." He just sat there. But the university did not then divest.

Meanwhile, I had been working on getting heavier clout on our side. Governor George Deukmejian was my man. Now, Deukmejian in 1985 had vetoed the bill sponsored by Maxine Waters that would have prohibited the state from doing business with South Africa, so he didn't seem an especially promising ally.

But I had begun working on my relationship with Deukmejian. It involved a steady diet of one of my least favorite foods, tuna sandwiches. That George Deukmejian and Willie Brown would ever become buddies seemed very unlikely. He was suburban; I was urban. His idea of a good time on a weekend, someone once said, was cleaning out the garage of his modest home down in Long Beach. My idea of a good time was a weekend of clubbing around the nightspots of San Francisco. His clothes were ready-to-wear; mine, of course, were bespoke. We were completely different animals.

I loved fine dining. George, although the governor of California, ate his lunch alone down in the statehouse cafeteria. That's where the tuna sandwiches came in. I noticed George sitting in the cafeteria by himself one day when I was leaving the capitol for lunch. It looked to me as if he could use a friend. So I began strolling down to the cafeteria and if I saw George there, I would join him. His favorite lunch was tuna on white bread. That's what I ate as well.

We talked of many things during those lunches, including the genocide of the Armenian people at the hands of the Turks in 1915—a horror that was present in Deukmejian's life, since members of his own family had suffered terribly then. I pointed out the parallels between the condition of the Armenian people then and the black citizens of South Africa now. This struck a chord with Deukmejian, who felt far more acutely than did President Gardner of the University of California that public policy could be a powerful weapon against oppression and atrocity elsewhere. Deukmejian had been horrified by the actions in South Africa in 1986 by which three thousand people were arrested and a "state of emergency" was declared through which the white regime assumed dictatorial powers. That changed Deukmejian's mind. Up until then he had vetoed Maxine Waters's divestiture bills, arguing for a case-by-case treatment of the state's investments in companies doing business in South Africa. After the mass arrests and the state of emergency, he was a changed man. He joined the divestiture forces. And he moved quickly. Some have said he also felt political pressure from my friend Tom Bradley, the black mayor of Los Angeles. Bradley was running against Deukmejian for governor and had already backed divestiture moves by the city of Los Angeles. But I can tell you this: my conversations with Governor Deukmejian covered all sorts of topics, including the purely political. Whenever we spoke about South Africa, however, he spoke only about the issues and the moral right. His own staffers have said the same: Deukmejian was not a spin artist; he was a big man.

Deukmejian used his influence with the university and also agreed to support legislative action by Maxine Waters. In July 1986, the University of California's Board of Regents, acting under Deukmejian's persuasion, voted to divest from South Africa. The next month on the floor of the assembly, a daylong debate took place on Waters's bill to have the state pull its pension funds out of companies doing business in South Africa. I spoke last and with feeling. In closing, I praised Governor Deukmejian, saying, "It takes a big man to recognize that circumstances and information should now dictate a decision different from his previous one." The vote passed fifty to twenty-six. In September, Deukmejian paid me, and the people of the Bay Area who had worked so long to effect this policy, the ultimate compliment. He signed the bill in San Francisco. He did more as well. He lobbied President Reagan and the California congressional delegation on divestiture. Our California legislation became the national standard for bills in other states.

It also had an unforeseen and beneficial effect in the corporate world. U.S. companies began to sell off or close their South African holdings. The companies actually started to divest! They wanted California's money in their coffers and realized they wouldn't get it so long as they were allied with South Africa. So they began to pull out! Far from hurting our portfolio, divestiture helped. And because of the corporate pressure, the South African government moved more quickly to end apartheid than it might have.

Nothing would have happened were it not for the perseverance of Maxine Waters over seven years, but she knew she always had my support. Her agenda was my agenda. And nothing would have happened either if it weren't for the fact that a governor who ate lunch alone in a cafeteria liked to listen and learn. Once again, as is often the case in politics, it took a combination of the principled and the personal touch persevering together to make needed change. Principle isn't enough, alas. You've got to find that niche, that crack, that small opening, to get things done. Sometimes you lead by finding the path through which the visionaries can go. You can say that finding the way to George Deukmejian's signature was pure politics. I say being political is also being principled.

And then sometimes when you are acting at your most principled, you are accused of being merely political, as was the case in 1992 when, in a fight over the budget, the State of California went broke and couldn't pay its bills for two months. I was accused of playing politics with people's lives and pay. Actually, I was fighting hard, and rather alone, for the one thing that I believe is above politics: education.

In 1992, the Republican governor, Pete Wilson, made two mistakes in trying to make a budget for California, then in the midst of the worst economic recession since the Great Depression of the 1930s. In facing a budget deficit of fourteen billion dollars, he erred in: a) trying to balance the budget by cutting funds for public schools, and b) trying to be the czar of the budget-making process all by himself. The latter was foolish because both houses of the legislature were in the control of the Democrats, and Wilson wasn't going to get the two-thirds majority votes he needed to pass a budget without some cooperation. And in trying to balance the budget by cutting school funds below the amount mandated by the voters when they passed Proposition 98 in 1988 (which set a floor of public spending for schools), he was flying in the face of public opinion, the constitution, and the only thing really sacred to voters and to me: support of the public schools.

You can compromise on spending for the environment, you can compromise on money for prisons, you can compromise on raising taxes, but you can't slice away the money for education without upsetting me.

So as we went into the budget-writing process in the spring of 1992, we faced a rocky path. The state constitution requires a budget to be enacted by July 1, and while that deadline has often been breached, it was never before breached quite the way it was due to Wilson's intransigence in 1992. Unwilling to support school funding, he was unable to get a budget passed on time. Without legislation to continue spending, and with puny cash reserves, the state was broke within a day.

Not even legislators were being paid. The state controller, Gray Davis (who in 1999 became governor), started issuing IOUs, or "registered warrants" as they were formally called. Between July 1 and September 2, 1992, he issued $3.4 billion worth of them. That was bad enough, but by midsummer, banks were growing nervous about cashing the IOUs. Nursing homes and hospitals, dependent on state money to stay in business, took out private loans to keep running. Patients feared eviction; caregivers felt abandoned. The situation was dire.

I was under enormous pressure to cave in to Wilson, let him cut school funding below the constitutionally mandated minimum, and get the state back into business. I simply would not abandon the schools, though. It was an extremely lonely fight—even within my Democratic caucus.

A lot of my old team—former assembly members like Mike Roos and Richard Alatorre—whom I could depend on to hold the hands and boost the morale of wavering legislators—had left the assembly. The members, the civil servants, the public were full of panic and urged me to compromise. But cutting the floor out from school spending was unacceptable. So the budget crisis went on and on. Radio talk shows and TV were full of games and gimmicks castigating me, the legislature, and the governor for the impasse. One time a reporter questioned me about a deli across the street from the capitol that had a sign in its window announcing it would refuse to sell food to legislators until the budget passed. I was completely honest with the journalist. "I've never eaten there," I said. "The food is at reporters' level." Not a wise thing to say, but it was a dumb question about a fight that was over dumbness itself.

My only allies were the members of the California Teachers Association, who were of course behind me. But not everyone in the general public, or at least that portion of the electorate that was Republican, was fond of the CTA. The Republicans in the suburbs believed in good public schools, but they also wondered if in fact they weren't simply being hornswoggled by a powerful union. Would the cuts really be so bad? What actually would the money have been spent on? Classrooms or bureaucrats? They were reasonable concerns. Then Pete Wilson himself gave the game away: it would be classrooms that would be cut. He did it by announcing that in order to balance the budget, he'd be cutting public kindergartens.

I jumped up and down when I heard that. He made my case for me. The cost of his budget cut was not in the bureaucracy—it was right in the classroom. More than one hundred thousand young-sters would be denied admission when they were due to go off to school. Forget about the programs for preschoolers called Head Start. Wilson's idea of proper schooling could have been called "Late Start."

You could hear every mom in the state get furious. They had been planning on getting their kids into school when they were five years old, now Wilson was saying no. Every time a mom called to complain about the kindergarten-reduction plan, I had my re-ceptionists route the call through to Wilson's private phone line. Let him bear the brunt of his cuts. As a matter of fact, I had my re-ceptionists route *every* call complaining about the budget crisis on to Wilson.

If it had not been for Wilson's shocking announcement, the public would have vilified me. But the voters certainly seemed to understand that it was Wilson, not I, who was playing politics with their kids and their state paychecks. The game turned. Wilson began to get real, and we made headway in our negotiations. Even-tually around Labor Day, we got a budget passed. It wasn't a great budget, but through a complicated series of financial moves, it kept the schools from falling even further behind. Wilson paid for his foolishness on Election Day. He had been predicting that Democrats would lose control of the assembly as angry voters sup-posedly punished us for the budget fiasco. But came Election Day, and I didn't lose the house. The voters kept it in the hands of Dem-ocrats. I actually improved my majority, albeit by one vote. It was not the rout Wilson prayed for. You can't go wrong when you back the schools. So sometimes you lead by being a bulwark, by refusing to bend. I call that being principled.

CHAPTER TWENTY-FIVE

Sustaining Speakership: Most Magnificent Moment

IN THE SUMMER OF 1994, a Republican assemblyman named Paul Horcher came to see me in my office. Horcher was thinking of doing the unthinkable: renouncing the Republican Party and running for reelection as an Independent.

He had good reason to be disenchanted personally with his fellow Republicans in the assembly. He was being treated as an untouchable by the newer sort of Republicans who had taken over their caucus in the assembly. These people believed only in cutting taxes, increasing prison time, and wreaking partisan vengeance on their opponents within the party and without. They called themselves conservatives, but they were really just bullies. They had no talent for making politics work; they were intent on mayhem. They hated problem solvers like Horcher.

Horcher had excited their fury to such a degree that no Republican would even sit next to him. If another Republican walked into a hearing room where there was only one vacant seat but it was next to Paul Horcher, the other Republican would stand. On

213

the floor of the assembly, he couldn't even be seated in the Republican section. His neighbors would refuse to take seats around him. I finally had to reassign him to a place over by the Democrats.

Horcher had incurred this childish wrath of his Republican mates by voting to pass the budget of a Republican governor. In 1991, Republicans in the assembly, bent on hatcheting taxes and cutting state services (except for building more prisons), revolted against their own Republican governor, Pete Wilson. Wilson's budget, shaped by the horrific recession California was then experiencing, made the kinds of cuts they liked, but it also raised taxes. I didn't much like the budget either, but after weeks of negotiation with Wilson, the state senate, and the assembly, we produced one that we could live with, one that would let the state continue to operate. So in its service, I helped put together a coalition of Democrats and Republicans that would just about achieve the two-thirds vote necessary to pass the budget. We needed one more vote. Governor Wilson himself called Horcher and asked him to vote for the bill, saying, "Please do the right thing."

Horcher did and became the fifty-fourth, and winning, vote in the budget fight. Wilson's budget passed, but the right wingers hated it and hated him for providing the passing vote. Things didn't get better for him with his party mates in 1993 when I appointed him to the vice chairmanship of the Ways and Means Committee. This important spot on the assembly's budget-wrangling committee was one that I liked to reserve for a Republican, but it was also one that I insisted go to someone who was committed to passing a budget. We needed a player, not a photo op seeker. The Republican leadership had wanted me to appoint Dean Andal, from Stockton, who had voted against the budget the rest of us, including the Republican governor, had hammered together at last. I wasn't going to have a die-hard obstructionist in the leadership of a committee that had to be results oriented. So I appointed

Horcher instead. Then Republican leader Jim Brulte told Horcher to step aside for Andal. I told the Republicans, "No way." Horcher stayed as vice chairman. With that, the Republicans in the assembly increased their war of taunts on Horcher.

Now, Horcher was a proud guy, sensitive even. So this treatment must have hurt him terribly. But he was courageous as well. Back in 1979, he had been in Iran, working on oil refinery construction for the Fluor Corporation, when Iranians began taking Americans hostage. In what was a horrifying ordeal, he managed to escape from Iran without being captured. "I resolved then," he once told me, "never to be frightened again." I believe that to have been the case.

So when he came to see me in the speaker's office in the summer of 1994 to talk about leaving the Republican Party, it wasn't because they were frightening him into leaving. He had been taking the taunts for years. I believe that he decided simply that he didn't want to be part of a group that engaged in such degraded politics any longer.

My advice to him that day, however, was that he not leave the Republican Party. His own district, Diamond Bar, in the rapidly growing Inland Empire of Southern California, east of Los Angeles and west of Palm Springs, was becoming increasingly Republican—conservative Republican. I told Horcher that in such a district an Independent, even an incumbent, stood no chance against a Republican. My advice was to stay in the party, take the taunts, win reelection, and wait for a better day. He stayed in the Republican Party, won reelection, and shortly thereafter had his revenge on the party mates who had treated him so shamefully. It was a revenge that, when it came on December 5, 1994, would help me, even though it meant that Horcher would have to leave the assembly that day under the guard of the sergeants at arms because death threats were being made against him. The mean, dysfunctional condition of Republican politics was a concern to many, including sane Republicans. We were worried that as the bashing rose and the bipartisanship declined we'd all be hamstrung from doing the public business. It was like facing jihad and the Taliban. The bullies wanted to destroy not only Democrats and fellow Republicans; they wanted to rip up the process of doing the public's work.

It was clear to me that summer that the Democratic majority in the assembly, which had lasted in one fashion or another for twenty-six years, was threatened. Two reasons in particular were responsible. One was the impending arrival of term limits. The other was what I've alluded to: the wave of Gingrichism, of right-wing hate politics, which was sweeping the country.

Term limits wouldn't come into effect until 1996, but already some members were deciding to leave the house, either to run for different office or to get out of politics. Five Democratic incumbents in the assembly had already decided to give up their seats. We wouldn't have incumbents running in those districts, which meant hard, expensive fights to try to hold on to those seats. I figured we Democrats might lose five or six seats, but I figured that I would be left with a majority of one or two.

One of the most frightening aspects of Gingrich fever was the viciousness and the amount of negative campaigning. Democrats were being assailed as never before. In particular, my name and image were being dragged into scores of local races. I—black, urban, flamboyant, politically adroit, from San Francisco—was used as the poster boy by Republicans. It was as if Willie Brown were running in every district. I was being used to frighten voters in every rural and suburban district in California. It was shameful. I was being used as the Willie Horton of the 1988 presidential campaign. You remember Willie Horton? He was the convicted murderer serving life without parole who was given a weekend furlough from his Massachusetts prison. While on furlough, he beat and raped a woman in Maryland before being captured there. George Bush the Elder's campaign used the story and Horton's frightening mug in a TV ad to enormous effect against presidential candidate Michael Dukakis, who happened to have been governor of Massachusetts when Horton, an African American, was furloughed. The ad, unfair to Dukakis, was also incredibly racist. The ad's producer, Larry McCarthy, said that Horton had become "every suburban mother's nightmare." That's what the Republicans were trying to do to me and our candidates: paint us as every suburban Califor-nian's nightmare.

The smear ads and mailings in California were supported by a fund of hundreds of thousands of dollars especially contributed by corporate special interests. Big Tobacco was part of the game.

Now, I've been criticized for accepting large campaign contributions on behalf of Democratic candidates from Big Tobacco myself. Indeed, I took their money. But I was not their boy. I raised Tobacco's taxes on them. They didn't like that and they didn't like me. In 1994, they were intent on eliminating Willie Brown and the Democratic majority in the assembly.

At first in the 1994 campaign it seemed that Big Tobacco was content to play its usual game—spreading their contributions around to both parties. They contributed a total of about $125,000 to the entire Democratic war chest. It was just a tactic to lull us.

On the Friday before the election, the game was revealed. Philip Morris USA, as the company is called, itself poured $125,000 into just one race. In a kind of middle-of-the-night ambush, Philip Morris went after one Democratic member, Betty Karnette, a retired schoolteacher and political moderate from down in Long Beach. Without Betty's vote, they reasoned, my career as speaker would be over. If they beat Karnette and took seven Democratic seats that were clearly vulnerable, Big Tobacco could cost me my majority.

Karnette had been sailing through her election campaign until this money suddenly came in against her in the last five days of the campaign. Her opponent spent the money on negative advertising and mailers. Pure smear. Betty Karnette lost. In total, we Democrats lost eight seats, some by slight margins. So on the day after the election, the Republicans held the majority with forty-one seats. I had thirty-nine. But it wasn't over. I was determined not to hand the assembly over to the gang of untalented misfits that constituted the Republican majority.

Immediately after the election, Jim Brulte, the Republican leader, confidently predicted he would become speaker, ousting Willie Brown. The *Los Angeles Times* reported, "Cheered by erasing the Democratic majority in the assembly, Republicans said Wednesday [Nov. 9] that they are poised to oust their longtime nemesis, Speaker Willie Brown, and take control of the lower house for the first time in 25 years." George Skelton, the *Times*'s premier political columnist, wrote, "Brulte is destined to be speaker." I, of course, had been asked for my opinion. I merely told the truth. I told the press that I would sustain the speakership.

A reporter asked if I was nervous. I replied, "Joe Montana [once a great San Francisco 49ers quarterback] is never nervous. With two minutes to go and his team behind, he simply does his job and wins the game." I set about organizing my play. Jim Brulte and the Republicans did the same. Actually, he set out to organize premature celebrations. Before the actual vote to elect a speaker, he held a ball in honor of himself. These guys were really bush league.

On December 5, 1994, when the new assembly met, the first thing I did was object to the participation of one Republican member in the election for speaker. This was Richard Mountjoy of Arcadia. On November 8 he had been reelected to the assembly all right, but he had also been elected to the state senate (in a special election held to fill a vacancy). State law forbids any one person from holding two offices, and since it was obvious that Mountjoy had participated in meetings with the senate's Republican leaders about the organization of that house, we argued quite correctly that he could not also participate in the assembly's business. I didn't win in that first effort to stop Mountjoy, but it had the right-wing Republicans growing nervous.

Then came the roll call to elect the speaker. The members had started voting when they noticed that Paul Horcher, the outcast Republican who had come to see me the previous summer about leaving the Republican Party, was not in the house. Then just before his name was to be called, Horcher, who had been lying low for the previous weeks, entered. He took his seat. When the clerk asked him whom he was voting for speaker, Horcher slammed his fist down on his desk and shouted, "Brown." I was not surprised. But his party leaders were stunned as he bolted. They foolishly assumed that he would just go along with the opportunity to elect the first Republican speaker in twenty-six years despite their years of affronts to him. With Horcher voting for me, the Republicans failed to win a majority in the election. The final vote that day was a tie: Brulte, forty votes, and Brown, forty votes. I had stopped them. And if I could go on to eliminate the "hybrid" Mountjoy from the floor, I would win and the assembly would not become an asylum.

The Republicans were not on their game. But perhaps that's simply because they were outplayed. I had anticipated earlier, of course, that they would go after Democrats and try to get one to join them in their battle to make Brulte speaker. I had addressed that question in the Democratic caucus in purely pragmatic terms. I said that if any Democrat were to be approached by the Republicans, he should insist on becoming speaker in return for his vote. Why give Brulte, who would punish all Democrats, a free vote? Make him agree to back you in return for your vote. I said I would happily step aside from the speakership for any Democrat who could summon forty-one votes, even if thirty-nine were Republicans. Obviously, they didn't follow up on the idea of backing another Democrat. I also let a few Democrats who were vulnerable to Republican appeals see that I already had Horcher's vote. That was enough to keep them in the fold.

Our fight in the California assembly had also become a national story. While Gingrich and Gingrich fever had taken over the U.S. House and other state legislatures, we in California were refusing to bow. We would not be bulldozed. The national attention and the pride shown in us by Democrats across the country was a huge morale builder with my members. It helped them understand that we were fighting over something more than Willie Brown's power to assign parking spaces. This was a fight for democracy. It took much ingenuity, obviously. It always does.

My old friend former assemblyman Mike Roos stood with me as we stopped the Republican assault, as did assemblywoman Maxine Waters of Los Angeles and members of my family. As the Republican dream ended in a nightmare, Roos said of me to a reporter, "This is a monumental moment for a true legend in American politics."

Luck would intervene on my behalf as it so often has. When the assembly met the next day, there was technically no speaker. So following the law, the assembly's chief clerk presided. This was a man who had been like a son to me, E. Dotson Wilson. Years earlier he had been on my staff, and I took great pride in seeing to his election in 1992 as the first black chief clerk of the assembly. Republicans had voted against him. Yet as he presided over the stalemated assembly, he would do me dirt.

In a difficult, exhausting session on Tuesday, December 6, Wilson in effect ruled against us as we tried to remove Mountjoy. But the next day, Chief Clerk Wilson failed to show up for work. He failed to preside over the assembly. He had been hospitalized overnight for stress, according to a physician's note that was sent to the capitol. The doctor forbade Wilson from doing any work for at least the next few days. So, who would preside in the absence of the chief clerk?

The rules dictated that in such a situation, the dean of the assembly, the member with the longest tenure in the house, would preside. Who was this dean of the assembly who would now make the rulings on Mountjoy? He was a man with thirty-one years' membership in the body. He also was a man with encyclopedic knowledge of the rules of the house. He was me. That's right, I, Willie Brown, turned out to be the man who would ultimately make the rulings on Mountjoy.

As presiding officer, I promptly ruled against Mountjoy. I was right. It was completely illegal for him to remain in the assembly. The only reason he wanted to was to bury Willie Brown. I told a reporter, "Mr. Mountjoy has made it clear that he intends to be a state senator. He only wishes to participate in the Forest Lawn [an iconic California cemetery] ceremony for Willie Brown. Once he has done the Forest Lawn ceremony, he will wash his hands of that dirt and move over to the senate." But the game was not yet over.

The Republicans then left the field. They physically abandoned the assembly to keep it from having a quorum. They decamped the capitol entirely, going across the street to meet in the Hotel Senator. This paralyzed the assembly, making it impossible to act. For a while I toyed with the idea of ordering the Highway Patrol to go over and arrest them and bring them back. But that seemed too melodramatic. No question, though, in abandoning

221

the capitol, the Republicans were highly irresponsible. Nothing could be done absent a quorum. No one was even being paid.

I tried negotiating with the Republicans, offering to share power with them as speaker. But they refused to talk to the speaker who had been the fairest to Republicans even about a better deal. Finally, the money, or the absence of money, got to them. They wanted to be paid. That was what brought them back to the capitol. Money! They wanted those tax dollars in their pockets.

Democrats, of course, were suffering too. But for those in real need, we directed them to resources—family, friends, supporters who could tide them over. It always astonishes me on thinking back about this that the Republicans went out on strike, but they didn't even have a strike fund. We Democrats know better.

Meanwhile, the Republicans busied themselves working their revenge on Paul Horcher, who had registered as an Independent. They filed papers for a special election to recall, or oust, him from office. (Eventually on May 16, 1995, that election would be held, and Horcher would be ejected from office. He was a talented guy and when I became mayor of San Francisco in January 1996, I put him to work on my staff.)

Finally, on Monday, January 23, in a session that started late in the evening and went on until 2:00 a.m the next day, we went on to elect the speaker. I received forty votes, and Jim Brulte got thirty-nine. I had sustained my speakership. (I did not need the usual forty-one votes, a majority of the full house, because with the departure of Mountjoy, the size of the assembly was reduced to seventy-nine members.)

As a matter of good politics, I did share power. I shifted some of the speaker's powers to the Rules Committee, which was evenly divided among Democrats and Republicans. (But I kept myself as the trump card: if the Rules Committee didn't resolve an issue within fifteen days, the matter would revert to me.) And I divided the money available to support the assembly evenly between the two parties. In no way, though, did I bargain myself into a diminished speakership. I was determined to remain strong and to keep the house from degenerating into the kind of politics that had caused the Republicans' own demise.

I would remain in the assembly for all of 1995. But I stepped down as speaker on June 5, 1995, to run for mayor of San Francisco. The Republicans finally got to elect one of their own as speaker. But it wasn't Jim Brulte. It was a feisty lady from Orange County named Doris Allen. So contentious and irascible was the Republican majority, so ungovernable, that she stepped down three months later, saying she was "glad to get out of Dante's inferno." As I said earlier when I justified my efforts at sustaining my speakership: under Republican rule the house and government would spiral down into pure hell. I prevented that for at least another few months. Believe me, I didn't wage that ordeal-filled fight for entertainment purposes.

CHAPTER TWENTY-SIX

The Godfather and the Father of the House

IT PROBABLY DIDN'T HELP matters much as the FBI continued its lengthy investigation through the '90s that I appeared in Francis Ford Coppola's *The Godfather: Part III*, released in 1990, playing a shrewd, flamboyant, and corrupt politician. But I couldn't resist taking the part.

In the movie I have a scene with Al Pacino as Michael Corleone in which an envelope passes hands and I offer him some cagey advice on handling a delicate political deal. Originally, I hadn't been cast in the role. However, the actor who had been cast was having trouble delivering his lines the way Coppola wanted. In exasperation, Coppola said to him during one of many takes, "Do it the way Willie Brown would do it." The actor, clueless, had no idea what Coppola was talking about. After a few more frustrating takes, Coppola in a moment of genius decided to get Willie Brown himself to do the role. He called me from Rome and I was off as soon as I could be, packing suitcases full of very elegant suits.

Hollywood travels first-cabin, so on the flight over I found myself sitting in one of those upper lounges that were then part of first-class travel on Boeing 747s. There weren't many people there so I had plenty of opportunity to overhear the worried conversation going on among three big guys who from their talk and the cut of their expensive suits were obviously Hollywood studio officials. They were talking about Coppola. I listened intently. They were on their way over to take him to the woodshed about cost overruns on *Godfather III*. Coppola was in for a stern couple of hours at the very least. They were even talking of firing him. I don't think these studio suits would have talked so freely if they realized that an actor about to go to work for Coppola was on board, but then Willie Brown never looked like a mere actor.

When I got off the plane, I was driven to the set where Coppola briefed me on the role and gave me a script. I briefed him on what to expect from the studio suits. He laughed and thanked me. At that point the three suits walked in and were horrified to find that the elegant black man who had been on the plane with them was then in a very intimate conversation with the director they were about to admonish. I used the feel of the whole thing as my guide to how to approach my scene with Pacino.

I went off to wardrobe to get fitted. The costume designer produced a couple of suits she thought were right for the role. They might have been right for someone playing the part of a gin-soaked Chicago alderman in a 1940s comedy, but they sure weren't right for Willie Brown. I argued with her for a while, but finally just took the suits and went back to my very swank, studio-paid-for hotel suite. When it came time to shoot my scene, I showed up in my own clothes. Coppola was delighted with my wardrobe selection. It fit the part. After *Godfather III* was released, the costume designer won some award for her work on the film. I was mightily annoyed. I should have at least shared in the prize.

Some friends were horrified that I could play the part of a dishonest, money-grubbing pol in a movie at a time when I was being subjected to an FBI investigation, no matter how screwy. But as you know by now, those sorts of considerations—i.e., this would be impolitic—just don't bother me. This was going to be fun being in a major Hollywood movie directed by the greatest director of his era. And anyway, who knew the type better than I? Of course I did it. Many more people today remember that I was in one of Coppola's *Godfather* movies than remember the investigations. It was a wonderful experience and I was glad that I could help Francis with a little advance info on his studio bosses' plans. I support the artist any day and my friends every day.

When I left the speakership after having been termed out and was elected mayor of San Francisco, I had to endure criticism when I hired two former Republican assemblymen, Paul Horcher and Brian Setencich, to work in City Hall. Horcher had voted for me for speaker in 1994 after the Republicans had won control of the assembly. Setencich helped as well. Their party turned on them, but I didn't. I hired them for real jobs and they did them well. I never abandon a friend, no matter how extreme a difficulty he or she is in. I try to keep in mind something another fine actor, W. C. Fields, once said. Fields was asked why he would not be attending the funeral of his old-time friend and boon companion, John Barrymore, where he had been asked to be a pallbearer. Said Fields, "The time to carry a pal is when he is alive."

My having been elected speaker of the assembly for the last time—with Republicans in the majority party—speaks not only to my skills as a politician but also to one of the hallmarks of my fourteen-and-a-half-year reign as speaker: I was a members' speaker.

I did much as speaker to help the lives of the people of California because I (unlike some other speakers) was intensely interested in the subject matter of the legislation we were considering. But I maintained my power for so long because I was also intensely concerned about my members.

Many speakers didn't much care about the members. During Leo McCarthy's reign, for example, an ordinary member couldn't easily get to see the speaker. You had to go through layers of whips, leaders, and assistants. You'd be put off. McCarthy himself didn't even like the Sacramento scene; he didn't hang around after hours, as I or speakers Unruh and Moretti did. As I said earlier, Leo drove home every night to San Francisco to have dinner with his family, a feat and a goal that I respect very much but that indicated he didn't regard the membership as family.

I was a strict disciplinarian and, as you have seen, a member who crossed me would have to pay. But I was not a tyrant and I certainly was not uninterested. My interest crossed party lines. It didn't matter to me if you were a Democrat or Republican (I don't think Speaker McCarthy even spoke to Republicans), if you were a member, you and your needs were important to me. I regarded the members, all the members, as my constituents and I lavished on them the kind of service politicians usually reserve for their constituents back home in the district.

I tried hard over the years to make the experience of being in the legislature, of being in Sacramento, fun and exciting. I wanted the members to look forward to coming to the capitol and to enjoy the time there. Sometimes, it just meant doing something to relieve the stress we all felt at difficult times. In late June, the budget was due, for example. But because of the intense wrangling over items, the process could often extend into July and become vexing and personally (as well as publicly) taxing. When this happened, I would throw a Fourth of July cookout and party for all the members, staffers, and their families on the statehouse lawn. I don't think you could do that today. Partisanship has taken such a toll that members don't even like to mix. Hell, we made them mix, and they invariably had fun. We could get back to the budget tests a little refreshed and not so knotted up.

I also made sure that the assembly was the center for a constant parade of distinguished and exciting visitors, from Sammy Davis Jr. to the Queen of England. All of them came over the years, at my invitation, to entertain, meet, and instruct the members. When I could, I would take these visitors out on the nightly rounds of Sacramento watering holes to meet the legislators in relaxed surroundings. I still regret, though, that I made Sammy Davis Jr. endure the karaoke singing of some of our members in, of all places, an Irish bar. I turned the assembly into a showplace and university. No member was excluded.

And in the political arena, while I exercised tight discipline and concocted some incredible vote-getting deals to pass various bills as father of the house, I never once asked a member to cast a vote that he couldn't live with.

I was very happy to have been the members' speaker.

PART FOUR

Da Mayor

From Soccer Moms to Sacred Cartels:
Tales and Triumphs from My Imperial Mayoralty.

CHAPTER TWENTY-SEVEN

Why Would You Want to Be Mayor?

IT'S NOT SURPRISING TO ME that politicians quickly find another job to run for as soon they're term-limited out of their current office. Frankly, the holding of elective office—almost any office—is a powerful high. There's nothing like it. It's an addiction. Once you've tasted it, you've got to have it. Even if you're trading down in terms of what office you might hold, you want the gig. You figure you'll make the position give you whatever it is you've craved, be that a podium, respect in the big picture, a chance to be productive, or just powerful. You want *position*.

So I can't blame people for thinking that as soon as I was term-limited out of the assembly in 1995, I decided to run for mayor of San Francisco. The truth is somewhat different.

True enough, though, back in the mid-'70s, long before I rose to power in the assembly, I had daydreamed about someday running for mayor. Ideally, I would have succeeded my pal and fellow political daydreamer George Moscone in 1984 after he completed two terms in that office. George's assassination in 1978 tore apart the San Francisco political landscape like one of our fiery earthquakes. The sour political atmosphere that followed the murders of George and of Harvey Milk turned me off city politics. Instead I concentrated on my legal career and made my way forward in the assembly. I didn't give the fractious precinct politics of the city of San Francisco much more thought, though I continued to love my city and did much for it in the assembly.

It'll be another hundred years, if ever, before anyone discovers some of the formulas, gimmicks, and tricks I insinuated into the state's budgets and appropriations to maintain the city. I enjoyed that work. I just wasn't sure that I wanted to administer a city hall.

So in 1995, running for mayor wasn't on my agenda. I thought I might run for a state senate seat from San Francisco, work my magic on the other house in the California legislature, and become part of the leadership of the senate. But I was also thinking that perhaps I ought to just close out my political career when I left the assembly. Perhaps what I really needed to do was go back fully into private practice and, for the first time in my life, concentrate on making money, on building assets. I was sixty-one years old at the time and hadn't made any money. I had raised almost $100 million over the years, but it wasn't for me.

Then early in 1995, Jack Davis, the reigning genius of the world of political campaign consultants in San Francisco, visited to show me some polling he had done. The figures demonstrated that I could be elected mayor of San Francisco. They also showed that either I or my longtime friend John Burton could be elected to the state senate. Jack clearly wanted me to consider making the run for the mayoralty. This was fascinating because Davis had been the man who had elected the then current mayor of San Francisco, Frank Jordan, in 1991. Davis put Jordan, who was not a politician but who had been the chief of police in San Francisco, into City Hall, running him as a man who would be a "citizen mayor," whatever that meant. During his visit to show me the polling numbers, Davis revealed that he would not be backing his 1991 candidate for reelection.

Davis said to me of Jordan, "Frank isn't dumb, but sometimes when you talk to him he gets this kind of glaze in his eyes and you wonder if he knows what you're talking about. That's not good in a mayor." Davis and many other political people were pining for a politician mayor. I represented hope to them—whatever that meant!

I did think about making a run, made some inquiries, but still found myself with further qualms about running.

One qualm was about the job itself. I really couldn't envisage myself refereeing fights about stop signs, zoning permits, and leash laws. Those parochial concerns seemed such a far cry from the grand games and issues that I dealt with routinely in the legislature. In fact, we spent half our time in the legislature trying to abolish local government. I had been where the real genius of politics was, and now I was expected to run for a job in local administration? Arbitrating neighborhood fights? Spending four hours a day signing my name to bond extension contracts and resolutions in honor of Mother's Day?! I hated pen work. A part of my nimble mind warned me that concentrating on such negatives was more a reflex, an expression of my disappointment at having to leave the big world of the speakership than it was a dispassionate, disinterested insight, but in those early days I was disappointed and grouchy.

A more significant negative was the actual mess the city of San Francisco was in. My friend Rudy Nothenberg, who had worked for me in Sacramento years earlier and who had just retired as the city's chief administrative officer (he was CAO when he brought me the news that George Moscone had been assassinated) was baleful about the city. "There's no money in the treasury," he told me in 1995, "and the next mayor will have to make deep cuts. Why should you be the one to make them? You'll just find yourself disappointing yourself and your supporters. Being mayor would be a thankless task." He urged me not to run.

Then there was the matter of my lifestyle. Could I live on the mayor's salary of $137,000? Even when you added in the $57,000 pension that I would receive for my thirty-one years in the assembly, the two together would just about cover my basic obligations to family. It'd be tough because I would be prohibited from earning an outside income and I had no built-up assets. I had invested only in things like my Porsche and my clothes and my lifestyle. If you couldn't wear it, drive it, or eat it, I didn't have it.

To come up with the money to subsidize being mayor, I'd have to sell my law practice, sell my Porsche, and hope (unsuccessfully, as it turned out) I could persuade the city to provide me with a mayoral home! (San Francisco, unlike New York City and Los Angeles, has no mayoral mansion, though there are a few fine publicly owned residences like Admiral Nimitz's old home on Yerba Buena Island or the stately McLaren Lodge in Golden Gate Park that would have done nicely.)

Parochialism, fiscal disaster, personal sacrifice—they all cautioned me against running. Then Louise Renne, the able public-spirited citizen and political maverick who was then San Francisco's elected city attorney, came to me. Louise is a formidable person. Appointed city attorney in 1986 by Mayor Dianne Feinstein, she was subsequently elected and reelected to that post, ultimately serving fifteen years as city attorney. She transformed the office from a sleepy nook of rubber-stampers into an activist, aggressive center. She went from the defense to the offense. As city attorney she took on the tobacco companies, electric power companies, gun manufacturers, big banks, and slumlords.

Previously, she had been a deputy California attorney general and had served on San Francisco's elected board of supervisors. She herself had run for mayor in 1987 against Art Agnos and a popular old-time conservative named John Molinari. Her motto was "Not one of the boys." She was definitely not one of the boys, but she lost. Louise laid it before me: the city was indeed a mess, as Rudy Nothenberg had said. Spending decisions were being made politically, not intelligently, and as a result city services and institutions were falling apart.

In Muni, the city's bus, cable car, and streetcar agency, maintenance, for example, was being deferred to keep spending down, and as a result both daily service and the physical fleet were failing. Pay raises hadn't been given. As a result, drivers were taking out the missed raises in time off, often unscheduled time off. Operations in this and in many other city departments were haphazard and hazardous. And that was just on the day-to-day front.

There had to be better ways to solve these problems. But Louise had no faith in the administration of Mayor Frank Jordan to provide intelligent solutions. City Hall was running on panic. City Hall was flailing, and Jordan, hoping for reelection, was avoiding tough solutions. Frank was a decent guy, but whenever there was a problem, he'd cut corners, come up with what he thought was a political, not a substantive, solution. Louise was so disgusted with the Jordan administration that as city attorney, she refused to represent his office. She disqualified herself from representing her number one client, the mayor. Renne had told Mayor Jordan he'd have to get his own representation.

Then she made it very clear to me: if I didn't run, she would have to run for the job. Louise was never afraid of a fight and she would have made a terrific, if stern, mayor. But she didn't want the job and wasn't sure she could win. She felt deeply that someone else with vision and skill must run.

After Louise's first entreaties, others came to see me with the same message. Their appeals were also to gallantry and honor: it would be a singular distinction for me to finish out my career as mayor of the city I loved, to serve it well, and to solve some of its problems. I agreed, and in late May 1995, I decided to run for mayor.

CHAPTER TWENTY-EIGHT

Running for Mayor

I OPENED MY CAMPAIGN on Saturday, June 3, 1995, at the Peace Plaza in San Francisco's Japantown, where I had announced my candidacy for the assembly thirty-one years earlier. Before five hundred people, I shouted, "I want to be your mayor!"

"When I came here in 1951," I said, "San Francisco had a magic about it. It was a city of vision. A city of risk takers. George Moscone, Mayor Jack Shelley, Congressmen Phillip and John Burton, the great politician Gene McAteer, and planner Justin Herman. This is a magnificent city for political leadership.

"But I've watched this city change, especially over the last years, and I'll tell you this: it is being led by people who are merely caretakers." And by that I meant Mayor Frank Jordan. "We need strong, vibrant, risk-taking leaders," I told the throng. "Everything I am I owe to this city: my public education, my credentials, my ratification as a worthwhile human being. I owe this city a lot more than I have given it so far."

I was in the race.

I went completely into Willie mode. When someone asked me why I was running, I'd say, "Well, the job seemed at least halfway vacant. Mayor Jordan doesn't seem completely to fill the chair." Or when someone asked how it felt to no longer have a car and driver (one of the perks of being speaker), I'd reply, "Why do you think I'm running for mayor?"

But frankly, when I started out, I knew next to nothing about local government. I was in a panic when the first candidates' debate took place a few days later on Friday, June 9, at the venerable San Francisco Italian Athletic Club out in North Beach, right opposite lovely Washington Square Park.

CNN and every other network and local TV station were there because I, the one-million-pound gorilla, the King Kong of California politics, would be there, coming back to run in this playground called the city and county of San Francisco. They were looking for great revelations about housing, health care, and matters involving potholes and public parks. I didn't know shit about any of that! I knew nothing. Absolute zero!

I was also in a panic about the program and protocol of the evening. It was a debate. Even though I knew my opponents had trouble communicating, which I did not, I did not have knowledge—which is of course part of communicating. But that was the deal. I was in a panic.

When we took the stage, I immediately started praying, "Lord, please, don't let me get the first question . . . on some issue involving local government." And sure enough, the Lord answered my prayers. The Lord gave incumbent mayor Frank Jordan the first question.

And then He gave Roberta Achtenberg, the assistant secretary of Housing and Urban Development in the Clinton administration and one of the new generation of politicians to come out of the gay and lesbian political world, the second spot.

The Lord continued to bless me. He gave Angela Alioto, president of the board of supervisors and daughter of the much-beloved late mayor Joe Alioto, third spot. I was number four.

The two people below me, number five and number six, were

absolutely stone idiots—so they wouldn't have been able to provide me with any information in their answers. But the three people ahead of me would. Thank God, the first question was about housing; I would be able to crib from Jordan, Achtenberg, and Alioto, all of whom had some knowledge, presumably, on the issue.

But Frank Jordan, instead of answering the question, spent all his time—I mean full time—castigating me. He talked about damn near every contribution I had ever received. He talked about every vote I had ever cast. And some lady in the back yelled out, "Did you do all those things, Mr. Brown?" So I said, "I will not answer any questions on issues uttered by Mr. Jordan." The lady yelled back, "Well, why not?" I said, "Because I probably did half of what he said, but I don't know which half. So let's not engage in that. Let him make his presentation." I got some good laughs, deflecting Frank.

Meanwhile, Roberta Achtenberg, who was sitting next to me, had been busy the whole time writing on a legal pad about the official question: housing. She made copious notes; I mean, it was absolutely amazing to see how quickly she could write as she thought about what the answer should be to this housing question.

And sure enough, her presentation was flawless. I mean, it was incredible. But in answering, she never looked up from her notes. So nobody in the audience heard a word she said. There was only one person listening to her. Me! Nobody else could hear her, and she gave a perfect answer—a textbook answer. It was one that in law school I would have copied if I had been seated next to her in order to ensure getting a good grade.

Next to answer was Angela Alioto. Angela turned to me, after having been somewhat inattentive to what was going on—she had been waving and smiling to everyone, blowing kisses—and in something of a stage whisper said to me, "What was the question?" Oh, Angela! The moment for mischief was present.

Well, I really wasn't under oath, so what I gave her was a formulation of what I thought the question should be. And she answered that question. It wasn't the one that had been asked, and everybody in the audience thought that she was some kind of uninformed person.

Then they came to me. And I co-opted Roberta's words, twisted them into my phraseology and my delivery system. I sounded like the genius I was supposed to be.

The rest of the night went equally smoothly. The next day the reports were glowing. And I really felt good, ready for more. Well, in this town you go from an Italian social club one night to something like the United Irish Cultural Center the next night. It was another full house. It's amazing, I thought, how this town is so interested. But what was more amazing was the fact that the same people who were at the Italian social club were at the Irish Cultural Center!

Usually you change your answers event by event to suit the new audience, but instead of a brand-new audience we had the same one. This phenomenon continued throughout the campaign. This was one of the first oddities of mayoral campaigning I discovered: the press would write about how another debate had attracted a full audience, but in fact it was the same audience. Little wonder politicians sound bored. They're often giving the same speech to the same audiences over and over again.

It's not that the people of San Francisco were apathetic; it's just that in these formula events that loom large in coverage you got formula audiences. The real battle for votes would be on the streets, sidewalks, TV spots, and in mailed advertisements.

As our campaign continued, the Jordan people attacked my integrity. In all encounters, stagy or spontaneous, I tried to emphasize my ability to get things done and to understand the city's gridlock. I could tell that voters were flocking to my truthful approach. The Jordan people attacked every dollar I earned, and they accused me of being beholden to the interests from whom I seduced campaign contributions for my side in the assembly. They even suggested that I was personally pocketing campaign contributions. But every penny I ever earned was on the record. People could look and see whom I had worked for and what I had earned.

As to the charges that I was the political tool of Big Tobacco and its campaign contributions, I answered simply, as I have stated in these pages. I pointed out to the voters that for every dollar in campaign contributions I took from Tobacco, I took just as much from the health care industry. The interests balanced. Furthermore, I pointed out that California's strict antismoking legislation had originated in my assembly and had been passed by my assembly. I appointed every committee member who first approved it. If I were owned by Tobacco, I sure picked a mean way to pay them back.

As far as my widespread network of connections was concerned, voters regarded it as a plus that I was in touch with so many players and forces. That could only help. It showed I had experience dealing with all sorts of forces. It showed that I had an awesome speed-dial list to place at the service of San Francisco.

I repeatedly emphasized that I did understand real politics. I had practiced the actual wheeling and dealing in political life, and, just as importantly, could close a deal—in contradistinction to the frightened meanderings of a bumbling administration.

Of course, it isn't enough to be a deal maker. As a matter of fact, you don't want that to be your major claim to fame. Be known as just a deal maker, people think that's all you know and that you are prone to making side deals. You have to demonstrate that you make deals only in the context of public service. Your deals are for the city, not for the day's boodle.

Did my levity hurt me? When I joked in the debate that I wasn't sure which half of the things Frank Jordan accused me of doing I'd actually done, it didn't hurt. If you do make a joke about such things, people tend to believe that you are innocent—otherwise you wouldn't make jokes.

Anyway, it's one of my failings that I can't resist a quip. I like hearing myself say shocking things. An ability to joke and parry and take a joke has never hurt me. At the worst, people wonder about you: "Who is this lunatic?" Conversely, no one remembers a word Frank Jordan ever said during the campaign. And I won.

We had hard political work to do, though, in that campaign beyond the jokes. And, as usual, it involved building a coalition of the clubs and forces that could be relied upon to deliver votes. With the help of my campaign chief, Jack Davis, I built a federation that included the old coalition of progressive and populist voters that had elected Art Agnos mayor in 1988. Agnos served one term until Police Chief Frank Jordan beat him in 1992. Agnos's progressive coalition had dissipated amidst much internecine squabbling when he was mayor.

I didn't have the support in the 1995 election of San Francisco's old labor establishment, but I did have the crucial support of one key union: the cops' union.

Frank Jordan was not only an unpopular mayor with the police; he had been an unpopular chief of police. The rank and file felt that as chief and mayor Jordan had denied them the quality of equipment they needed. They howled at the cheapo motorcycles he made them ride. And they also felt he had dealt unfairly with one brother officer—literally, Frank Jordan's own brother. Frank's brother, Jack, was a captain and very popular with the street cops. But they felt that Frank hadn't been loyal to his own brother. That's death in an organization built on feelings of brotherhood.

So in a race against a former career cop, I had the support of the cops themselves. That created a lot of resonance in San Francisco, to my advantage.

Of course, I had a lot of support from the African-American community, but not all of it. About one-third of San Francisco's blacks supported Angela Alioto, who was a real populist and who as an attorney would represent scores of black litigants in antidis-crimination lawsuits.

I also worked hard to build up support in San Francisco's other ethnic communities. I had lots of help from activists and leaders. In Chinatown, leaders such as Rose Pak, Julie Lee, and Leland Yee organized their constituencies for me, while Jeff and Sandy Mori organized Japantown, and Dennis and Linda Normandy brought together Filipino voters—thanks to their efforts I received just about 100 percent of the Filipino vote. San Francisco's massive Hispanic community came together for me under the leadership of Dennis Herrera, who is now San Francisco's elected city attor-ney; Susan Leal, who now runs the city's Public Utilities Commis-sion; and Carlotta del Portillo, now dean of the Mission Campus of the City College of San Francisco.

Herb Caen and a politically active genius of a florist and party planner named Stanlee Gatti helped organize San Francisco's posher neighborhoods. I was already popular as a stylish figure in that world, but Caen and Gatti really talked me up in the socially rarefied air of Pacific Heights and Russian Hill. The voters on the hills were members of the First Families of San Francisco, with fortunes as old as the Gold Rush and as new as Silicon Valley. Be-cause they're smart and vocal, they're opinion leaders. They also had cash to contribute to campaigns.

While at first I didn't have much support from San Francisco's conservative middle-class neighborhoods, the city's poorer neighborhoods like The Mission and the South of Market district were largely for me. These constituencies had all benefited from my time in the legislature.

People remembered, especially in immigrant communities, things that I had done as a legislator. Many voters told me that they wouldn't have been able to get an economic start in this country if it were not for me, despite the fact that they came here with good professional and educational credentials. What they remembered was my legislation that made it possible for them to use at least some of their credentials in assembling their petitions for professional licenses in California. Thousands of good nurses, to name just one group, were able to get a start in their professions again once they got here because of what I did.

I also had strong support, of course, from gay voters, though some were tempted at first to go with one of their own, Roberta Achtenberg. But after Achtenberg was defeated in the November election, she threw her support behind me for the runoff election between Jordan and myself in December. I didn't even have to ask her.

Foolish good luck also intervened in the 1995 campaign. One day, Frank Jordan agreed to do a radio broadcast with two shock jocks—from his shower. Yep, Jordan and the two jocks jumped naked into the shower, had pictures taken, and did their broadcast. It was supposed to have been a joke, but the Jordan people, humorless, couldn't tell a good joke from a dumb one. That's another reason for having and utilizing a sharp sense of humor—you develop a sixth sense for when the joke is not zany but stupid. Frank's morning shower was a horrible embarrassment to Jordan's conservative voters. Needless to say, he became the butt of jokes, which were slow to disappear. It did him in completely. I don't think his Irish Catholic voters were offended out of prudery or modesty— but the escapade encapsulated the dubious judgment, the lack

of sophistication and intelligence that marked his whole administration.

People asked me if I ever would do such a foolish thing. I gave
it the Full Willie, so to speak. "Never," I said, "unless it was with
two women." Once, I said I would never appear publicly in a
shower because I simply disliked one-button suits. Poor Frank. He
never lived down the jokes. He even had a new nickname in the
Castro: "Shorty."

I made my share of bloopers, but nothing like that. The worst,
in the days before I became mayor, was to promise to fix Muni (the
transit agency) "within one hundred days." It was the typical sort of
dumb thing that a politician says when he doesn't know any better
or isn't thinking. Saying you were going to fix Muni in one hundred
days was like saying you were going to fix Medicare overnight. It
was an impossibility. It took me years to straighten out Muni, but
eventually I did get service and the fleet back to better levels. I even
opened a new streetcar line: a sparkling new light-rail line that ran
along the beautiful new waterfront and served the new ballpark and
opened up new neighborhoods. What I would learn about Muni
and how to fix it, as you shall read, was a revelation to me about the
limitations and challenges a big-city mayor faces.

During the 1995 campaign, I also had some secret support. I
went to a Labor Day rally in Oakland at which President Bill Clinton spoke. After the rally, Clinton said to me, "Willie, I have something to show you." He reached into his trousers pocket and pulled
out a "Brown for Mayor" button. "Mr. President," I said, "I
thought you never got involved in local politics. Where did you
get that?" He winked and said, "A president has his ways." To show
my gratitude, I tried to set up a golfing date for the golf-loving
president. There was a gifted amateur I wanted him to meet and
play with: a young man named Tiger Woods who was then at Stanford. Alas, I was never able to link up the two for a tee-off.

What I loved during the long days of the campaign, moving up and down the streets where I shook more than seventy thousand hands, were the surprises, especially learning the city's political customs. San Francisco's myriad Chinese groups had their own rituals involving candidates, often carried out in shrines and temples stuck away in nondescript buildings in San Francisco's two Chinatowns: the one near North Beach, and the other, newer Chinatown out in the Richmond district, off Clement Street. People who were interested in sponsoring you or your candidacy required you to go through a little fortune-telling ceremony. In an incense-scented room, they would have you toss yarrow stalks or sticks while a soothsayer looked at the results. In my case, I could tell from the smiling faces of those around me, the first results were auspicious. My candidacy looked good. That opened a world of support for my campaign.

Some politicians were not so lucky. One young woman running for another office always seemed to draw baleful results when she tossed the yarrow stalks. When she did so, her sponsors looked impassive, not discouraged, though. Then they would have her toss the sticks again. And again. And again, until she came up with a configuration that was pleasing. But I could tell her hosts were not enthused. They just kept her at it until it could end on a good note. But she didn't garner the support, money, or votes.

The Chinese voters also consulted soothsayers back in the old country about the campaign, analyzing numerical figurations of your name. I didn't have to go to Shanghai, Hong Kong, or Macau, but the consultations were thorough and important. Even the numerical values of the letters in my name, combined with the title of the office I was seeking, were scrutinized. They looked for auguries everywhere.

Another group that fascinated me were the Irish builders of San Francisco. San Francisco was full of small contractors, often just off the plane from Shannon or scarcely one generation re-moved. Under the direction of Joe O'Donoghue, a political genius originally from Limerick who started out as a labor organizer but grew into a master of the building and planning codes. Joe was able to make the rules work for him (and he reorganized the perti-nent city departments via a ballot measure). These builders had joined forces and become a kind of Knights of Malta combined with an Irish village football team. Remember the line Sidney Greenstreet, as the character Kasper Gutman, utters in that classic book and movie of San Francisco, Dashiell Hammett's *The Maltese Falcon*, when speaking of the Knights of Rhodes, fabricators of the Maltese Falcon? "Have you any conception of the extreme, the immeasurable wealth of the Order at that time?" "Well," said Humphrey Bogart as Sam Spade, "I imagine they were pretty well fixed." That was the Residential Builders Association. They didn't have many votes, but they could schmooze and support—and fight. At a moment's notice in the campaign, when we needed money, a couple of pickup trucks would pull up beside us as we were cam-paigning down a street. It was like telepathy. They must have had an incredible information network, for they often knew of a need remarkably early on. From the trucks, young builders would hop out. Then they would hand over a bundle of small checks, each one perfectly in order, each one properly made out to the campaign, each one containing all the information about the donor that the financial-reporting laws required. Joe O'Donoghue's squads could put one hundred thousand dollars on the street with only a day's notice.

Over time, I would have my share of disagreements with the builders over one project or another, but they never bullied or de-manded. They never invoked the argument of quid pro quo. They, like the Chinese voters, recognized the limits of relationships. They were very understanding, recognizing that you had many constituencies. They also understood that you had nothing to sell. A contribution didn't buy you anything but leadership.

I enjoyed the way that San Francisco's various political and ethnic groups, despite political differences, showed respect and comity to other groups by supporting each other's charitable events and social celebrations. All differences were set aside when it came to helping with an annual banquet or charity event. This was part of the etiquette of the political establishment. You would see them all at all the Chinatown feasts, at the Assyrian Society's gala dinner, at the golf tournaments for small hospitals and schools. They built relationships.

At the time of the lunar new year, Asian groups, especially the Chinese, not only held myriad events built around the New Year and San Francisco's Chinese New Year parade—the largest and most glamorous outside of China—but they also handed out red envelopes to all they encountered, from waiters to bishops. The red envelopes, embossed with gilt calligraphy, contained a shiny new bill, usually a five-dollar bill. It was a good-luck omen. In the course of a day around the New Year, I would receive scores of these. They were meant as good luck, not as hooks. But it was too risky to accept cash from anyone. Even a good luck token, in today's political atmosphere, could be construed as an illegal contribution or bribe. So I promptly recycled them unopened, passing them back into the community. They went right back to the next person I saw. I never kept them.

Although the city's populace was highly interested in the election, the city's chief newspaper, the *San Francisco Chronicle*, was too Pecksniffian to even bother endorsing a candidate in the race. But the day before the election, something better happened. The *Chronicle*'s chief columnist, Herb Caen, my old friend and formidable critic, wrote a column about me that essentially was an endorsement. Herb's column argued, "You'd be a fool not to vote for Willie Brown." It encapsulated much about the contest and me. I'm immensely proud of it and reproduce a portion of it here. Caen wrote in the November 6, 1995, *Chronicle*:

Yes, once more unto the polls, dear friends. On the face of it, tomorrow's Election of the Century, not to be confused with the [O. J. Simpson] trial of the same name, should be a no-brainer. Willie Brown is in a class by himself—and a bargain by any standards: For a piddling $137,000 a year, we have a chance to get a $1-million-a-year superstar. Not only that, he'll work 24 hours a day, seven days a week because the man is an insomniac. As politics is his life, San Francisco is his love and he'll be burning the midnight oil at noon and vice versa. If elected, Willie Brown will be all over the place, shaking hands, turning on the charm, listening carefully to your problems (he has impeccable manners) and trying to solve them. . . . I wrote years ago, thereby stirring up a minor controversy, that most people won't vote for candidates they think are smarter than they, and that's one of Willie Brown's problems. . . . For people like that, and we have many in this city, Willie Brown is "a bit much." He appears to be having too good a time. He makes no excuses for his occasional excesses. He seems unperturbed by the kind of media criticism that would drive the thin-skinned up the wall and perhaps into exile. He enjoys a good fight: The eyes dance, he goes into his boxer's crouch, he comes up with the zinger that befuddles his opponent.

The next day at the polls Roberta Achtenberg was eliminated from the race, leaving Frank Jordan and me in a runoff. Five weeks later in that runoff, I defeated Frank Jordan, 57 percent of the votes to Frank's 43 percent, and became mayor of San Francisco. I was hope to a lot of people.

On election night, as my supporters and I celebrated, a lady friend came to the podium and in front of the crowd presented me with a baseball cap on which had been embroidered the words "Da Mayor." Those words became a catchphrase for me over the next few weeks and on January 8, 1996—with my wife, Blanche, as she had predicted, standing on the podium next to me holding the family Bible—I took the oath of office. I had come a long way from Mineola, where oath-spitting men tossed nickels in a cuspidor for me to fetch out after I shined their shoes. I was "Da Mayor."

CHAPTER TWENTY-NINE

Slick Willie: Da Mayor

"I'M NOT INTO DOOM AND GLOOM," I told a reporter as I walked into San Francisco's Yerba Buena Gardens to take the oath of office as mayor of San Francisco on January 8, 1996. I chose the outdoor Yerba Buena Gardens, an urban esplanade built on a redevelopment site downtown, as the site of my inauguration because the gardens were so pretty, so hope-inducing, such a symbol of what San Francisco could be. But there was an echo of sadness too. The gardens are just opposite the Moscone Convention Center, named for my old friend, Mayor George Moscone, who was assassinated in the mayor's office on that gloomy, doom-filled morning of November 27, 1978. I was determined, though, to bring happiness and glamor back to the city.

But the reporter had been castigating me, as we walked from a church service to my swearing-in, that my inaugural festivities were too grand. I had included parties for one hundred thousand guests, free meals from San Francisco's best kitchens for our ten thousand homeless, entertainment by Carlos Santana and Huey Lewis, among others. There was also a phone call that came directly to the podium during the swearing-in. It was Bill Clinton calling from the White House. I remember he put me on hold in front of thousands of people—something only a president would dare do.

Jesse Jackson was there as well, along with attorney Johnnie Cochran and thousands of others of my pals. The party that night, titled "Soul of the City," cost a fortune. When we were planning the inaugural fest, I told Stanlee Gatti, the superprominent party producer and florist, the budget would be about $300,000. "Is that for flowers?" he asked. Stanlee obviously knows the Willie Brown style. In fact, $300,000, originally the budget for all the inaugural festivities, in the end just about covered the cost of the flowers.

The parties were paid for privately—through donations from San Franciscans so wealthy and so well established there was nothing they could wish for from a mayor. During the inaugural itself, the San Francisco Symphony Youth Orchestra played. According to one paper, their leading piece was Aaron Copland's *Fanfare for the Common Man*. According to another they were playing Mussorgsky's *Pictures at an Exhibition*. Well, that tells you that reporters don't get out to the symphony very much. I led the orchestra in a spirited rendition of "The Stars and Stripes Forever" and gave an inaugural address that was full of surprises, and still offers a few political lessons.

In the address I appointed the city's first black fire chief, Bob Demmons, and put the police department in the hands of minorities for the first time. I named Fred Lau to be the first Asian chief of the San Francisco Police Department. I also appointed legendary homicide inspector Earl Saunders, an African American, assistant chief. Both the police and fire departments had been previously notorious for discriminatory practices against minority officers. Years earlier, black police officers couldn't even drive police cars. Chief Lau, when he first applied to join the force, had been rejected because he wasn't tall enough—a regulation that really was a stricture against Asian Americans and women. When I became mayor, the fire department was still under federal supervision to overcome its years of discrimination against minorities.

In my inaugural address, I also named Charlotte Mailliard Swig (she is now Charlotte Shultz, having later married, as a widow, former Reagan secretary of state George Shultz, then a widower) as my protocol chief. She's from Texas, like me. She set up the inaugural festivities, so she deserved the position. Later she became an integral part of my plan to market San Francisco to the world. She still serves San Francisco today as a protocol advisor and serves Governor Schwarzenegger as his current protocol chief for Northern California. She is one Texas party gal.

Not one of these people knew until I announced their appointments that they had been promoted. I've learned over the years to keep appointments a secret—even from the people you're appointing—until you're ready to act. Otherwise, the news is leaked and you're fighting critics before you or you appointees have had a chance to perform.

After the inaugural, the parties began. San Francisco had soul again. As I've often said, I believe that politics and civic life should be fun. The city certainly needed a lift, a boost to its morale. I was eager to overcome the torpor that seemed to have laid the city low. It was more than just a mood thing. The place seemed physically dull and vacant.

As I walked from St. Patrick's Church over to the Yerba Buena Gardens, my mind was on my speech and on managing the festivities for later in the day, but it was impossible not to notice the gaping holes downtown. A one-hundred-yard-long lot on one side of the gardens lay empty and full of mud. On the other side, more sites lay vacant. The giant holes were stalled construction projects. Indeed, I knew all about them, having at various times in decades past represented petitioners and developers who wanted to build downtown. But why were these projects stalled? I no longer had any clients in the game, but it was hard not to notice that whatever game had been going on had come to a halt. The city was full of sites, lots, and projects upon which people had taken a chance but where little action had resulted. Everything was caught up in committees, in "process." I realized that among my priorities would be to get downtown San Francisco thriving again. The city really needed a mayor. It needed an advocate—one with connections all over the place.

Shortly after I took office, President Clinton telephoned me again. He wanted to wish me well.

"Is there anything I can do for you?" he asked. We had a lot pending with the federal government, but it was better to let things take their normal procedural path. I told him I had everything in San Francisco under control.

"Good," he said.

"But," I said, "there's something you can help me with back in Mineola." There was a second's silence.

"Where in hell is Mineola?" the president asked.

"Mineola is in Texas," I said. "It's a small town, about four thousand people in eastern Texas. And it's my hometown. I come from Mineola."

"And how can I help you with Mineola?" he asked.

"I think the Amtrak train should stop there." That was my request of the president of the United States. He may have thought I was a sentimental lunatic, but I don't think so. He laughed and was, I think, curious. But he quickly said, "Willie Brown—for you, not a problem."

Sometime later Bill Clinton called me back. He had spoken to the head of Amtrak. "Willie Brown," said the president, "you know, this guy at Amtrak is pushing back. 'We're not going to stop in Mineola at all,' he told me. Willie Brown, he's resisting."

"Listen, Mr. President," I said, "you're the president of the United States. Order him to do it." There was a second's pause.

"When are you coming to Washington?" President Clinton said next.

"In a few weeks," I told him.

He said, "Fine, I will have the head of Amtrak in my office. The three of us will meet."

A few weeks later, lo and behold, we had that meeting in Washington. I made my presentation about Mineola and what a wonderful little place it is. Pinto beans are processed there . . . and there are antique shops, and old railroad hotels left from the days when it was an important stop where train crews changed. I described an industrious but isolated little town.

The Amtrak boss stood up and said, "With all due respect to what the mayor has said, we've done a market survey and we have not been able to find one passenger who wishes to stop and get off in Mineola. We measured this over a three-month period and there's no reason to stop in Mineola."

The president then looked at me and said, "Do you care to respond before I rule or make a recommendation?"

"Absolutely, I want to respond," I said. "What the hell is the matter with that guy? The reason to stop in Mineola is not to let anybody *off*. It's to let the people *on*. It's not that great a place. Look at me! I left!"

The president of the United States turned to Mr. Amtrak and said, "You lose your job if you don't stop in Mineola." Then Bill Clinton turned to me and said, "You are the real Slick Willie!" We had a relationship.

CHAPTER THIRTY

A Mayor Is Actually Supposed to Solve Problems

IN AMERICA, A MAYOR IS the only elected official with actual responsibility for the direct day-to-day lives of people. Governors, legislators, senators, congressmen, state officials all have responsibility for general policy, but only a mayor is actually supposed to solve problems. That's not necessarily something politicians like doing.

When I came into City Hall scores of administrative operations were languishing, falling apart. The city had a huge structural deficit, and money for capital improvements was being siphoned off to meet day-to-day operational needs. Furthermore, those mainstays of any city government—the police and fire departments—were under court decrees that saw them essentially run by the federal government to redress years of discrimination and abuse against minority applicants.

At the Redevelopment Agency, I found that the agency was also using bond money to cover day-to-day costs. Had the bondholders known this they surely would have called in their bonds.

At the Housing Authority, responsible for thirty thousand tenants, things were so bad that a takeover by the federal government seemed imminent. Already grants and other funds from the federal government were threatened because of the rotten condition and abysmally bad safety record of the housing projects.

I realized that I had about six months to resolve these problems before I began to experience pushback from the feds and other interested parties. The situation in the Housing Authority was made no easier by the fact that it was a black-run agency.

The solution I devised was one that only Willie Brown could have come up with. The Housing Authority had gone through three directors in four years. The current director, Shirley Thornton, an African American, had experience only working in schools. To my mind there were questions about her job performance.

The federal government was ready to intervene. I went to Washington and got them to intervene—in a more creative and less punitive manner. In January 1996, I went to visit the secretary of housing and urban development, my old friend Henry Cisneros. Together, and with the help of former San Francisco mayor and assemblyman Art Agnos, we put together a plan by which the federal government would send in a team of advisors to help with the management of the Housing Authority. This way we managed to get help while also staving off penalties. I quickly removed Ms. Thornton from the agency. It was funny to me that whenever I appointed an African American to high office, it was always played up as "Willie Brown rewards a crony," but when I removed or disciplined an African American, the news as such was scarcely mentioned.

Officially, the Housing Authority (the biggest landlord in San Francisco) and the Redevelopment Agency were quasi-independent. They weren't municipal departments and were governed by commissioners chosen by the mayor. But I regarded the authorities as integral parts of my administration. I made sure that the board members whom I appointed, with the involvement of the city's legislature, understood that I wanted them to hire top staffers that I could work with and that their votes on policy were to reflect my policies only. That's the only way to get results.

I also made sure that my appointees to the commissions overseeing city agencies understood they worked for me. Some I removed from office. Some I remonstrated with. Some I, ah, reasoned with. One day Stanlee Gatti, whom I had appointed to the Arts Commission, took my call about a piece of business pending before that commission. Stanlee knew I wanted the vote to go a certain way. A frank fellow, he said to me, "Mr. Mayor, I don't think I can be with you on this one." I said to him, "Stanlee, you're a genius, but you're also my commissioner, and as such you don't think unless I tell you you can think." I hated doing that to a dear friend and a sensitive man, but when you sign on with Willie Brown, you sign on to go along when I need you. After all, it was my mayoralty and I had the big picture.

At one time, I found it necessary to see that a recalcitrant manager of one agency go. I didn't have the power to do it myself, but I conveyed this message to the board: "I am succeeding here. I am succeeding there. The only place I am not succeeding is with this department. The manager is not executing my plays. He's calling audibles. I won't put up with this. The manager must go. I want to send in a new quarterback." The director went. This was not only good for the city, it was good politics as well. You can't allow people to operate too independently. Insubordination is not acceptable. It leads to fissures and factionalizing. There is only one boss. That's the mayor.

Of course, this approach got me in enormous trouble with the city's legislature, the board of supervisors, which was constantly trying to trim my sails, especially during my second term. Some supervisors really were resentful of the fact that I stopped City Hall from becoming and operating as an oasis for every little political faction to refresh itself. They deeply resented that in San Francisco when Willie Brown was the mayor, the mayor's office was where you went to do business.

In fact, everybody wanted to do business with Da Mayor.

CHAPTER THIRTY-ONE

The Selfish: The Killer Dynamic of City Politics

ONE NIGHT SHORTLY AFTER I began serving as mayor, I was scheduled to drop in on a neighborhood hall in the Noe Valley section of San Francisco. Noe Valley is a lovely neighborhood of old Victorian and Edwardian homes—"painted ladies" they're called in San Francisco because of the colorful paint jobs given to the elaborate gingerbread trims that adorn their façades. Its main shopping street is packed with cafés and fancy shops of one kind or another. It's also a family-oriented neighborhood. I could see the problem dramatically when I arrived in the hall. To my left the seats were full of young, attractive people in jogging clothes wearing expensive running shoes. Nike did well out there. These people also had dogs with them.

To my right, the seats were packed with more young, attractive people. They looked no less fit than the others, but their clothes were not so athletic. They wore trim, comfortable clothes and looked as if they ran busy households. These people had their small children with them. The kids and the dogs looked as if they wanted to play together, but their respective adult custodians just sat there glaring across the aisle at each other. The soccer moms versus the dog lovers.

The specific problem was that the soccer parents were mightily annoyed at the dog owners because the dog owners had been using the soccer fields as places to run with their animals and the dogs were doing things on the field that weren't being picked up and cleaned after. The moms wanted the dogs and their guardians gone. The dog owners wanted the parks open to all. And they all wanted the mayor to resolve the dispute between them.

Now, I'm very skilled at dispute resolution and mediation. I've even been called in to mediate disputes within the gigantic Los Angeles Unified School District, which was like to trying to solve the fights in the Balkans or in Northern Ireland. But, looking at these two furious sides, I recognized right away that if I were to be at all effective in resolving this dispute, the first thing I had to do was to get out of there that night. This fight wasn't going to be resolved with the two sides sitting in there, swimming in fury.

So I made a short presentation about the things we were going to try to do for the city with our Recreation and Park Department. Then I told the crowd that the director of Rec and Parks had been studying their specific problem with his staff all day and that he would talk to them about the issues that seemed to need resolving. I pleaded the busyness of my evening's schedule and left the meeting to the director of the parks department, who didn't look too happy about that. But I knew that he could and would lay down and lay out the specific problems and issues their dispute involved. That at least would get a set of talking points out there that they could focus on.

I left the meeting but returned to the problem. The way to handle it was, first, to get representatives of each side in privately to tell me their complaint. It meant a lot of listening, but you can learn a lot when people are there yelling their litany of complaints.

In a dispute, people often don't address their real issues, anxieties, and hopes directly. But by noticing what points they keep returning to, you can discern what was really on their minds. And you have to let them listen to themselves. They're hearing. They often won't come to reason, but they and you will get an idea of what's really at stake.

Then you pull the two parties together and let them argue across the table. Do this long enough and enough times and you'll get a sense of what issues are truly at stake and which ones people might cave in on—not that they're being explicit about any of that. Dispute resolution isn't a key function of a mayor—you have bigger fish to fillet. But I found that by doing neighborhood dispute solving, I began to develop key insights not only into the issues bothering people but also into the odd dynamics of city politics, which are so different from state politics, and so much more deadly.

Normally in a dispute resolution, you'd then let parties stew for a while, what oddly enough is called a "cooling-off period." In this period people usually can find themselves trying to figure out what they'll jockey for, what they'll demand, and where they won't give. In this part of the process, they usually realize that they are in a true negotiation process. There's going to be a deal. They'll have to come to terms. They can't continue just to spout, outraged, about the grievances done to them.

A funny thing happens then. Each side gets a little frightened—frightened that they'll be the side to give way first. No disputing party wants to be the first to say uncle.

As a mayor you have to figure out how to get someone to go first and who'll be willing to take the plunge. To them, you rather subtly offer a carrot on some other issue. Arrange carrots and someone will give but will do so feeling they also got something. Nice if exhausting process. That's eventually what happened in the dogs fight. People gave. But I was struck and concerned about the moral outrage each side felt. Self-righteousness in less pliable situations would become a real obstacle to process. It also was a factor in my understanding of the strange situation of city politics: politicians often wouldn't take on special interests, which is what many advocacy groups were. Why face the fire?

Sometimes when parties are warring, you can even forge an alliance between the two of them that makes them want to resolve their differences rather than face the fury of an even angrier outside force. In labor disputes, such as an impending garbage strike or Muni strike, I was able to get the two parties, labor and management, to settle down and come to an early agreement. I pointed out to them that if they didn't agree, they both faced even bigger trouble: an outraged public. I didn't mean just the wrath of public opinion. I meant the fury of an outraged public as expressed by a mayor taking action on behalf of the betrayed public, say, by example, canceling the contracts, getting the work done by a third party, and suing the hell out of both parties. That they didn't want. So they moved out of the fear of being the first to fold and their own selfishness, and they settled.

Once I was able to forge an alliance out of more than twenty neighborhood groups that were fighting over an allocation of scarce city money. The city had a program for creating open spaces and recreational facilities financed by money that would be divvied up among the city's various neighborhoods. Since community control is an important ideal, the decision about how to spend the money was left to a kind of task force composed of representatives of the city's many districts. The problem was that although this program had money, nothing was being built. The reason was that the politicians, frightened of offending neighborhood groups, and the neighborhood groups, unwilling to let one get ahead of the other, appropriated the money annually in a rather stupid way.

What they did was cut up the money evenly among the various district groups. So each got a small annual appropriation that was never enough to do the work of completing a project. Naturally, they were furious that things weren't getting done. But captivated by their own selfishness, they couldn't see why this was the case.

I forged an alliance among the groups. I pointed out that at the rate they were going, it would take each district thirty or forty years to complete even one of the projects they had in mind. In the meanwhile, they weren't getting anything except mud holes and shut-down construction sites. I showed them that if they could get their heads behind the idea of letting each neighborhood in turn get a hefty appropriation, they could get things done. They agreed, and they also agreed that the most underserved parts of the city should go first. Soon, in one of the most neglected neighborhoods of the city, we built and opened a new park.

This was strenuous work for me and my staff. While we found that when people wanted to build parks for their kids you could appeal to their sense of public spirit and their profound wish to help all the kids of the city, with other special-interest groups— say, bicycle advocates or free-transit promoters or nonprofit housing advocates, righteous organizations—it was sometimes impossible to get people to move out of their own selfishness. It was what they clung to. Their moral outrage was, as I've said, their food. It was the capital that kept producing the dividends that enriched their lives. And they would make it grow. Oppose them and they'd try to beat you at the ballot box.

As mayor there were plenty of times when I could have used the help of other politicians on issues. But most politicians just want to survive. They could see the wrong, but they wouldn't dare oppose the wrongheaded but self-righteous.

It was this dynamic, or dys-dynamic, at play that produced and produces the gridlock characteristic of city politics. No wonder problems don't get solved; no wonder we don't get results. The combination of the selfish and the survivalist is guaranteed to bring things to a halt, a halt surrounded by heavy criticism and badgering.

If you're going to succeed as a politician, though, if you're going to get things done, you can't give way to this dysfunction. You have to understand it, which is why I describe it. But you have to have the confidence to weather the storm and in the end let results be your protector. Give good results and the general public will remember. That's what guided me every day during my years as mayor.

Sometimes negotiation didn't work. The interest whose hegemony you were opposing was so selfish that you had to find just the right moment, the right crack, to break through and achieve results.

Consider the case of a new parking garage for the busy North Beach section of San Francisco, the restaurant-and-nightlife remnant of the city's old Italian neighborhood. It may have lost many residents, but its vitality has not been hindered. When I became mayor it lacked parking places. It had for years. I wasn't trying to bring in *more* traffic to North Beach, but simply to construct adequate parking for what was there. That was a goal a lot of people shared, though they had different agendas and fears, especially about destroying homes or businesses to build parking. I got most of the parties—Italian neighbors, Chinese neighbors, merchants, planners, traffic experts, tourism types—together. We managed to find a solution. We found a dilapidated building then owned by the state, opposite a police station, which then had room for thirty or forty cars. If we fixed it up or put in a new building, it could hold 350 to 400 cars. That would help.

Although we had built this coalition of all the truly affected stakeholders, we were still blocked by the Telegraph Hill

Dwellers, who lived on an entirely different hill blocks away. But the Hill Dwellers, who had organized themselves into a group by that name back in 1954, regarded *all* of North Beach as part of their mountainy kingdom. They didn't then and still don't want any other living human beings coming to live, work, or play in North Beach. They don't even want them passing through.

The Telegraph Hill Dwellers are resourceful, dogged, and have money behind them. I have a great deal of respect for them. But, alas, they'll do anything to achieve their ends and they'll do it sanctimoniously. They tie up ideas for years in City Hall and in the courts. No plea is too outrageous for them to make. But like the Gang of Five who had tried to unseat me from the speakership years earlier in Sacramento, the Telegraph Hill Dwellers had never run into a real shark before. And this shark, with the backing of the majority of the community, was determined to get that garage built.

Eventually we proceeded through the permitting process and won permission to build the garage. But that would mean nothing to the Hill Dwellers. I figured their next move would be to block any demolition permit to tear down the old building. It was with the demolition permit I outsmarted them.

We secured a demolition permit on a Tuesday. But I told my operatives to block the issuing of the permit until the next Friday afternoon. That was perfectly ordinary.

Then I hired a contractor and told him to have a crew in place on Friday afternoon to tear the building down. At City Hall, this bewildered them. The refrain I heard from the bureaucrats was: "Don't start tearing it down on a Friday. The overtime for the crew working Friday night and all weekend will be enormous. You've got the demolition permit, just wait till next week and you can pay a crew regular rates to demolish the building."

But I knew what the Telegraph Hill Dwellers would do as soon as they heard a demolition permit had been issued. So I said to the bureaucrats, "Oh, no. It's essential we tear it down this weekend. We'll work Friday night, Saturday, and all day Sunday."

Sure enough, on the following Monday morning, the Telegraph Hill Dwellers, having seen that a demolition permit was issued on Friday, showed up in court seeking a restraining order to stop the demolition of the building.

Then someone shouted out to them that the building had disappeared over the weekend. They've never recovered from that little maneuver.

We built the garage; a nice structure decorated with San Francisco–style murals full of neighbors' likenesses. It has not intruded on anybody's sensibilities. And there has not been one word of criticism of it. Most people can't even tell it's a garage. It fits in really well. And is quite busy.

Who do you think showed up to cut the ribbon at the garage opening? Aaron Peskin, a member of the city's board of supervisors, himself a former head of the Telegraph Hill Dwellers and their key strategist.

Sometimes interest groups bullied not only the process and the politicians, but also each other. A central icon of San Francisco, right up there with the Golden Gate Bridge, is the Ferry Building downtown on the waterfront. Built before the earthquake of 1906, it boasts a campanile with a handsome clock with faces beaming in all directions. Today, the Ferry Building, which was hidden for decades behind the now happily removed Embarcadero Freeway, is still a major ferry terminal. It is also a grand public market, a foodie's dream that attracts thousands of visitors and food tourists daily to its stalls, shops, and restaurants. The city's largest-grossing locally owned restaurant, Charles Phan's Slanted Door, is there along with other stellar places such as Boulettes Larder, Lulu Petite, Taylor's Refresher, Cowgirl Creamery, and Hog Island Oyster

Company. "Meet me under the clock at the Ferry Tower" is a common phrase among San Franciscans setting out for a day's shopping or night's dining.

When I became mayor, the building was being seismically retrofitted, following the 1989 earthquake and, of course, being remodeled into the triumph it is today. While the restoration was under way, the giant clock in the campanile had been stopped. As it came time to reopen the building and thus restart the clock, a group devoted to helping patients at San Francisco's much-praised hospital of first and last resort, the San Francisco General Hospital, a county-city institution, wanted to auction off the rights to restart the clock. It was a brilliant idea to raise money to purchase small comforts like toiletries for the patients in the General's wards.

But the society of friends of the patients in this old hospital didn't have the cachet of other social or charitable groups. I wasn't surprised when a club connected with a more glamorous hospital announced, without checking with anyone first, that it would auction off the rights to restart the clock. They did not even check with me first. This was a terrible blow to the General and the struggling group of people trying to make life easier for that hospital's lonely patients. But the chic, well-connected group obviously expected the smaller organization from General Hospital to give way. It turned into quite a fight on the social scene. No matter how I intervened, I would be the demon, the devil. For once I decided to relish the role. I came up with a seemingly Solomon-like decision: I, Willie L. Brown Jr., would myself restart the clock. I did so on June 15, 1996—but not before making sure that the friends of the patients in General Hospital received a generous gift from an anonymous benefactor that I solicited. If you're going to be cast as a devil, you might as well be an angel at the same time.

Generally speaking, few politicians are willing to take on real problems in a city because they fear doing so would end their careers. Fighting groups intent on their own survival and righteousness becomes a suicide path. Amid a swamp of special interests, the survivalist politician becomes paralyzed.

The key is not to be paralyzed, but instead steadfastly work on what you can do. The first step to success in dealing with problems is to approach them not as a survivalist, but with some courage and nerve and a sense of what's best for the city. You won't win them all, yet you can make a difference. But don't expect thanks.

I had to figure out every day how to make things happen, how to get things done. That's the question I asked myself every day. How do I fix Muni? How do I build this stadium? How do I deal with this broken bridge? How do I get the necessary number of new homes built?

You can't look at these questions through the prism of "How do I do this to help me get reelected?" Once you do that, you've compromised any real solution, and you've compromised yourself. If you're thinking just about reelection, you start to make all sorts of accommodations—to people who literally don't want the project in their backyard and to people who don't want the project on their political turf. Think that way and you won't get a thing done. You can't think survival. You've got to engineer real solutions every day. I just wish I had Chicago mayor Richard Daley's power. He really has Chicago politics organized. I was in a den of lions.

I served eight years, or two terms, as mayor. But my own view is that a mayor should serve one term, and that term should be ten years. It takes that long to bring politics under control and to achieve results. For example, my own belief is that public transit should be free; riders should pay no fares. But it would have taken me ten years to build a coalition, to create the consensus to allow that to happen. I had eight years, but they were two terms. And when the second term started, it was like starting all over again.

A single ten-year term would eliminate much of the political gy-rating.

Yes, indeed, I believe in an imperial mayoralty. It's the only way to get things done, to get product moving. Otherwise it's just incessant inside politics and reelection planning. Awful. The people deserve better.

To be an effective mayor, you've got to decide you want nothing from the system. You don't want survival from the system. If you're constantly thinking of the next election, of being reelected, you're going to make one mistake after another.

What voters really respect is not the fey compromise, but the completed deal. You shouldn't go for the photo op announcing a new study; you go for the photo op announcing the completion.

In New York, Rudy Giuliani and later Mayor Michael Bloomberg decided they wanted nothing from the system: forget the political nibbling, let's get going.

That's why they're successful mayors. And that's why I was as well. Indeed, on November 11, 1996, *Newsweek* put Rudy Giuliani and yours truly on the cover of the magazine: America's two outstanding mayors.

CHAPTER THIRTY-TWO

Traction and No Traction: Muni and Homelessness

SAN FRANCISCO IS A CITY that really cares about people. It wishes to be as generous, as socially conscious, as it can be. So for twenty-five years, ever since the closing of state mental facilities and the influx of addictive drugs began to drive afflicted people out onto the streets where they lived homelessly, the city has tried to do its best for these people. Cash grants, a vast array of social services, and a lenient attitude about people camping out in parks and on streets marked San Francisco's approach. Instead of ameliorating the condition of these afflicted people, this policy seemed only to increase their numbers and the danger, distress, and demoralization of the whole population.

In 1993 my predecessor (and in 1995, my opponent for the mayoralty), Frank Jordan, began a program called Matrix to get the homeless off the streets. Reflecting Jordan's origins as a career police officer, Matrix was essentially a police action, an aggressive police action designed to displace the homeless from their spots on the streets and in the parks. It was unsuccessful and also awfully unpopular with much of the city's population, who saw it as nearly brutal and not much of a social solution. Matrix was a major issue during the 1995 mayoral campaign.

I campaigned honestly and accurately against Matrix. Matrix helped defeat Jordan. It seemed to me and to thousands of others that homelessness could be more effectively addressed through something more helpful to the homeless than law enforcement. I earnestly believed that we could do more than displace already placeless people. I was sure we could in fact do the job of freeing people of the horror of having to live on the streets. I thought there was a real possibility we could do that. I was naïve.

Once I became mayor, it soon became painfully clear to me that three-fourths of the folk living out there on the streets were out there without any possibility of ever getting off the streets. Not because there was not opportunity. Not because there was no shelter or housing available. Not because there were not enough mental health programs. Not because there were no drug abuse programs. We were providing those and, of course, we could do more. The will to provide services and shelter was there.

I discovered factors—some bureaucratic, some political— working in a kind of evil synthesis with each other that really prevented the long-term homeless from entering the system. For one, the rules and regulations of the welfare system wouldn't let us require people go into the treatment protocols or processes that could lead to their maybe breaking out of the cycle of poverty, hopelessness, homelessness. To me this was tantamount to condemning people to a prison of the streets.

Backing this up was a collection of so-called activists with heavy political clout who absolutely believed (and still believe) that homeless people should have a right to live on the street. They believed that homeless people had an absolute right to do everything they were doing, no matter how harmful to themselves or to the rest of the citizenry.

Opposing them was an army of businesspeople, small and large, who didn't want the homeless anywhere near them. Shop owners in the neighborhoods were furious, frustrated, and fiery. Hotel owners and managers, of course, didn't want the homeless within sight of the tourists who come to San Francisco. These people wanted draconian action, they wanted law enforcement.

You had all sorts of deep division within the polity and no side capable of budging. It was a nightmare. Here was a more dire example of the situation I encountered on lesser problems: selfishness and self-righteousness preventing people from coming to serious dialogue. They wouldn't budge and you couldn't wedge them.

In the legislature and in general political conflicts, I usually had been able to nudge sides out of their selfishness by showing them how outrageous they were actually being. In this situation, especially with the so-called homeless advocates, they were feasting on their outrage. Their moral indignation was their very food. And self-righteousness is not on the menu at the bargaining table. The selfishness was astonishing to me.

Of course, I addressed the issue as best as I could—over years. You just couldn't have any dialogue, however. Activists would storm meetings. The businesspeople would flee. Without dialogue you can't reach a solution, no matter how many people are suffering however horribly on the streets. For trying, I became the object of outrage.

The criticism was heavy, political and personal. People raised questions about my commitment to my core values. Even my friends like John Burton and Gavin Newsom raised questions about whether or not I really cared. Had I not almost become a Republican because I was raising questions? People accused me of abandoning the problem when I was working daily to try and get a solution going. It was brutal.

People who really understood the problem were pilloried as well. My friend the Reverend Amos Brown, whom I had appointed to the city's legislature, came up with a program in 2000 to help people get out of the cycle of madness that was life on the streets. It would have provided shelter and services, and in return would have cut the monthly cash grants (then $395 a month) that homeless people got from the city. The cash, which was to help with rent and food, often was spent on drugs and booze. Amos Brown's plan redirected the cash to provide housing and help. For this he was roundly castigated. His plan failed at the polls. And his advocacy was crucial in ending his reelection bid.

But less than two years later, Gavin Newsom, also in the city legislature, came up with a similar plan. He gave it a sharp name, Care Not Cash. By then, chaos was on the streets as the plight and dangers presented by homelessness produced anger and disgust so great that the very people, in and out of the political establishment and the media, who had opposed Amos Brown's plan were supporting Newsom's. Care Not Cash passed and became law.

So in the end, the outrage moved. But by that time, I had become demonized, and my own efforts belittled. Despite Care Not Cash, homelessness persists as a great and serious problem on the streets of San Francisco. My own belief is that it will be a problem for San Francisco long after Mayor Newsom is reelected and completes a second term. The problem of homelessness is not going to be solved, in my opinion, until one major drastic change takes place in public policy: we have to be able to impose help and treatment on people. The homeless face major challenges, but they'll never get succor, support, or a chance until we are able to force them into treatment. We all suffer today because of policies based on the premise that the homeless have a right to live in misery. That's not a right. That's cruel and unusual punishment. For us all.

Muni, or the San Francisco Municipal Railway, the agency that runs the city's cable cars, trolleys, buses, and streetcars, was another massive nightmare. I had better results with Muni, but I didn't start out well. As I have already written, in the middle of the 1995 Mayoral campaign I announced that I would fix Muni in one hundred days. Muni handled over 750,000 boardings a day, but the ninety-five-year-old system was deteriorating right in front of everybody's eyes.

I was convinced that everything that needed doing could be done within one hundred days. I knew the public, frustrated by ever-worsening service, ever-deteriorating equipment, and increasingly indifferent employees, desperately wanted Muni to be fixed. Even the employees were desperate for improvement. Most had pride in their work and in Muni, and they hated dealing with a frustrated ridership. But my "hundred days" announcement was a line that I would live to regret.

At the time I said it, I believed it. I wasn't just reaching into the air. Before saying such a thing, I had met with passengers, workers' stewards, management officials, transit experts. I honestly believed that within one hundred days of diligent work I could get the system and the experience up to par. No one would be able to call Muni, as Herb Caen often did, "the Muniserable Railway."

Even though I had studied with and consulted the experts and the stakeholders, it wasn't until I took office that I discovered I was totally uninformed about the intimate problems associated with Muni.

Consider just the problem of customer complaints about operators. When I took office, I found there was a backlog of eight hundred complaints against drivers. These were statements of dissatisfaction so serious that the customer had taken the time to file a charge and ask for a review. I wanted to know why these charges were not being acted upon. It seemed a fairly simple matter to do so. So how come eight hundred of them were backed up?

Well, it wasn't lassitude or indolence on the part of the complaint office. The rules said that Muni could not complete a review of a complaint unless the operator involved had been present at the hearing. Yet at the same time, there was a rule governing operators' behavior that, as incredible as it may seem, allowed each operator to take a large number of days off from work each year without warning. You just didn't have to show up for work if you didn't feel like it.

You can guess what happened: whenever a hearing was scheduled, the operator could choose not to show up. He or she took the day off. The complainant would appear, but the charged operator would not. Do that two or three times and the complainant, who probably wasn't being paid by his employer to take time off, stopped showing up. The result: you could never get the two parties in the same room at the same time, so the matter of the operator's behavior was never adjudicated. The complaint went unresolved and the passenger had another reason for regarding Muni as the Muniserable.

I found a way. I recruited a prominent lawyer, Susan Mosk, to clean up and manage the complaint system. She brought in a fulltime hearing officer—someone who did nothing but hold reviews on these complaints day in and day out. Then I got the television studies department at my alma mater, San Francisco State University, to provide students to videotape the testimony. The complainant could come in only once, testify on video, and leave. The customer didn't have to keep coming back. And after a while a recalcitrant operator who was ducking the hearings through his right to take a certain number of unscheduled days off would run out of days off to take. Eventually the operator would have to show up. The new system worked just fine. Through taped hearings going on full-time we soon cut the backlog down to nil. And we terminated abusive operators.

As a mayor you find yourself devoting enormous amounts of energy trying to figure out ingenious little solutions to problems like this. You've got to think creatively about problems, little and big. It helps to have a lot of experience in the real world. My years as a lawyer came in handy with many situations, including problems at Muni. We had a problem once when a Muni operator, off duty but in uniform, was riding a bus. This operator assaulted and beat a passenger because the passenger was gay. The operator was charged with a crime.

I told my executive director at Muni, Emilio Cruz, to remove the operator, to fire him. But the union, called upon to represent the operator in the termination matter, imposed the idea that the question of termination should not be acted upon until the criminal case was resolved. Frustrating and wrong to my mind, but fair is fair.

Several months later, after the criminal case wound its way through the courts, the operator was sent to jail. So we started removal proceedings.

This time the operator and the union objected again. They said the removal proceedings now were untimely because it had been so long since the incident occurred and that witnesses' memories were fading or gone, and that there were judicial issues. To me this was absolute pettifoggery in the service of a bad apple. This guy should not be a Muni employee. That was it.

One day, while I was in the middle of something else, the answer hit me. I called Muni director Cruz on my cell phone and said, "Look at the rules. Do the contract rules permit you to be absent from your Muni job while serving time in prison?" He said they do not. I told Cruz to issue an order to the operator telling him to be at work the next day. Of course, he didn't show up. We filed AWOL charges against him and removed this bad apple that way. This time he was gone without a whimper.

How to remove an operator, how to handle complaints—these are the sorts of intimate problems you don't know about when you're a first-time candidate. You think you know—there are the rules right there—but what you don't know is the gaming of the rules. Mastering them is just part of your job. It's not an achievement; it's just your job.

Achievement comes when you can get all the stakeholders together who are part of a big problem and work out a plan. You can't just broker a compromise either; you have to get people together in the service of a vision, the right plan. When it came to Muni's big problems—essentially figuring out what its place in the city should be and getting it there—we had to deal with a score of warring and interconnected parties representing different interests. There were the union contracts to consider, the limitations imposed by the civil service system, the demands of the very active bicycle coalition advocacy, the antiautomobile club, the advocates of free public transit, the problems of aging infrastructure and rolling stock. You couldn't get those together in one hundred days.

Eventually, though, we did a lot to improve Muni. We opened new rail lines. We obtained the money and authorization to start a new subway line through Chinatown, whose residents use Muni in unbelievably large numbers. We got new rolling stock. And we improved the riders' experience. It didn't get done in one hundred days. It took two terms. And some of these big projects, like the Chinatown subway, won't be completed for fifteen years. Muni was better when I left than when I arrived. It's still very important to me. Muni, when it works, is a great system. No matter where you live or work in San Francisco, you're almost never more than two blocks from a bus stop. I ride it often.

There were other operations, some quite unexpected, that required vast amounts of ingenuity and thought. One of my crowning glories was the restoration of a public building. It faced the same kind of political problems homelessness did. But buildings at least in San Francisco are more flexible than people. That's how this whole thing started—with a building being too flexible in an earthquake.

CHAPTER THIRTY-THREE

Restoring the City's Crown Jewel

AMONG THE STALLED, confused projects that greeted me on inaugural morning in 1996 was City Hall itself, a magnificent 1915 edifice designed by architects Arthur Brown and John Bakewell in the Beaux Arts style. Occupying two full city blocks, City Hall is the centerpiece of San Francisco's Civic Center, an array of public office buildings, courthouses, and cultural venues like the Opera House and Symphony Hall, all built in a similar architectural style. City Hall, with its breathtaking dome—one of the five largest in the world—is the focal point of the Civic Center, which was begun as a monument to the resurgence of San Francisco after the 1906 earthquake and fire. The 1989 earthquake literally undid City Hall, though. The five-hundred-thousand-square-foot building swung like a heavy pendulum under its dome. Over the years, bureaucracy and politics had taken its toll on the building as well. Once a palace of light, an inspiring monument, it had become a dark, stultifying place, grimy and gloomy. The building was a mess.

The story of its restoration became a case study in daring and capers—a textbook example of the pressure a big-city mayor faces. But it wasn't originally on my agenda. As I tried to restore City

Hall, I was subjected also to personal attacks from politicians, many of whom were defending their weak treatment of City Hall's plight by accusing me of grandiosity. I also received plenty of support, though, from citizens of all stripes. To most San Franciscans, the glorious City Hall was a civic monument, an emblem of pride and beauty as well as the seat of government.

When I became mayor, City Hall was being worked on, following the damage of the '89 earthquake. But it was just being rehabbed, not being restored the way it should have been done. Nor was it really being wired for the age of streaming video, email, and the internet. Nor was the building really being refitted in a way that made it accessible or safe for the physically challenged. And its architectural features were also being ignored. The building was being rebuilt with total disregard for its existing attributes and the needs it would have to meet if it were to be a building for the twenty-first century.

Politically, I could have safely passed the buck on the restoration while focusing solely on other issues. I could have left the task to a commission or a committee, but I believed in it, and I believed that the grandeur of City Hall was worth protecting. And the only way to do that properly was to become personally involved. I spent immense amounts of time on the project. I became the restoration manager. When I looked into the rebuilding, I found that we had made another bad deal with the federal government. Following the 1989 earthquake, FEMA, the Federal Emergency Management Agency, had settled a sum of money on the city to restore the Civic Center, but the settlement contract was a terrible one—from the city's point of view. The sum FEMA was to provide under this contract was less per capita than what Oakland had managed to get for its city hall. It was not enough to get the job done right. We had $103 million from FEMA to work with for the entire Civic Center. But just the seismic refitting of City Hall would eat that up. I believed the building should be restored to its original status, not just reworked so it was a simulacrum of the tired old bureaucratic building that existed in the moments prior to the October 17, 1989, earthquake. I also believed that most San Franciscans, prominent and quiet, also wanted the hall to be glorious again.

I shifted almost everything not yet spent under the FEMA agreement to the task of restoring City Hall. You had to move money—that's how bad the contract was.

I also went back and through a laborious process of trying to prove that FEMA had taken advantage of the city by not assisting San Francisco in getting everything it might have been entitled to. FEMA had not been proactive on the city's behalf. The federal bureaucrats' defense was simple. They said, "Bullshit—the city made the choice."

I went to my old friend Jamie Lee Witt, the head of FEMA in Washington, DC, and thanks to that relationship, got the FEMA officials to agree at least to listen. Nonetheless, we had to establish that we weren't trying to scam the feds. We had to establish that we were due more money, that in fact the calculations had been wrong, and that the city, under its previous mayor, had been dumb or not fully informed as to its eligibility.

Fortunately for us, a disaster in Southern California—the massive 1994 Los Angeles–Northridge earthquake—helped. The feds were ready to appropriate money for that. My question was: how do I get into *that* money? There was pushback on that. Because when FEMA was spending that money, the standards of eligibility were designed just for facilities affected by the '94 quake; in other words, buildings in Los Angeles.

To get into *that* pot of money, we had to help FEMA and the state redesign the standards of eligibility to include buildings around the state. My friend, the Republican governor Pete Wilson, signed the legislation. I'm quite sure he must have noticed that although the new standards were statewide, there was only one building in the whole state that fit the criteria: San Francisco City Hall! It was quite a feat, since there would be no new headlines or credit for government officials in helping a building left over from the old quake. And I'm not sure the Democrats in Washington were especially anxious to help Pete Wilson get credit for helping a Democratic city.

Fortunately, because I had built up such relationships with the Clinton people and with the Republican Wilson people, so we got the dough. Obviously, there had to have been merit behind our claim. This wasn't a giveaway. We had a factual foundation, but I also had the relationships. That's what got us the dough. Also, I couldn't have done it without the help of San Francisco's congresswoman Nancy Pelosi and California's senior U.S. senator Dianne Feinstein, who herself is a former mayor of San Francisco and committed to helping restore City Hall. They helped us enormously with legislation and by keeping after federal bureaucrats.

Locally, I had to build a coalition to protect our plans from my opponents. I also made some sacrifices—on my account. And then I had to fight. And a fight it was. Opponents on the city's legislature decried my efforts as pharaonic; they said I was building a monument to my greatness. One even called the City Hall that I envisaged as "Taj Ma Willie." Not true, but turnabout is fair play. I began to describe this opponent, a city legislator and otherwise decent fellow named Quentin Kopp, as "the town grouch."

But I was very careful to make sure no one could validly say the restoration was about my own glory. In all the plans we made to refurbish and regild the hall, only one department was left out of the reglamorizing: the mayor's office. I would have liked to expand the suite of offices available to the mayor, but I took no more territory. You never, as a rule, advance yourself.

Even when it comes to transportation. I love cars; when I was in the assembly I owned a black Porsche Turbo. I loved that car, but it was my own, not a state vehicle; it was not charged to the state. But every Highway Patrol officer in California knew my car and license plate. I made sure they did. Otherwise I wouldn't have been able to establish the land speed records I did, going from San Francisco to Sacramento, a ninety-mile trip, in just an hour.

Ed Rollins, the party operative working for the Republican minority in the assembly, was masterminding the deal for them to vote for me for speaker in 1980. When Ed first wanted to parlay, he phoned me in San Francisco from his office in Sacramento. He didn't believe me when I told him I'd see him in an hour to deal. I did, and he knew then that I was a serious parlayer, player, and Porsche driver.

When I became mayor, I was entitled to a city car and security. I would have preferred a Cadillac, not the civil service issue Lincoln Town Car traditionally offered to mayors. The Caddy, however, would have been an expensive item for the city, even if it's the only wheels truly fit for an American mayor. Rather than get what I wanted, thereby giving my enemies an opening to attack me as a princeling, I humbly accepted the Town Car from the city fleet. When I left office, my security drivers from the police department gave me a set of personalized license plates. They read "SFPDPAL." I put them on a Cadillac. I wanted to put that Caddy on MTV's *Pimp My Ride*. By the way, my security officers, whom I chose carefully from the ranks of the young, the minority, the smart, the discreet, and the ambitious in the San Francisco Police Department, were not without their own sense of humor. My drivers' code name for me was "Miss Daisy."

On my front I kept things modest. Indeed, during the reconstruction of City Hall, the only structural or even cosmetic change we made to the mayor's suite was to reconfigure the small anteroom off the mayor's formal office where Mayor Moscone had been killed. Frankly, the assassination site had become ghoulish, and it seemed right to take the horror off the room by rearranging the walls a bit.

I also worked hard to enhance the condition of the city legislature, the board of supervisors. I arranged for them to have, for the first time, private offices. I rebuilt the legislative chamber so it was equal both to the dignity of the public business and to the wonderful plans drawn up by architect Arthur Brown back in 1913.

Many politicians wanted something cheaper, a Formica forum for a chamber, not a suitable hall of state. They were afraid they would be accused of being spendthrifts. But their seeming parsimony would actually have been more costly and counterproductive—cheaper fixtures would need to be replaced every few years. What I proposed, which was what the architects originally designed and which was eventually built as I restored the building, will last a hundred years. Frankly, I believe that politicians should work in settings fit for czars.

I do believe that public spaces should be beautiful spaces and that the public's business should be carried out in space that connects with the past. In Sacramento, where I restored the assembly chambers, I was acutely conscious when speaking of all the great and historic names that had stood there before. Likewise when I have visited the United States Capitol, it thrills me to stand where the great debates of the past have taken place. I see no reason why in San Francisco, the legislators and public servants, and the public as well, should not feel the same continuity.

I also turned City Hall into a moneymaking building. The grand rotunda and staircase under the massive dome are imperial spaces (you can catch a glimpse of the same on the cover of this book which shows me seated near one of the interior arches of the City Hall dome) that make wonderful sites for parties and weddings. Today couples, families, and corporations love to hold events under the great dome. I also opened up two large spaces, called light courts, on each side of the dome. Over the years the spaces had been divided up into cubicles and their glass roofs had been covered with concrete. Now they are places for public festivities. And everybody who uses them pays rent for them. Indeed, my idea was that City Hall should not only be a public building, it should also be a center of revenue for the public. "Taj Ma Willie," indeed.

One thing I regret is this: I should have ensured that revenue from the use of the hall stay in a lockbox to be used only for the upkeep of the hall. Now those funds generated by the use of City Hall are raided by other departments to help with their budget problems.

Fortunately, in the work of reconstructing City Hall, I had the assistance of San Francisco civic leaders like architect Jeffrey Heller and Gap founder Don Fisher. We also received assistance from Silicon Valley tech firms who saw the chance to provide for the city's future—and showcase their wares by providing the expertise and equipment to wire and cable the building for the internet age.

My opponents persisted, however. At one point they instituted a rule that would have required me to get a 75 percent approval from the city legislature to make any further changes in the plans to restore City Hall. Fortunately, I got the votes I needed.

Winning my battles required ingenuity not only on the political level, but also right down to the real rat level. I had been bothered by a plaza of olive trees and benches outside City Hall that had become a nuisance. The trees, dirty and oily, had become a cafeteria for rats. The rodents loved the olives. And the benches had been taken over by people hovering around a nearby methadone clinic. It was a scary place. It also was out of keeping with the original plans for the plaza. Looking through old photographs, I noticed that the original plaza was free of the olive trees and benches that were becoming a daytime adult druggie playground.

So I gave a city official, Bill Lee, the job of restoring the plaza to its original appearance, adding as well some new amenities for the children in day care at City Hall. We'd build playgrounds for children, not for adults. We also installed bright streetlights that also replicated the original street lamps.

All went well, but Bill stopped short of removing those trees. So we still had the mess, the stink, and the rats. I asked Bill why he hadn't cleaned out the trees. He said he couldn't: to remove a tree you had to go through all sorts of public hearings. Every tree lover in the city would be out protesting. He was right: in San Francisco it's easier to remove an elected official from public office than it is to uproot a tree.

I did some research, which gave me a solution. The law, I learned, provided that if trees were diseased or had become a hazard they could be removed without public hearings. So over one weekend I had all the trees quietly—very quietly—removed. If you go look at the record you'll see that a tree doctor signed certificates saying the trees were diseased and must go. Maybe his signature isn't terribly clear, but he was a legitimate tree doctor and he made a legit inspection.

I also kept the removal project secret from the permanent non-political staff in City Hall, the civil servants. I've found that in today's political climate, many civil servants love playing the role of whistle-blower, leaking things even if there's nothing in them to whistle about. There was nothing wrong in what I was doing, but why look for trouble?

The proof of the correctness of what I had done came in an ironically disappointing occurrence the Monday following the removal of the olive trees: not a soul noticed the trees were gone. To this day no one has asked, "What happened to those trees?" People are now so proud of the Civic Center and the plaza, they overlook what's gone.

Now, if we had gone through the rigmarole of publishing our intention of removing the trees and asking for public hearings, every defender in the world would have come out. We'd have to prove—beyond the level of proof you'd need to execute a condemned, vicious murderer—that the trees should go. I didn't give the tree lovers who constitute the primary jury in such matters any opportunity to block the actions. The trees were diseased and they were removed—for their own good.

I was vaguely upset that no one ever asked what happened to the olive trees. For I didn't just uproot them, I took good care of them. I had them transplanted. They are now in an arboreal assisted-living center in McLaren Park, a 317-acre public reservation in the southern portion of the city. I was so looking forward to telling unthinking tree lovers they could go visit the olive trees out in McLaren. But no one ever asked after them.

The plaza is beautiful, and I have no regret about finding a way to get results. You have to be unconventional and, when necessary, ruthless. History proves you right. Ruthlessness is part of being a master pol.

Finding enough cash to properly finish the restoration and upgrading of City Hall was always a problem. The settlement with FEMA was inadequate, and even additional bonds supported by the voters were insufficient. While we had found enough money to finish the interior of the building, there wasn't enough money to literally gild the massive dome, which rivals the U.S. Capitol dome (ours is taller) and St. Peter's Basilica dome in Vatican City.

There was originally no money for the dome from FEMA. To my mind, the whole building had been damaged by the quake, but FEMA said the dome itself had not been damaged in the quake. This was the mentality I was fighting.

I was desperate. On February 13, 1998, I received a call on my cell phone from City Hall: the dome was on fire. A welder had left a blowtorch on and the scaffolding around the dome had begun to burn. When the staff called me, I was tempted to say let it burn for another twenty minutes, then the dome will be truly damaged. But they already had called the fire department. Some of my opponents found the blaze suspicious, but fortunately I had an alibi: I was in Washington, DC, trying to persuade FEMA to help with the building.

Fortunately, frustration can sometimes be a good thing. A nagging problem can create new opportunities.

That opportunity to finance the restoration of the dome came from out of the skyward blue. Architect Jeffrey Heller, who has designed many distinguished buildings in San Francisco and who also happens to be a proponent of good outstanding public architecture, called me on a seemingly unrelated matter. It seemed that a client of his who wanted to construct a building downtown was vexed by one planning regulation. It was a rule that required the developers of certain new properties to appropriate a small percentage of the cost of construction for artwork that could be seen by the people using the building.

No developer deeply objected to having to add to the visual delights of the city, but they did object to the rigmarole and criticism that any public sculpture or artwork proposed or constructed in San Francisco seemed to face. In San Francisco, everybody is an art critic, so developers hate the process by which they have to find art and then be criticized for it.

Heller's client was wondering if there might not be a better solution. Couldn't he just donate the required sum of money to the city government and let the city government choose some art project to spend it on? A light went off in the dome that is my brain: why not use such private funds to gild the dome and finish the hall?

It was the perfect solution: a) the job would get done, and b) we would avoid the criticism, sure to come, of spending public dollars on pure gold to go on the roof of City Hall. Also, it would be beautiful, a true piece of civic art for all to behold.

It worked and City Hall was regilded without having to get additional funds. Now everyone, including those who opposed me, wants to take credit for what is surely one of the most gorgeous and successful public buildings in the world. It's a beautiful space. It's a smart space; it's a compliant space.

We did everything perfectly. Thanks to the careful use of matching granite walls, the ramps provided for wheelchair users blend in seamlessly with the exterior. The elevator cages, which were not to have been restored, are now perfect chambers from an age when elevators were not just linoleum-covered utilitarian vehicles. The building is fixed up for the video and the electronic age. Yet it looks as it did the day it was first finished in 1915.

I spent vast amounts of personal time on the restoration—from building the coalition of support to checking out the supporting columns. Like so many things worth doing, the project required that I be a personal project director. I had much help, especially from people like Tony Irons, who loves City Hall and who was the manager of the restoration. But in the end, if you're the mayor and you want to do it, you've got to do it yourself.

When it came to raising money, I'm sorry I didn't use a device that hospitals, universities, and museums regularly employ in fund-raising: I should have sold naming rights to City Hall. Imagine walking through the Google Dome, or the Oracle Chamber of Legislators, or even the Chuck and Helen Schwab Office of the Mayor!

Then—finally—those who accuse me of having sold the mayoralty would have had an actual basis for their charges.

CHAPTER THIRTY-FOUR

A Football Stadium and a Sadomasochistic Birthday Party

CARMEN POLICY, THE PRESIDENT of the San Francisco 49ers, and I, two of the most dapper gents in the city, were walking together through The Castro, San Francisco's celebrated gay neighborhood, one day early in May 1997, smiling and waving at couples and singles. We weren't soliciting pickups, looks, or leers. We were soliciting votes.

On the ballot for the June 3 election was a question for the voters, what in California is called a "proposition." This particular ballot initiative, called Proposition D, would authorize the construction of a new pro football stadium in San Francisco to replace the municipally owned, decaying Candlestick Park, which had opened in 1960, making it one of the oldest parks still in use in pro football. Without a new park, the future of pro football in San Francisco was severely threatened.

What was interesting about Proposition D is that it would have built the stadium, and an attendant shopping mall, without the use of any tax dollars. The city would provide $100 million of the esti-

291

mated $525 million construction cost via revenue bonds. But the bonds would be repaid out of the money generated by the shopping center.

This was an ingenious solution to the problem of building a stadium without handing over tax dollars to a private company.

Carmen and I had been campaigning for the new stadium for weeks. Of course, some of San Francisco's gays and lesbians are among the most ardent sports fans in the country so we had made it a point to stop at Castro bars like the Pilsner, one of the city's gay sports bars, looking for votes. There was a lot of partying going on in the bars as we moved through our tour. But we didn't know that later in the week a party that would shock even the unshockable partying set of The Castro and of the rougher gay scene of South of Market, would perhaps kill the proposition.

First the background. The 49ers were the first West Coast pro sports franchise. Initially owned by two brothers, Tony and Victor Morabito, who were in the lumber-hauling business, the team and its owners in those early days of the late '40s and '50s were pure San Francisco. They played in Kezar Stadium, a high school stadium nestled in a corner of Golden Gate Park near the Haight-Ashbury neighborhood. What San Franciscans did in the '50s was to go out to Kezar on Sunday afternoons and watch this incredibly entertaining bunch of guys lose. But we loved them. There were all sorts of players and coaches like Frankie Albert, still much beloved in the city.

I had always loved football. I had played it in high school, despite my small size. I actually lasted just one play in a scrimmage before I was knocked out cold. But I continued to love the game and reported on Mineola games for the local paper. In San Francisco, I joined the crowds at Kezar. In 1958, when I was twenty-four and had just become a lawyer, I bought season tickets. The seats I had were wooden and rough on the 25-yard line, but I loved them, and loved being at the games. Forty-nine years later I am still a 49ers season ticket holder and go to all the home games.

Tony Morabito, one of the team's founders, was a much-admired, tough old-timer who battled to build a football team in San Francisco at a time when no one else believed there could be West Coast pro franchises. But in the late '40s Tony foresaw the coming of air travel that would allow teams to fly, and he beat back a rough coalition of sports team owners, journalists, and league officials to create the 49ers. Tragically on October 27, 1957, he died of a heart attack midway through a game. When Tony died the 49ers were trailing the Chicago Bears 17–7. At halftime, Coach Frankie Albert was handed a slip with the message, "Tony's gone." Albert conveyed the news to his players who went back on the field to beat the Bears 21–17 to win for Tony.

Tony's widow kept operating the team for many years. But in 1977 she sold the team to a man out of Youngstown, Ohio, a contractor named Edward DeBartolo Sr., who made a fortune by virtually inventing and constructing the first modern shopping centers.

Edward DeBartolo also allowed his young son Eddie DeBartolo to take a big hand in the running of the football team. Eddie and his constant friend Carmen Policy really took over the team. Early on the two decided to turn this franchise into a winner. They did.

They settled things down, then hired a fabulous coach from Stanford University named Bill Walsh. Walsh of course put together an operation that included many coaches who would go on to become NFL head coaches on their own. More importantly, he revitalized the game on the field via what was called the West Coast offense, a short precision passing game designed at first just to augment the running game, but which then developed into a torrid game-winning offense in its own right.

Eddie, Carmen, and Bill drafted players like Ronnie Lott, Joe Montana, Jerry Rice, Roger Craig, and others who would become Hall of Famers. They really built a popular team, but because windy Candlestick Park, where the team had moved to, was so inhospitable a venue, Eddie was thinking of moving the team to Arizona, where the city of Phoenix was contemplating building a stadium for them.

Dianne Feinstein, a formidable football fan in her own right, was then the mayor of San Francisco. She stepped in and made an eleventh-hour handshake agreement with Eddie that convinced him to keep the Niners in San Francisco. In return, the city made certain commitments to further remodel, renovate, and reconfigure Candlestick.

By this time I had moved my season tickets over to Candlestick. I had gone from the 25-yard line to the 50-yard line, right under the press box. I was there for every game.

We thought the handshake would be enough. Dianne did make the city live up to its end of the agreement, but when she left the mayor's job, Art Agnos, who had no interest in either football or baseball, succeeded her.

By the early '90s, however, the 49ers were really hot, in their glory days. They had been in five Super Bowls! In 1995, the 49ers were feted by a downtown parade featuring fans cheering Jerry Rice and Steve Young! The NFL made a commitment to play a future Super Bowl in San Francisco. The NFL's commitment to a Super Bowl, however, was contingent upon the city's promise to do something about Candlestick: either build a new stadium or remodel the rattling 'Stick into condition suitable for a Super Bowl. The issue bounced around with no ground being gained because there was no positive leadership on the issue from city hall.

Then I became mayor.

For me, resolving the Candlestick Park problem was a major

priority. I knew we had to have a new stadium by 2006—since that's when the handshake deal that Eddie DeBartolo and Dianne Feinstein had made to keep the Niners in town would expire. More pressingly, what were we to do about the proposed San Francisco Super Bowl, an event that could bring three hundred million dollars into everyone's favorite city?

Did we ask the NFL to postpone San Francisco's next Super Bowl until we built a new stadium? Or did we keep to the original schedule, remodel the existing park again, and hope that was sufficient for the picky NFL?

Eventually we decided to build a new stadium. We were guided by the experience of San Francisco's baseball franchise, the Giants, who had just managed to get ballot approval to build a stadium in downtown San Francisco. The new stadium would not require a layout of tax dollars. They had been trying for years to get a new stadium built, but every time they went to the voters with a proposal that would use public money, they were turned down.

By the early '90s, the Giants, tired of the frustration and of Candlestick, where they also played, were all set to leave San Francisco for Florida. But a new collection of owners under Peter McGowan saved them in 1992 and kept them here. But to secure the Giants' remaining in San Francisco, they had to have a new park. After all the previous ballot failures in the '80s, they got creative and came up with a new ballot proposition to build a baseball park but without any public funding beyond what was needed to hook up city services and connect the park to public transportation. There would be no taxpayer help for the team's owners, who would have to pay for the stadium themselves.

That proposition passed in 1996. The Giants set out to build their new stadium, now a magnificent edifice on San Francisco's waterfront. And learning from them we focused on building a new football stadium.

We came up with a plan to build a complex including a stadium and shopping mall. The new stadium and mall would cost about $525 million and would be built in an impoverished, neglected corner of the city called Bayview–Hunter's Point, just around the corner from Candlestick Park. Although no city tax dollars would be used in building the complex, to get the project going, the city would provide $100 million in bonds, to be repaid out of the proceeds from the shopping mall. If the voters approved the plan, San Francisco would get a new Super Bowl–worthy football stadium, and a poor neighborhood would be revitalized. We even agreed that 50 percent of the construction jobs on the project would go to the unemployed in Bayview. This had a lot of appeal to San Franciscans all over the city. So one day in May 1997, Carmen Policy and I found ourselves out campaigning for votes for the 49ers and Bayview.

Our campaign was perking along until May 6. Then Jack Davis, the political consultant who was running the ballot campaign, held a birthday party for himself. It became a scandal. I got caught up in a terribly inconvenient truth, and the whole stadium project looked threatened.

You can get a sense of the party by reading what the *New York Times*'s Tim Golden wrote about it in the May 10, 1997, *Times*:

> There is no shocking the citizens of San Francisco, it has been argued; it takes some doing just to entertain them. Or so they apparently thought at a party last weekend where the mayor, the district attorney, the president of the board of supervisors and dozens of other local notables gathered to celebrate the 50th birthday of the city's most powerful political consultant, Jack Davis. Then the "entertainment"

got under way: dancers from a local strip club, male and female, gyrated in the smoke of a fog machine. A topless, mustachioed woman clad in parts of a cowboy outfit wandered merrily through the crowd. Inflatable plastic penises bobbed here and there.

There was even a display of sadomasochistic sex involving penetration via a whiskey bottle. It was called an Apache sex ritual. This was totally unacceptable behavior, even by San Francisco standards. What was weird was that I didn't see any of this—I had been to the party, but so early the band hadn't even set up. In fact, I was the only politician who readily admitted he had been there. But my admission and acknowledgment of my presence there had been made without the knowledge of the notorious events that had taken place during the party. But as you shall read, by behaving as a typical politician, I just got myself deeper into a jam.

This was one of those evenings, typical when I was mayor, when I was going to ten or twelve events a night. Early in the evening I started over in North Beach at a party for a respected art school. From there I went to Chinatown and various other stops. Ironically, on this night of outrage, my last stop was at the very conservative United Irish Cultural Center way out in the Sunset district, just two blocks or so from the ocean and worlds removed from what was going on at Jack Davis's party.

My third of twelve stops had been downtown at the Jack Davis party in the San Francisco Mart. I was there so early that only the caterer, a decorator, and the band were present. I even helped the band set up their equipment. Jack Davis himself hadn't even arrived.

I had to go, so I left word with the band to tell Jack that I would be back after I finished my night's schedule.

Sometime after 10:30 when I finished at the Irish Cultural

Center, I was about to head back to Jack's party. But on my phone was a message from Eleanor Johns, my chief of staff, calling from the Davis party. Eleanor's message was simple: "Skip the party, go ahead and have dinner. I know you haven't had dinner." I realized later Eleanor was warning me. But she gave no details of the lurid goings-on that prompted her sage advice. For all I knew, the party was a dud. But I took her advice. I went to my late-night hangout, Lorenzo Petroni's North Beach Restaurant, and had supper. Then I went home to bed.

The phone rang at 5:30 or 6:00 in the morning. It was KCBS, the all-news radio station. That's where I began to get myself in trouble.

The reporter said to me, "How was the party?"

"What party?"

"Jack Davis's party."

I said it was a great party.

"Did you enjoy it?"

"Oh, yes, I did enjoy it. I had a great time—watching Jack turn fifty."

And I went on and on about the party. Typical political expansion without lying: raving about watching Jack get older, joshing about him. I should have kept my mouth shut. Or at least have been suspicious.

And at the end of my comments, the reporter asked me, "What did you think of the entertainment?"

"Well, what entertainment? I didn't exactly see any entertainment."

Then he proceeded to tell me what the entertainment was. And I proceeded to tell him, "You're kidding me. You're full of shit; there's no way that was the entertainment."

"Oh, yes, it was," he said. Oh dear.

Well, lo and behold, by 8:00 a.m., my normal arriving time at

City Hall, I was all over every news channel and organization as the only politician who acknowledged being at this party.

And the assumption was that by virtue of the report and my quotes to KCBS that I had in fact witnessed all of this incredible show—a show I knew nothing about.

Since I had spoken so profusely in typical political fashion about how wonderful the party was, I didn't have much credibility when I denied having seen the goings-on.

So my convenient lie had trapped me into an inconvenient truth, as Al Gore's prone to say.

Needless to say, worldwide attention was lavished on this political consultant's party. And local news attention was focused on what it meant that the host of this outré extravaganza was running a campaign to build a Super Bowl–worthy stadium and to bring some economic justice to a neglected neighborhood.

Frankly, even before the party, our polling had showed the chances of the proposition's succeeding were iffy—particularly since it was being opposed by a whole host of people who didn't believe we had gotten the right deal to ensure that no public dollars would be used.

And we now had the scandal of the party, a party at which people believed that the mayor and the leading proponent of the stadium campaign had been present. The more I denied it, the more the broadcasters aired the tapes of me raving about the party. Never mind I didn't see a thing, people figured I approved. Some probably thought I was up on the stage as part of the show.

Over the next two or three days Carmen Policy and Eddie De-Bartolo peppered me with questions as to whether or not Jack Davis should be dramatically terminated from the campaign.

Jack volunteered to leave. And I of course had (and continue to have) the reputation of never abandoning any friend, no matter what their plight, so I was opposed to Jack's having to walk the plank. Furthermore, he and his associates, like the late Ed Cana-pary, were geniuses at identifying people who probably wouldn't have voted and then giving them a compelling reason to get out there on Election Day. We needed Jack's political expertise, if not his entertainment sense.

Eddie DeBartolo Jr., Carmen Policy, Ed Canapary, Jack Davis, and I agreed quickly to meet in the Prosciutto Room in the base-ment of the North Beach Restaurant.

From the ceiling hung about one hundred hams being cured for the restaurant. In the middle of the room was a corrugated tin table on which they sliced the hams. It's also a room in which the temperature is really low because you have to keep it cool for the curing of the hams. But it was a favorite meeting place for me, both for work and celebrations. They'd cover the table with a wooden top and a tablecloth, and serve a few people there. The room also had an upright piano. We didn't use the piano that day.

It was surreal: the four of us sitting around this cave full of hams discussing Apache whiskey rituals, sodomy, scandal, and the iffy condition of our stadium proposal—but no one from the press thought to look for us down where the hams are cured and the hams sing the old songs. The press was looking for us, but they probably thought we were meeting in a rough bar or perhaps a fu-neral home.

During our long meeting, we made the decision that Carmen Policy would appear on the top local breakfast TV show, *Mornings on Two* on KTVU. When asked the question what would the 49ers do if they didn't get this stadium approved, Carmen would say, "Leave. The team will leave San Francisco."

Following that, from City Hall, I would blast Carmen Policy for threatening to take the 49ers away.

Well, that was the drill. It was a healthy solution to a still-hot toxic problem. It worked: we shifted the conversation away from the party to the potential loss of the Niners. We shifted the dialogue.

We also would continue to emphasize the economic benefits to the city and the neighborhood of building the mall as part of the stadium complex. We also started really enforcing another economic message: the NFL had a made a commitment to us that as soon as the new stadium was up and operational, probably in 2005 or 2006, San Francisco would get the Super Bowl. And it would get the Super Bowl again, again, and again—every five years the Super Bowl would be played in San Francisco, bringing in three hundred million dollars each time. A lot of this strategy was based on what Ed Canapary was learning through his exhaustive polls and focus groups about what was acceptable to voters.

So suddenly we had lots of firepower—and Eddie DeBartolo Jr. agreed that there was no limit on what could be spent to carry that message. Jack and the geniuses on the campaign side redid the whole campaign, graphics and everything. And we embarked on a new twenty-one-day campaign to secure the stadium. Carmen appeared on TV. I countered from City Hall. Then we all hit the speech-making circuit arguing on behalf of Proposition D. Paul Tagliabue, commissioner of the NFL, came out and spoke to voters as well. Indeed, every significant figure that we could get our hands on who had any cachet with the public went around town making speeches, visiting house parties, appearing on talk shows to get the votes for this campaign.

We did everything that you could possibly do. But as late as the morning of Election Day the polls showed it still only as iffy. So Jack and his colleagues superintensified their get-out-the-vote effort. It was a Super Bowl try. That night, we readied to watch the returns.

DeBartolo, Policy, and Davis were in a brain trust room at a hotel near Fisherman's Wharf. I was at the nearby International

Longshoremen's union hall, with the campaign workers and football fans.

It was a long night. With 55 percent of the ballots counted, we were trailing. With 65 percent, we were behind. With 75 percent of the vote in, we were still behind. With 85 percent counted, we were still trailing. With 90 percent, we were still behind. I was left in front of this massive collection of television cameras and reporters to explain what looked like a defeat, though I was not sure we would lose. But when we got to 91 and 92 percent, we were still trailing. The brain trusters, who had come by the union hall, left.

Well, I climbed up on the rostrum with the express intention of saying what a politician says when it's been a long night and he is about to lose a close race. As I was climbing up, preparing my encouraging bromides and asides, I began to take off the jacket of my brown suit. I wore a pink shirt and a pink tie, and just as I reached the podium, removing my jacket and about to take the mike, Eleanor Johns, my chief of staff, pushed her way through and handed me a little note saying 95 percent of the vote had just been reported in, and our side was ahead!

People thought I had been bullshitting all night as I had uttered the formulaic explanation, "Our votes haven't been counted yet." But in reality I was right. Our votes hadn't been counted until late in the evening. They didn't really register until seconds before eleven o'clock.

When Eleanor handed me that note and I had to make that announcement—it was wonderful.

I let out a three-minute scream and began swigging on a jeroboam of champagne. Barbara Taylor of KCBS, the doyenne of San Francisco city hall reporters, still has that tape of me squealing with delight for three minutes. We had won with just over 1,500 votes.

This was one of my most joyful nights in politics. There was nothing more joyful to me than that moment—having put together that ballot proposition for something I believed in, having campaigned so hard and fought against so many weird obstacles (like the outrageous birthday party), and then coming out on top with just over 1,500 votes. There was nothing like it.

What had happened? Why did we suddenly pull ahead? It all had to do with the manner in which the votes came into City Hall. The first votes counted, which were very early in the evening, were absentee ballots. They were definitely against us. Many people who vote by absentee ballot are conservative in social attitudes— so Jack Davis's birthday party had hurt us with the absentee voters.

It wasn't until late in the evening that the votes from outlying and undermanned precincts, chiefly Chinese neighborhoods and African American districts, were brought in. These were for us and turned the tide.

Ultimately the proposition passed because the Chinese community, where I had campaigned heavily and where I was enormously popular personally, and the African American community in the housing projects, many of whom would have benefited from jobs in the new mall, were for it. The heavy participation in this ballot of these two communities really was an affront to the political establishment. The so-called progressives in San Francisco were opposed to the proposition, as were many conservative types. And they were used to being the only ones voting.

Years, months, weeks, and days of paying court to the various Chinese community groups and to black churches really paid off. It was a magnificent experience. No one had ever seen such a thorough job of campaigning in San Francisco. And many didn't believe it could produce the results it did. Oh, it was magnificent!

Naturally, after the election we were investigated by everybody and anybody with an axe to grind. But they lost and we won.

So now we were ideally situated to produce a stadium and get a mall built. We had a developer lined up for the mall and an investment-banking firm to ensure and guarantee the one hundred million dollars as revenue to be generated. We were on a roll to produce the stadium.

Then came the roadblocks. Eddie DeBartolo got himself in trouble down in Louisiana. He pled guilty to a charge of providing Governor Edwin Edwards with a solicited four-hundred-thousand-dollar bribe to get a casino license (which he never obtained). Eddie was barred from active control of the 49ers for a year. By 2000, in return for a settlement, he gave up control of the team to his embarrassed sister Marie Denise DeBartolo York and her husband, Dr. John York, who suddenly found themselves owners of a football team they hadn't much personal interest in. Carmen Policy left the team as well.

The economy changed about the same time. The Mills Corporation, which was going to develop the shopping center planned for the stadium, refocused its attention on other projects it planned in San Francisco.

And as a result, the energy went out of the effort to produce a stadium in the southeastern corner of our city. That the stadium was not built is an enormous disappointment to me. But I still thrill at the thought of that election night and my three-minute scream of victory.

I think if either Carmen or Eddie had remained connected and retained their authority, the stadium would have been built.

Stadiums, like the 49ers park and the Giants park, are part of a mayor's legacy. It's true they're complex deals taking years to complete. But the mayor who gets them done has shown a lot of leadership and drive. I would have been thrilled to be the father or at least the guardian angel of two new pro sports franchise stadiums for San Francisco.

It wasn't to be, however. Sometimes, no matter how much talent, resources, and skill you throw into a project, it won't come off. The stars are not aligned. As a mayor, as a politician, you have to learn to live with that. Sometimes you are not going to succeed. But in this case, it wasn't because we didn't do our level best.

What the future holds for the 49ers is hard to say. I am convinced that the NFL wants a franchise to remain in Northern California and that they want the team to be known as the San Francisco 49ers. But the games will probably be played in a suburban field, just as the New York Giants and Jets play outside of the city. So we may find that in five or six years, the Niners play in Hayward or Fremont.

I don't believe they will play on the site in Santa Clara now proposed by the 49ers. There are just too many encumbrances and economic problems with that site of land to make it a viable place on which to build a stadium. But while I believe the 49ers will remain and will remain as the *San Francisco* 49ers, it's a sad fact that I don't believe they'll be playing their home games in a new stadium in the city that gave them birth.

That's unfortunate because it lessens the appeal, the variety, and the fun of the city. We willingly and amply support the opera and the symphony, the ballet, the zoo, the waterfront, the parks, but we should make room for tailgaters as well as for white-tie crowds.

They are a part of San Francisco too, but I fear we have pushed them out. It's our great loss.

CHAPTER THIRTY-FIVE

Schemers Scorned

"DOESN'T IT BOTHER YOU," someone asked me when I was mayor, "to be sitting in City Hall and know that somewhere someone in the giant operation of city government is up to no good?" Well, of course, it bothers me that anyone might be up to fiscal mayhem or political stupidity, but I don't believe that it is healthy for you as a mayor to sit in City Hall every day of your life and try to figure out who is doing something wrong. You'd be totally reactive. You'd spend valuable time trying to figure out where and when the next shoe is going to drop. Instead, operate on the theory that all the people in City Hall are honest and that they are there to do their jobs. You'll be about 98 percent right. And as for trying figure out who the bad 2 percent are, well, they will alert themselves to you. If your instincts and intelligence systems are working, you'll get the signals.

Signals do appear because you can't corrupt the system without tinkering with the rules. If you're alert, you'll see the signs that someone has been playing with the rules here or there. Sometimes you see them in the defensiveness of people's behavior. More often you discern it in the unusual way a normally routine process is taking place or isn't taking place. It's as subtle as an application moving too quickly or too slowly through the system. If something is going out of sync, you ask questions. How is it that this permit application hasn't been acted upon yet? Did they file it on time? Or is someone sitting on it?

Now, when I found something odd like that, I didn't believe I had the responsibility to pick up the phone, call the cops, and say, "This nine-month delay on this grocery store planning permit application is unusual. There may be somebody in the department who's on the take from a rival grocer. You ought to check it out."

But I did have the responsibility to look closely and ask questions, just little insignificant questions, about why the process is taking such an unusual turn. Look for nervous answers, look for pushback, look for resistance. Then nose around. You'll get answers. If people reveal that they are on the take, that they have sold themselves, that they are part of a corrupt, greedy operation, then you get rid of them. You get them out of your life. You defang them forever. You eliminate them from the system. And you make sure that everyone associated with them gets the word. No harm to the institution, no black eye, and you move forward.

Of course, there were people, special interests, who were looking for favors or breaks. They could be quite subtle. A large developer called me one day to announce that he had become a "Green." He was thus committed to more open space, more green space in the city. Highly laudable, I told him.

I knew that behind his conversion to the tree people was simple economics: he was trying to enhance the value of his existing properties by denying to others, under the protective shading of green, the opportunity to put up new office and commercial buildings.

I had to be careful with this new Green because he was also a heavy contributor to not only me but also to national and state Democratic politicians. Despite his new green coloration he showed no signs of walking away from the Democratic Party. Nor would I want him to. I think he really believed, in his heart, in the principles of the Democratic Party. He couldn't be cut loose. But he was used to having his way. Of course, what he really was doing was gaming the system. He knew just what he was up to.

I listened to him carefully as I listened to everyone, contributor or not, who came to me for intercession. But as mayor, responsible for the well-being of an entire city, I listened as well to my sense of what was good for the city. I measured the requirements of his new faith against the requirements of a city. There were many interests that had to be balanced and then weighed against the public interest. For example, to grow the tax base we needed new commercial development, new office development. We also needed more green space to maintain the quality of life in San Francisco. We also needed new housing units to accommodate the new residents that a booming San Francisco was attracting. We also needed to create that housing without displacing existing residents, especially those absent the resources to find their way in a housing market growing ever more expensive. Much of what the city could get in new so-called affordable housing would depend on deals made with developers of luxury or market-rate housing. In return for permits to build their valuable, highly profitable new properties, they typically also had to pay for some affordable housing. So I felt I had to encourage new development, both commercial and residential.

In this case, however, I was stuck with this political genius who insisted he wanted only to make San Francisco a greener city. I had to take a chance with him. I sat him down and told him the facts of life: we're not going to hold back new development. Then he intimated he'd take his business to the suburbs. I smiled at him. "You know how things are," I said. "This is what the good of the city requires." I didn't have to tell an old pro like him that while I appreciate his strong financial support, all that his campaign contributions bought was a commitment to the best possible public policy.

His contributions wouldn't buy what he wanted, even though he couched his desires in terms that made attractive politics.

He was angry with me for a while and stayed icy for even longer. But eventually he acquiesced. There was still plenty of money for him to make in San Francisco—without the city's subsidizing his moneymaking just to say it was a green city. Anyway, when I was mayor we did plenty to green the city as well.

Sometimes I ran into the reverse situation, where people had gotten what they wanted but it blew up in their faces. A fairly recent ordinance in the city allowed the building of something called "live-work lofts." The original idea was to encourage the construction on small lots here and there of cheaper housing in the loft style for artists and craftspeople who worked at home. The builders and the owners of these new homes got a break on the requirements that usually encumbered the construction of small residences. For example, they didn't have to contribute to certain school funds.

For a while there wasn't much construction along those lines. But then my friends, the well-organized, largely Irish Residential Builders Association led by Joe O'Donoghue noticed something new. With the coming of the dot-com era and the new biotech industry, the city was becoming increasingly attractive to young single people. They needed housing, often telecommuted from home, and they didn't need much: a bath, tiny kitchen, bedroom, and computer space. The Residential Builders saw opportunity in the legislation allowing the building of live-work lofts. They began buying up options on small lots of land throughout the city. In the SOMA district, a previously empty former industrial part of town located south of Market Street (hence the acronym: SOuth of MArket), they began constructing live-work housing. The units were an immense hit. People moved in by the thousands; they didn't displace people from existing housing, and they added more of that key element in a successful city: density. Within a couple of years the former desert of SOMA was a thriving neighborhood of residents, street life, shops, and restaurants. An entire portion of the city had been revitalized.

But the original sponsors of the live-work lofts, who wanted just piecemeal construction of units that were then to be reserved for a few craftspeople, fought the new construction all the way. They were unsuccessful, but they fought hard. Had they won, San Francisco's suburbs and Oakland across the bay would be full of these young residents who have added and continue to add so much to the city's life. We might have had a few more craftspeople, but SOMA would still be a dark, empty place, not the vital, lively neighborhood it is today. Building hundreds of live-work lofts for new telecommuting citizens helped give birth to a renaissance in San Francisco.

I soon realized that as mayor I would become the repository of every fear and fantasy conjured up by those whose petitions and plans had been rejected. The lady whose variance on a planning permit was denied soon spread rumors that I had demanded a kickback, a payback, for the permit. Not so. But when rejected, people misrepresent things. Hell hath no fury like a schemer scorned.

Occasionally, you had to deal with people trading on your name. One day a contractor came to me and said, "Look, I realize you don't go around soliciting money from people looking for city contracts. But as you know, I am trying to win a contract from the city to do a certain deal.

"Well," he continued, and here he named an aspiring black broker from the Bayview, "this Mr. X has come to me and said for a fee he can get you to deliver the contract to me. For a fee paid to him, you'll give me the contract."

Essentially he said this Mr. X was representing himself as my agent, and that for a fee of $25,000 to be split between Mr. X and myself, I would steer the contract to the guy who had come to me. It was all nonsense—upsetting, but not surprising.

Here is how I dealt with it. I told the contractor first that the reviewing boards would automatically reject any contract that had Mr. X's name or even scent attached to it. Then I instructed the reviewing boards that were set up to scrutinize petitions and requests for services to watch for Mr. X and to be wary of any contracts that he might be connected to. He was soon iced out. He was unable to get anywhere. My other option was to call the DA and ask if they had cases involved with this guy. I wouldn't have needed to say anything more. They would have opened a file on this guy and begun an investigation.

I was satisfied at the moment with icing the guy from my end. It worked while I was mayor. But he was incorrigible. Once I left the mayoralty, he was back—and this time he was getting contracts and subsidies. I'm waiting for the day when one of his enterprises collapses. Investigators will discover that the public funds that supposedly went into this minority business didn't go into the project at all, but into Mr. X's pocketbook.

CHAPTER THIRTY-SIX

Sacred Cartel

KEEPING CITY POLITICS ON THE LEVEL really means keeping the processes of city government fair and not subject to private advantage. To most citizens, I suppose, this would seem to be largely a matter of guarding against what you might call "classic corruption": payoffs of one kind or another to city officials to influence decisions or alter public policy. But as I've said, I actually found relatively little of this kind of behavior, since most public servants are indeed honest. Furthermore, people knew that as a mayor I was very attentive to process and could detect the little burps and bumps, the bits of arrhythmia, in the daily procedures of departments that are inevitable when things big or small are not functioning the way they should. Classic corruption almost always reveals itself.

Not so obvious was behavior in San Francisco that I regard not only as really detrimental to fair process and good government but which also is not much noted—in part because I think survivalist politicians, who are trying to avoid potentially damaging fights, just won't take it on. Yet it involves millions of dollars in public money and the lives of the city's most vulnerable. So it was a big concern to me. It also involved some unlikely suspects: a group of nonprofit corporations involved in the building of housing for the poor, and thus surrounded with the odor of sanctity and bearing enormous credibility. I came to call them the "sacred cartel."

Building and managing housing that the poor, the aged, and the disabled in San Francisco can afford is, obviously, an important business. It's so important for the city that all three levels of government—city, state, and federal—offer a variety of financing instruments, from subsidies to tax credits, to entice people to build it. And in San Francisco at least a dozen nonprofit corporations do so. For-profit developers, whose bottom line would be helped by their involvement in putting up nonprofit housing, also want to do so. But what I found in San Francisco was that this cartel of about five nonprofits seemed to have an edge over all others. Not all nonprofit builders of housing were involved. But overall this sacred cartel was more successful at the game than any of the others. They were getting what they wanted: much of the money available to build affordable housing, institutional heft, and the enrichment of a select few, such as pet suppliers and executives who enjoyed much political power as well as fine lifestyles. I happened upon all this by doing what I do best: asking questions about ordinary things—that's an important attribute in a mayor. As a mayor you have to be a curious person if you're going to be at all effective. Noticing what's going on on the streets and asking questions about it is simply being conscientious.

So one day, as I was driving around the city, I noticed a plot of vacant land. I asked my staff, "Could we build housing on it for low-income or disadvantaged people? Who might want to build the housing? How could we finance it?"

Land in San Francisco is so scarce and the demand for affordable housing so great that I expected to find a large number of builders who would be interested in the few vacant lots available in town. But what I found out when I questioned my staff was surprising. This lot was in the purview of this nonprofit; that lot was in the purview of another.

Had this been determined through the bidding process? I asked. No, I was told: bidding hadn't even been started. It was just understood from the get-go that properties around town were reserved for members of the cartel, and the project would go to the cartel member that held sway over the neighborhood. It was just politics, I was told. And I was expected to accept this. Instead I investigated further. It seemed implausible at best.

But the data that my staff compiled on previously completed projects filed with the San Francisco Redevelopment Agency and other offices strongly indicated there was effectively something of a cartel operating—it was nothing illegal, it was just damn unfair, and, to my mind, an abuse of process.

Not so nice, you might say, but what's the problem, Willie Brown? Wasn't affordable housing getting built? Yes, it was. And weren't these nonprofits building it? Yes. Wasn't that better than letting greedy for-profit developers take the land? Of course. Aren't you just complaining about the fact that a group of people who are apparently very good about doing something that's undeniably a real social good have seemingly arranged things among themselves so they can each get on with their work?

Well, first, no private arrangement should be allowed to hold sway, as this appeared to do, over the goals of a completely fair process. Second, this arrangement seemed to make it harder for anyone, nonprofit or for-profit, who might have a better idea about how to utilize this financing to get a project.

There were (and are) for-profit developers who wanted to build affordable housing in San Francisco. They wouldn't try to make a profit from the affordable housing—they couldn't by law—but by being involved, they could get credits and tax breaks that would help their corporate bottom line. There were also many developers in this socially conscious city who felt they should, as a matter of moral obligation, help build affordable housing. But they were often frozen out. And the cartel also disfavored contractors, architects, and landscaping companies who were not among their pet suppliers. The interest and creativity of others was not encouraged.

Then there was the question of the work itself and the management style of the cartel members. There were many reasons to believe that the nonprofits in the sacred cartel were quite inefficient when it came to construction. They could be slow in getting their buildings up. The buildings themselves were often of inferior quality.

And the cartel could be rough on their tenants, especially those with the temerity to complain or voice concerns about living conditions. Yet the cartel could be plenty noisy and powerful at the ballot box with politicians who might oppose them on one of their pet projects. They'd just clobber you with demonstrations and organize votes against you. A survivalist politician, bent on just winning reelection, won't oppose them. I found them to be unfair, inefficient, and harmful to the political process. But I admired their success—they were getting what they wanted, they knew how to arrange things, and they knew how to whale away at their enemies. They were also covered in sanctity for doing God's work.

But, frankly, they were also hypocrites, without the courage of the principles they espoused. Here's an example. In 2001, a parcel of land became available for low-income housing when we tore an old freeway down. It was on the edge of The Castro, the gay and lesbian neighborhood I've supported and advanced ever since the days when I battled for the first gay-rights legislation in the assembly. My friend Bevan Dufty, a member of the city's legislature who happens to be gay, came to me with an idea about that land. He wanted me to use my influence to ensure that we constructed affordable housing there, but he wanted the housing limited to gay and lesbian senior citizens. Now, I've done a lot to support housing for the gay community, especially for people sick with AIDS, but I was surprised at this idea. "Isn't this discrimination?" I said to Dufty, putting it nicely. "We can legitimately build housing and limit it to senior citizens, but you know we can't limit it to a segment of that community. How would you feel if I said I was going to build a development just for black senior citizens, or Asian senior citizens or Latino?" It grew into a huge fight. But the nonprofits in the cartel, who should have been the first to fight against discrimination, were silent in this fight. They didn't push back at all. They remained silent.

I beat the sacred cartel, however. For one, I encouraged other groups to form new nonprofits to build housing. San Francisco's famous Glide Memorial Church, led by the Reverend Cecil Williams, for example, has built some and is building more. That fight was complex but relatively easy. The cartel was hard-pressed to bring its political forces against a church that has done so much for San Francisco's dispossessed and disenfranchised as has Glide, which feeds, houses, and cares for thousands of the worst-off every day.

Then, aside from these various small projects, I made a structural attack upon the sacred cartel.

Within the San Francisco Redevelopment Agency, the basic landlord for many of the sites available for building affordable housing, I created my own nonprofit called the Public Initiatives Development Corporation. To run it I hired the man who was the real guru for all the nonprofits in the city, Olson Lee, who knew the ins and outs of financing affordable housing like no one else. He had previously taught the nonprofits all they knew. So I co-opted them. I had the PIDC bid on a piece of property.

Unholy hell broke out around the project we bid on. We faced terrible demonstrations and horrendous criticism in the press. A Filipino American theater troupe that was being displaced by the new development brought drums and dancers and actors to City Hall to protest our proposal. They had been promised a replacement space in the new building. I offered the theater company, with the intriguing name of Bindlestiff Studio, an even better deal in our building. That ended the drums and performers—not that I didn't enjoy the creativity and artistry the Bindlestiff players brought to the demonstrations against us.

Our proposal was approved by the Redevelopment Agency, of course. And now it's built and occupied. It's a handsome home to 115 people, many of whom had been residents of the fleabag hotel it replaced. We used top architects, first-rate materials. And today, even though it is on the edge of Skid Road, people ready to pay market-rate prices for apartments come in inquiring about rentals or purchases. They can't get in. It's great affordable housing. And with it I penetrated the walls of the sacred cartel. A survivalist politician would have just gone along with the quiet game.

CHAPTER THIRTY-SEVEN

A Mayor Makes Friends with Warlords as Well as with Nice People

TO BE AN EFFECTIVE MAYOR you have to keep up relationships with all kinds of people. You can't just do seminars, policy sessions, and social events and hope to keep the peace or grow a city. San Francisco is a big city, not a laboratory at a political science institute. It's a city of the desperate as well as of the bejeweled. It's a city of guns as well as of basketball courts. And right now it's a city plagued with gangs, drugs, and guns.

There are scores of gangs in the city. Some, like the Latin gangs, are ethnically based. The Nicaraguans have their gangs; the Mexicans have their gangs; the Colombians have their own. They usually war just among one another. It's not acceptable, but it's comprehensible. Other gangs are strictly business. That includes the black drug and gun gangs. These are the most painful to me.

Drugs are a big business, and the gangs' various rivals defend their turf boundaries with guns and killings—usually of teenagers. Life is expendable to the gang leaders, and teenagers—impulsive, susceptible to the lure of money, guns, and flash—make good soldiers. A lot of life is lost and lot of pain is suffered.

Tragically, the number of gang killings has increased tremendously in the last few years. Frankly, guns are the root cause. You have a lot more guns around than you did even when I was mayor, and where you have guns, you're going to have death. You really want to cut down on crime in the city, and you can do it by eliminating guns. That seems unlikely to happen right now.

I was able to keep the number of shootings down, by some simple hard politics. Two kinds.

One way was to use my personal power and street authority with the people I knew to be the heads of the gangs. These are throwback guys, veterans of prisons, relics of the '60s, con men in many ways. My willingness to acknowledge these lusterless but powerful people was taken by some as a sign of corruption. It certainly wasn't. But as a mayor intent on keeping the peace, I had to keep in touch and keep the respect of people who are essentially the warlords of the gangs. I sat down with these people and told them, "You want to do your killings? Do it in Oakland. Do it in Richmond. Do it elsewhere. But don't do killing in San Francisco. It reflects badly on a black mayor."

It worked. It's realpolitik, as Henry Kissinger might say. Not pretty, but it worked.

The second thing I did was to utilize a group that had no respect from City Hall, the white establishment, or the do-gooders but who did do a lot of good and who had the respect of black people. That group was the black Muslims.

I developed positive relationships with the black Muslims and put them to work. The Muslims, instead of the uniformed cops, became the safety force in the public housing projects. Of course, it cost money, but no one else was doing the job.

Many of them were ex-convicts, but they had become true believers in order and social peace. We had them out there making housing secure, making the streets safe. And really laying down the law.

This had the added effect of causing the dope dealer types to find other places outside the city to do their bad stuff. Between giving the order to the heads of the gangs to stop the killings and building a positive presence in the housing projects through the black Muslims, we were driving the drug trade and the killings out of our area. Not solving the big problem, but driving it out of our location. That's what a mayor is supposed to do.

Of course, my friends in the San Francisco Police Department, whom I supported generously, claimed not to like this. But even more they disliked having to patrol the housing projects, so they were glad to let the duty go to other, tougher guys who weren't as bound by constitutional niceties. The black Muslims also put the younger kids to work—patrolling buses, working as peacekeepers. This was positive stuff for them to do.

So suddenly you had former outlaws and once outcast people usefully participating in society and carrying out their responsibilities and duties. And you had some of the drug traffic fleeing. All because as mayor, you make friends with people who aren't necessarily very nice.

Of course, you also want to keep up your relationships with very nice people, the movers and shakers in a big city. One of the tragedies of big-city America these days is that people like this, what I like to call the "leadership class," are disappearing. It used to be that in every big city, and certainly in San Francisco, there was a brigade of people of wealth and interest who could be counted upon to support the city, its institutions, and its needs. Often they came from the ranks of high society. In San Francisco we had people who looked after various causes. Some might support the opera; others might look after the ballet; some were interested in the symphony or the aquarium or this museum or that. Some came from old Gold Rush families, others were in banking, many were in real estate.

They also could be called upon by a mayor to help with other causes. Although Mr. Z might primarily give to the opera, you could call him to help with a building fund for a new museum. This they felt was their civic responsibility. In an afternoon, you could reach a dozen or so people and help a worthy institution get its special fund-raising under way. You really didn't have to explain very much. You just said, "The museum needs help. Everyone's pitching in. Will you? And will you call people you know?" They did.

But the people who feel this way are dying away with no one to replace them. It's not that fortunes are disappearing—we have more billionaires than ever in San Francisco. It's simply that this kind of local civic spirit is disappearing. You can still get people to help, but you really have to make a pitch these days. You have to run through the subject matter. You have to explain the cost benefits. You have to shame. It's a lot of work.

I suppose it's because there isn't much payoff anymore in being a part of the local inner circle. The wealthy today think of themselves as global citizens first, not as San Franciscans. They have homes around the globe, not just in Northern California. They aren't rooted here as they once were.

I used to keep a Rolodex of real estate developers, builders of big apartment houses and office buildings, whom I could call upon for help with civic matters. These guys have almost all disappeared. Very few locals are directly involved in local real estate anymore. They don't invest in buildings; they invest in global real estate investment trusts. They're not San Francisco landlords; they're market investors.

In time, I suppose the younger fellows who are making their money out of Silicon Valley and the internet may surface as local philanthropists. They certainly love living in San Francisco. But their philanthropy is of a different order, too. Call one and you are referred instead to a philanthropy officer in their company who'll want to put their money to work in a global program. I certainly don't quarrel with the good work they do, but I wish these younger people would get as much of a kick out of being a big deal at the opening night of the San Francisco Opera as they do appearing at a seminar in Switzerland with Bono. I fear for the future of local institutions.

CHAPTER THIRTY-EIGHT

The Scared Days and an Urban Legend

ON THE MORNING OF SEPTEMBER 11, 2001, I was at home packing and preparing for a short trip to New York City. I was going on a marketing jaunt for the city. I also had rare tickets to see the Broadway show *The Producers*, on September 12.

It was before six when my driver called me from downstairs; he was ready to take me to the airport. Then suddenly my private line rang again. It was my aide, Martha Cohen, who excitedly said, "Mr. Mayor, Mr. Mayor, turn on your TV. A plane has hit the World Trade Center in New York." I turned on the television and saw one of the towers smoking. Small aircraft were hovering about. Like most everyone else, I assumed that a small plane had flown off course and hit the tower. The same thing had happened once decades before to the Empire State Building. It seemed an awful but isolated incident. Then the unimaginable happened; a larger fixed-wing aircraft flew directly into the other tower. I knew that the icons of Manhattan and all of New York City were under some sort of attack. I thought of our own icons—the Golden Gate Bridge, the Bay Bridge, the Transamerica Pyramid, and the environmentally sensitive San Francisco Bay itself.

I called City Hall and convened an immediate meeting of our Emergency Services task force. We met within minutes at our secure location away from City Hall. Police, fire, hospital, and other emergency personnel gathered. Before we knew fully what had happened in New York, I wasted no time and declared a state of emergency in San Francisco. We closed the schools, closed City Hall, and put the city on full emergency alert.

We sent police cars to each city school to guide students, teachers, and parents. We called for Coast Guard help with the bridges and placed security around iconic buildings like the Transamerica office tower. We weren't sure what was happening in New York, but we wanted to be ready in case San Francisco was also a target, which seemed possible since we soon learned that a plane bound for San Francisco, United Flight 93, had been hijacked. It seemed best to shut the city down. Stores and offices were soon closed, but people were going to churches to pray. We kept them open.

And with that began a series of days in which the city grew really scared and I became the subject of an odd new urban legend that is still repeated on talk radio and on internet message boards. It's not terribly important, but I am asked about it all the time.

The rumor is that somehow Condoleezza Rice or an aide called me in advance of the attack on 9/11 and warned me not to fly to New York. Well, it's true, of course, that I was scheduled to fly to New York that morning, but no one from Condoleezza Rice's office ever warned me off. The reason I didn't fly was because I needed to stay home and mayor the city. Anyway, the airports were shut.

As to there being some sort of secret network of high black officials who communicate with one another, well, that's absurd. I scarcely know Secretary Rice, even though she once lived and worked just down the road from San Francisco at Stanford University.

I've met her and seen her a few times in my life, but always at public events. We barely have a nodding acquaintanceship, let alone a friendship. The idea that she or an aide had some advance knowledge of the attacks on 9/11 and called me to alert me is just preposterous. It never happened.

So how did this yarn begin? The only thing that I can think of is that on the day of September 11 as we went about on our preparations, a reporter, Phil Matier of the *San Francisco Chronicle*, accompanied me as a kind of pool reporter for the day, providing coverage for himself and for other reporters.

In the course of the day, Phil had asked me if the city had had any advance warning. I explained to him that at irregular intervals the airport would receive advisories from the federal government about safety and travel conditions. And that these reports, which included warnings when the feds suspected terrorist work was on high, were relayed pro forma to me as chief executive. The next day he printed that in his column in the *Chronicle*. I gather that eager minds read his report and extrapolated it to mean that my flight plans had been canceled based on some report sent to the city. And then the story escalated to Secretary Rice sending me a personal warning. Not so. Never happened. I guess I'll just have to live with this. One weird and goofy aspect of political life is that you become a character in other people's fantasies. This is one of those.

Meanwhile, I had a frightened and nervous city to reassure and to get back to work again. Within hours of the 9/11 attacks the streets of downtown San Francisco emptied; they would stay empty for days. Even real estate prices fell. New condos near the Bay Bridge went from six hundred thousand dollars per one-bedroom unit down to two hundred housand dollars. No one wanted to be downtown or near the bridges or the bay.

One of the first things we did once things calmed down was to encourage shopping downtown with a series of promotions and cheer-up events. San Francisco is lucky in that it is one of the few big cities in America with a still-thriving downtown shopping district. I wasn't going to let an isolated terrorist attack do to our city what urban renewal and suburban flight hadn't been able to do. Eventually we were able to pull people back into town. Promoting retail goods may not seem to be part of the job description of a modern mayor, but I had to get out there and sell if we were to save our city. By Christmastime things were back to normal.

One of the oddest facts that came out of the 9/11 tragedy was the revelation that Osama bin Laden, in his preterrorist days, had spent a few months living in San Francisco. Sometime in the early '70s, when he would have been in his twenties, he lived in an apartment owned by his family atop Nob Hill. No one seemed to remember him, and all connections to him were long gone despite the best efforts of the FBI to track them down.

CHAPTER THIRTY-NINE

The Political Life

WHEN I LEFT CITY HALL AS MAYOR, I was broke. This surprised people who assumed that a mayor who helped so many people become rich must have become rich himself. Actually, what I did for people was make sure that they had fair access to process and that the process handled them fairly. No one got anything from my City Hall that the merits of their proposals didn't entitle them to. If ensuring fair process is doing people a favor, then that's the favor I did for them and for the city I care about and think about so deeply. I was happy to use my power to get people what they were entitled to: fair dealing. But I wasn't in it for money. I was never an entrepreneur. I was, however, in politics for power. I wasn't in it to be a prophet. I wanted to achieve change and deliver product. For that you need institutional power, not just powerful rhetoric.

I achieved power obviously by becoming a master politician, servicing my constituencies. In the legislature that meant serving the members. That's how I got the votes. In City Hall, it meant serving the people and meeting the needs of everyone. And then putting my skills at negotiating, coalition building, arm twisting, and flattery in their service. If some mayors were the mayors of business interests and others were the mayors favoring labor and others served various other constituencies, I liked to think that I was the people's mayor. I liked knowing everybody, knowing what anybody needed or was worrying about. Anyone could come and see me. I made sure they all had access. Every month or so I held an open house so that those people who wouldn't think of trying to make an appointment with the mayor, or who didn't know how, had a chance to connect directly with me. I met a fair number of nuts. I also met some extraordinary common people—the most ingenious of whom I hired or put to work on city oversight commissions. I also made sure I spoke to all kinds of people. I did regular radio shows in English, Chinese, Spanish, and all the other languages spoken on the streets of San Francisco. I went to events and gatherings of people from high society to ordinary society to low society. If you're going to be an effective mayor, you've got to be curious and conscientious about everyone. I did the same in the legislature. I was available to everyone from citizens to lobbyists to bureaucrats to members. The best of their agendas became my agenda.

So it always disappointed me when critics would say I had no agenda, that I was not a prophetic leader with a vision or a set of guiding principles. My guiding principle was to place myself in a position of power so that I could help people with good ideas see those ideas realized. I was the leader as facilitator, a facilitator you didn't want to cross because then I became a shark.

Early on I learned, especially from my mother, grandmother, and mentors like Jesse Unruh and Phil Burton, that true power came not from mastering the podium (though I was terrific at that) but by mastering the rules.

In this I was especially guided by the example of a man I admire greatly, the late congressman Adam Clayton Powell of Harlem, who served in office from 1945 until 1970. The 1950s and early '60s were his heyday. I liked everything about him from his mastery of the system to his personal style. I learned from his downfall too. It's a cautionary tale.

It was his style that was first attractive to me. Powell was the personification of what you would want to be by way of his public image. His handsome appearance, his commitment to wardrobe, his skill in the pulpit, his knowledge of social issues, and his absolute, undying commitment to equality for African Americans. All this made him in his day *the guy*. He really was. Martin Luther King Jr. had not yet come of age. A. Philip Randolph was a distant aloof figure, as was Roy Wilkins of the NAACP. They were stodgy. But Powell was a rock star before there were rock stars. He had all the components of an ultimate politician. He had the lifestyle of royalty—before the Kennedys were on the scene. He really was the guy. And he had power. He used and parlayed the congressional rules as well if not better than Sam Rayburn or Lyndon Johnson. And Rayburn, that crusty old Texan, loved Powell for that.

Powell used whatever was in front of him. When it came to dealing with white people, he used the guilt that he saw right there, the kind of guilt that, however vague, was the basis of their relationship with him and black America. When it came to the House of Representatives, he saw that it was the rules of the house that drove the place. He used the rules rather than just railing about them. For example, back then seniority was the trigger to power, so he made sure he had seniority.

To ensure his longevity, by the way, Powell did something few politicians do, though it seems they obviously must. He built a base that was devoted to him and to him alone. One forgets that Harlem was politically active and filled with ambitious rivals. Powell secured his own base. He worked it assiduously, got himself elected and reelected. Thus, he obtained the seniority that was the path to power. At one point, as chairman of the House Education and Labor Committee, he controlled more than 60 percent of the domestic affairs legislation in the U.S. Congress. Under his chairmanship, in one term, his committee moved more bills than any other committee before or since. He was the ultimate.

And this was in a Congress where, until Powell came along, black congressmen couldn't even eat in the members' dining room, and where it was acceptable, until he stopped it, for elected officials to use racial slurs in speeches from the floor of the U.S. House.

He also suffered the ultimate downfall. This son of the House of Representatives was expelled by his peers. He thought that he had become invincible. He thought that "the system" that he had served so well would save him. But the system, like all political systems everywhere, saves only itself. It will jettison anyone who becomes a threat to its continuation.

Powell in his later years had become very arrogant. He stopped being a workhorse and was frequently absent. He was suddenly sloppy about the rules—especially those governing money. He got into tax trouble and personally abused congressional committee money. Perhaps, if he had been a little more observant, more cooperative, and then a little more contrite when he got in trouble, the system might have saved him. But ultimately he suffered because of his delusion that the system would keep him. It won't, if you disrespect it.

Wrapped up in a corruption scandal, his twenty-five-year membership in Congress was over when my friend Charles Rangel, who still holds the Harlem seat, defeated him in 1970.

A British politician once said that almost all lengthy political careers end in tragedy. They usually do. But mine didn't. I survived because I stayed on top of the rules. As a matter of fact, my political career isn't over. Though I have no intention of ever running for office again, I remain enormously active. I strategize, sell advice, and comment freely.

I've also set up the Willie L. Brown Jr. Institute on Politics &
Public Service, financed by campaign contributions left over from
when I retired from electoral politics. (I take no money from the
institute.) The Willie Brown Institute is dedicated to finding ways
to support cutting-edge issues like stem cell research in a hostile
political environment. We also try to teach politicians how to survive and how to figure out what their real role is in the world today.
That's a good question—for which I have an answer.

CHAPTER FORTY

What Is a Politician?

IS THERE AN ANALOGY for the role that a conscientious politician plays in today's society? There is indeed a curious one, but I think it's apt. In my own career, I've often analogized myself to a quarterback in football or a point guard in basketball. You're always working up plays, executing them, keeping the squad going and focused. You can't cheat, and if you do, you'll be exposed and punished. The sports analogy has worked because it's apt and easy for colleagues and citizens to understand. But a more appropriate comparison is to, of all things, nursing.

Indeed, that's really how I've often thought of myself. You're doing vital work, necessary work. You get to use your brains, your people skills, and you get to help people. The physicians are specialists with highly specific knowledge, but the nurse is the facilitator, the real practitioner. And often you have to get people to take medicine, medicine they don't want. So I leave you with that analogy. A real working politician these days isn't a prostitute, isn't a preacher, isn't a topic-specific expert, isn't a rabble-rouser. The good pol is a nurse for the body politic.

These days I think there's something else to be mastered by anyone aspiring to a serious life in politics. It's this: take care of your own and your family's economic needs first.

In older days, when campaigns weren't so dependent on fundraising, when politicians weren't having to spend three-quarters of every day begging for bucks, you could go into politics and earn a living at the same time. But today, unless you have taken care of your personal family money first, you're going to be under constant suspicion that you're on the take.

I worked as a lawyer during my time in the assembly—lots of members did. But in later years, as the media became obsessed with looking for links between money and votes, we were attacked because our clients supposedly hired us to work our connections on their behalf. Never mind that we were ethical enough and sharp enough to warn clients away from trying to get us to use influence improperly. Never mind that people hired us because of our competence, not our connections—we were accused.

For a black man trying to make a career as a lawyer and as a politician, it was an awful kind of double jeopardy. When I started out as a lawyer, no big, white-shoe law firms were hiring black lawyers. So I started out working for the only people who would hire me—people in trouble, like pimps, prostitutes, small-time crooks. I was attacked for having a sleazy clientele. But when I began to acquire corporate clients, I was subtly accused of going above my station: a black lawyer should defend only small-time criminal clients. Other lawyers in the assembly who had corporate clients weren't so accused. I was. And then when I achieved that status of being able to attract corporate clients, I was accused of influence peddling.

But if you have your own pile of dough, or at least have economically secured your family before setting out in politics, no one can accuse you of being on the take. You'll still have to raise money, unless you have done so well that you can afford to self-finance campaigns—like Steve Forbes, who inherited his cash; or Arnold Schwarzenegger, who made his in show business; or Steve Westly, a California politician who made his in Silicon Valley; or New York mayor Michael Bloomberg, who made his fortune in finance and communications. If you have your own dough, no one can credibly insinuate that your vote has been for sale.

So, my advice to young people contemplating a career in politics is follow the Ten Commandments, take care of the money, master the system, and comply with the regulations. You'll be safe on the ethical front.

Then, to be effective, learn the other lessons I have tried to draw in these pages: learn that consensus is what you have to build even to get the most righteous idea across; make friends and be loyal; instill and demand allegiance; learn the value of intelligence; be tolerant; keep the public interest paramount.

You also have to learn to have fun. This was easier when legislative chambers weren't so partisan. It was possible then for members to enjoy each other and life in the chamber. It still can be that way. It takes more work now to have fun, but it's the only way to make it bearable.

You also have to learn how to live without power, how to survive those periods when you may be in exile or defeated. Jerry Brown, who has gone from being governor of California at an early age to having become mayor of Oakland in his late middle age, and now in his sixties is California's elected attorney general, has certainly learned that. Al Gore has as well.

Each has kept old connections and made new ones while in exile. Each has attentively listened to the changing pulse of the electorate while keeping personal honor bright. Each has reinvented himself while remaining recognizable.

When elected speaker in 1980 after having been defeated six years earlier, I was said to have secured that victory only by becoming more humble. That was humbug. I didn't become more humble. I became, as I have said, more nimble. That's what you use the fallow years for. If you like the game and believe you can help the people, you don't quit because they throw you out or because the victors exile you. You don't want to waste the talent and skill that you have developed. So you work the talent, you work the skills; you wait carefully for the favorable moment. It will come to you; the people will come to you; the enemies will turn again toward you. They will recognize that your talent is needed.

You also don't keep grudges or alienate people permanently. Never make a permanent enemy out of someone you've defeated. Leave the vanquished their dignity; you may want to be partners with them on a vote someday. As my grandmother used to tell me: "Make enemies out of people, even people who insult you or degrade you, and you'll be very shocked someday to find you stand alone. You'll find you've made the whole world your enemy." That's not my way.

Acknowledgments

Bob Barnett, the literary lawyer of the age, has ably represented me and this book, for which I offer him many thanks. He took this project to Simon & Schuster where it received a warm welcome from David Rosenthal, Alice Mayhew, and Roger Labrie. For their incisive editing and true encouragement, I thank them. As I thank diligent editors Patty Romanowski and Jonathan Evans. I wish also to thank Elisa Rivlin, Simon & Schuster's able general counsel.

In my own office I am especially grateful to Song Schreiber, Eleanor Johns, and Susan Brown for their unfailing assistance in completing this project.

Scores of people have contributed time and stories to help with the work of this book. I could not possibly thank them all, but I wish particularly to remember the following, who went beyond the bounds of friendship to answer inquiries and share detailed memories and insights: Bob Agnew; Darius Anderson; Rusty Areias; Publisher Amelia Ashley-Ward of the *Sun-Reporter*; Bill Bagley; Wilkes Bashford; Geoffrey F. Brown; Jack Davis; Harry deWildt; Mrs. Ruth Garland-Dewson; Gene Duffy; Will Durst; Jeanette Etheredge; Michael Galizio; Leah Garchik; Stanlee Gatti; Terry Goggin; Mrs. Prentis Cobb Hale; Peter C. Haley; Nancy Hamon; District Attorney Kamala Harris; Warren Hinkle; Gale Kaufman; Steven Kay; Matthew Kelly; Susan Kennedy, chief

ACKNOWLEDGMENTS

of staff to Governor Arnold Schwarzenegger; Ken Maley; Phil Matier; Bobbie Metzger; Sonya Molodetskaya; Ed Moose; Joe O'Donoghue; Christine Pelosi; Speaker of the United States House of Representatives Nancy Pelosi; Paul Pelosi Sr.; Mike Roos; Andy Ross; Irene Roth; John Roth; Billy Rutland; Ginger Rutland; Kevin Shelley; Charlotte Mailliard Shultz; former U.S. secretary of state George Shultz; Martha Smilgis; Congresswoman Maxine Waters; Paul "The Lobster" Wells; and the Reverend Cecil Williams.

I owe a great debt of thanks to my family: My wife, Blanche Brown; my children Robin Brown-Friedel, Michael Brown, Susan Brown; and, of course, to Sydney Brown and her mother, Carolyn Carpeneti. My sisters, Gwendolyn Brown Hill, Lovia Brown Boyd, Baby Dalle Hancock, and my brother, James Walton, have never failed to assist me.

I would like very much to thank P. J. Corkery, who collaborated with me on this book, for his work, words, interest, and questions. P. J. is a shrewd student of political power, a lively wit, good company, and a fine journalist. He has long conducted a column in the San Francisco *Examiner* and his articles have appeared in *The New Yorker*, *Harper's*, *Rolling Stone*, *The New Republic*, *Spy*, and many newspapers.

Finally, I would like to thank the people of San Francisco, who have honored me for more than thirty years by electing me their representative and mayor. This life has been more than I dreamt was possible when I first stepped off the train in San Francisco as a wide-eyed Texas teenager in 1951.

Photo Credits

Dennis DeSilva, www.studioseven.net: 1, 34

Author's Collection: 2, 3, 4, 5, 6, 7, 8, 10, 11, 14, 20, 23

Art Torres: 9

© Kim Gottlieb-Walker, www.Lenswoman.com, "all rights reserved": 12

Eve Crane: 13

Rich Pedroncelli: 15, 16

Drew Altizer: 17, 18

Photo by Russell Collins Stiger: 19, 25

© Barry E. Levine: 21

Courtesy Jay Leno: 22

Walt Zeboski, AP Images: 24

© Photo by Glen Korengold Copyright Photo by Glen Korengold: 26

Ray Scotty Morris: 27, 29

Thomas John Gibbons: 28

Stanley Zax: 30

From *Newsweek* November 11, © 1996 Newsweek, Inc. All rights reserved. Used by permission and protected by Copyright Laws of the United States. The printing, copying, redistribution, or retransmission of the Material without express written permission is prohibited. Photograph by Nigel Parry/CPi: 31

William J. Clinton Foundation: 32

Sacramento Bee / Brian Baer: 33

Index

INDEX

INDEX

INDEX

INDEX

INDEX

INDEX

taxes:
  cigarette, 57
  property, 123–24
Taylor, Barbara, 302
Telegraph Hill Dwellers, 265–67
television:
  clothes and, 39–40
  1972 Democratic convention on, 111
term limits, 216, 226, 231, 269–70
Thompson, Steve, 113
Thornton, Shirley, 257
tobacco industry, 57–58, 217–18, 241
Torres, Art, 142, 144, 148, 156
Travis, Benjamin, 73–74
Tucker, Curtis, 148, 153

United Farm Workers, 171
Unruh, Jesse, 32–33, 108, 112, 151, 153, 155, 169, 170, 227
  WLB's relationship with, 89–90, 328

Van de Kamp, John, 199
Vanocur, Sander, 111
Vasconcellos, John, 144, 211
Vicencia, Frankie, 149–50, 152
Vietnam War, 14, 79
Villaraigosa, Antonio, 3
Voudou religion, 99

Wajumbe Performance Ensemble, 99
Waldie, Jerome, 115
Walker, Sandy, 2
Wallace, George, 108–9
Wallace, Mike, 111
Walsh, Bill, 293–94
Ward, Doris, 53
Watergate scandal, 152
Waters, Maxine, 39, 49, 53, 55, 220
  divestiture legislation sponsored by, 205–9

in plan to make WLB assembly
  speaker, 144, 146–47, 153, 450–51
Watson, Diane, 53
Watts, J. C., 46
welfare system, 272
Westly, Steve, 56, 333–34
Westminster Presbyterian Church, 72, 74
whistle-blowing, 64–66, 287
White, Dan, 127–31, 132–33
white community, black politicians
  and, 45, 53–54
Wilkins, Roy, 329
Williams, Cecil, 94, 316
Willie L. Brown Jr. Institute on
  Politics and Public Service, 94, 331
Willie L. Brown Jr. Music Scholarship, 94
Wilson, E. Dotson, 220–21
Wilson, Pete, 209–12, 214
Winfrey, Oprah, 54
Witt, Jamie Lee, 282
Wolcott, James, 49
women politicians:
  black, 53
  clothes and, 38–39, 42–43
  in Congress, 51
  as wives or daughters of male
    politicians, 52–53
women's rights, 14, 54–55
"Women's Summits," 54–55
Woods, Tiger, 245
World Trade Center, 323

Yaki, Michael, 78
Yee, Leland, 243
Yerba Buena Gardens, 251, 253
York, John, 304
York, Marie Denise DeBartolo, 304
Yoruba religion, 99
Young, Steve, 294

350

About the Author

Willie Brown has been at the center of California politics, government, and civic life for an astonishing four decades. His career spans the American presidency from Lyndon Johnson to George W. Bush. Today, he heads the Willie L. Brown Jr. Institute on Politics & Public Service, where this acknowledged master of the art of politics shares his knowledge and skills with a new generation of California leaders.